FIRST AMENDMENT STUDIES IN ARKANSAS

First Amendment Studies in Arkansas

THE RICHARD S. ARNOLD PRIZE ESSAYS

EDITED BY

Stephen A. Smith

The University of Arkansas Press
Fayetteville
2016

Contents

Foreword

My brother, Richard, would have been delighted by the essays in this book, for they are proof of a new generation's recommitment to the ideals of free speech, ideals that are central not just to the efficient working of our democracy but to the definition of what it means to be a free person in a free society. Richard knew these elementary facts, which accounts for his determination that speech and associational rights be afforded bounds so generous that there could be no doubt that they were fundamental bedrock. This latitudinarian outlook will necessarily license speech and expressive acts that are unpopular, offensive, and even immoral in the eyes of many, but that is hardly surprising: An inoffensive Caspar Milquetoast will hardly ever need protection from a government for what he says or does. As the familiar epigram would have it, freedom of speech sometimes means freedom for the thought we hate.

This elementary constitutional principle has lately gone missing in places where it was once fiercely embraced, namely, our colleges and universities, where truth must be supreme and the search for it must be a paramount object. Achieving a congenial environment for that search requires tolerating the fullest range of expression, even edgy and raucous expression, and providing that environment is an obligation that falls most heavily on state institutions, where the First Amendment has the force of law. An institution, even a state one, of course has a right to have core ethical values and to express them. It may, in some circumstances, have a duty to have such values. But that right or duty cannot extend to suppressing or punishing thoughts and speech that run contrary to those values: An institution's ethical views cannot trump its legal obligations. The numerous cases in which federal courts over the past few decades have had to hold university speech codes unconstitutional is proof enough that free-speech principles are in need of some significant rehabilitation.

It is not easy to describe the basic republican free-speech instinct as either conservative or liberal, nor is it necessary or useful to do so. In its neutral application over a wide range of expression, it is a manifestation of the classical liberal faith that free speech, in the long term, is both efficient and moral, that promoting it is both useful and just. The instinct is conservative in the sense that it preserves the basic values of restraint, civility, humility, and tolerance that have characterized western civilization since the Enlightenment. It encourages listening and counter-speech as the most appropriate response to speech in most instances and trusts rationality and good will to carry the day. These are large assumptions, but we as a country have staked our future on them. All in all, it is more than apparent that we made a good bet.

My brother's instinctive attachment to this faith is evident from his First Amendment cases. They attracted a lot of attention from the public and the profession, and in their even-handedness they were part of the reason that he was, as the expression goes, the liberal's favorite conservative and the conservative's favorite liberal. So it is not surprising that the Speech Communication Association's Commission on Freedom of Expression established the Richard S. Arnold Prize for Scholarship in Free Speech, describing my brother as "a jurist noted for his outstanding opinions in Constitutional and First Amendment Law." And the First Amendment Center bestows an annual award in his honor on a student who participates in its national First Amendment moot court competition. As Justice William Brennan, for whom Richard clerked in 1960–61, put it, "Judge Arnold . . . consistently vindicated the First Amendment guarantees of freedom of the press and freedom of speech, even in cases in which the protected expression was controversial, distasteful, or hateful."

Some commentators have guessed that Richard's robust attachment to the First Amendment owed something to Justice Brennan's tutelage. That is perhaps true: No doubt Brennan and Justice Hugo Black had a good deal of influence on his thinking and certainly their opinions offered a lot of guidance. But this misses the important beginnings of the story. Not every dinner-table conversation in our country devotes a lot of time to discussing political and philosophical matters, but talk around our table when Richard and I were growing up often centered on what a boon our bill of rights was to us because it set limits on what the government could do to us. The social and political milieu in those days promoted freedom as the primary organizing principle of our nation. The movies and the newspapers and the magazines were chockablock with paeans to the blessings of liberty. Our victory in World War II was largely framed as a victory for liberty over tyranny. As the old common lawyers were wont to say, we drank this law in with our mother's milk. Our mother, a vigorous anticommunist, was also a fierce foe of Joseph McCarthy's underhanded tactics. Our father, a lawyer, often expressed the fear that the bill of rights could not survive a popular referendum, so ferocious were the attacks on free association and expression when Richard was in college. So it is no surprise that Richard acquired a high regard for free speech that stayed with him his entire life. The habit of liberty, if acquired early, has a way of enduring and making itself evident in the best of our public servants. Richard's contributions to our little experiment in freedom, and especially his tenacious regard for the First Amendment, was a principal reason that Justice Ruth Bader Ginsburg of the United States Supreme Court could write of him, and rightly, that her "generation knew no finer federal judge."

MORRIS S. ARNOLD
United States Circuit Judge
for the Eighth Circuit

Introduction

It is an honor to present and introduce these essays, both because of their contributions to the conversation about the meaning of the First Amendment and because of my deep and lasting respect for Judge Richard S. Arnold. It was my pleasure to know Judge Arnold as a friend for more than three decades and to learn much from him in our many discussions of First Amendment issues. Moreover, he exemplified the best in what a judge should be in his decency, his honesty, his humanity, his brilliance, and his courage.

As Judge Arnold's biographer, Polly Price, said, "Judge Arnold was probably most noted for his First Amendment opinions. He believed that freedom of speech and association and the right to participate equally in the political process were linked."[1] The Richard S. Arnold Prize in First Amendment Studies was established in his honor to encourage and recognize student scholarship on freedom of expression and freedom of religion, and it was a fitting tribute to his legacy. Justice William Brennan, for whom Arnold once clerked, wrote, "Judge Arnold has consistently vindicated the First Amendment guarantees of freedom of the press and freedom of speech, even in cases in which the protected expression was controversial, distasteful, or hateful."[2]

This collection of fourteen essays presents a unique insight to how First Amendment issues have played out in Arkansas during the last eighty years. Most traditional examinations of cases focus on the particular legal issues and the constitutional principles enunciated by the courts. The approach found here looks at the stories of people and their struggles to express challenged or unpopular points of view. This is an important contribution because it reveals the way in which constitutional controversies arise from the actions of local officials and individual citizens going about making their arguments and searching for audiences to accept their claims.

These essays are also unusual in that they were written by graduate students in communication, rather than lawyers or legal scholars,
and they bring a unique perspective to understanding the parameters
of freedom of expression. While grounded in rhetorical and communication studies, they also bring an openness and candor in their
analyses that is often missing in formal legal monographs. The most
intriguing aspect of their contribution is that they draw on a wide
variety of legal, documentary, and oral history to tell their stories. In
our many conversations about the First Amendment, which I recall
warmly, Judge Arnold evidenced a genuine curiosity about the relationship between communication theory and freedom of speech that
included far more than constitutional doctrine. In his 1996 Madison
Lecture on Constitutional Law at New York University School of Law,
Judge Arnold noted that James Madison "was a Constitutional and
political scholar and magician of the first rank, though not encum-
bered by membership in the Bar, having studied law only briefly and
never practiced."[3]

I am certain that Judge Arnold would have enjoyed and appreciated the collected essays in this book. As he said, "My own view
is that history is important because it's intrinsically interesting, or,
to put it in plain language, history is fun. It may also be of some use
in the work we have to do in our own time."[4] These narratives are
important, because the stories connect the parchment promise of the
First Amendment to the lived human experience of striving for the
freedom to share and consider new and contested ideas.

We can learn from these essays that the First Amendment is often
important in small, or even forgotten, instances in our political culture, and not exclusively in those great questions that end up before
the Supreme Court of the United States. Even those landmark cases,
however, most often began with obscure citizens seeking to express
their views and invoking their constitutional right to do so.

Seven of these fourteen essays deal with events that transpired
within or concerning education and educational institutions. Paula
Killian Agee's essay examines the events at Southern State College at
Magnolia in the 1960s, when Students United for Rights and Equality,
a student group active in promoting civil rights and opposing the
Vietnam War, was confronted by college officials who sought to sup-

press these activities and maintain the status quo. The students and their faculty supporters eventually prevailed in *Pickings v. Bruce*, 430 F.2d 595 (8th Cir. 1970), before the U.S. Court of Appeals for the Eighth Circuit, but that vindication required time, money, and effort to secure rights guaranteed by the First Amendment, and several faculty members were dismissed for their steadfast support of the students.

The second essay by David Morris looks at the origins of *Neal v. Still*, a somewhat related case that developed after officials at Henderson State College disrupted a meeting of students and instigated the arrest of two speakers from the Southern Students Organizing Committee. The Arkansas Supreme Court eventually invalidated the state statute under which the speakers were arrested, but once again the prevailing individuals were deprived of time and money in defense of their rights against a state institution backed by a state prosecutor.

Carolyn M. Heintzman and Josh Bertaccini offer analyses of two very different controversies on the campus of the University of Arkansas, Fayetteville. Heintzman revisits the atmosphere that led to the case of *Gay and Lesbian Students v. Gohn*, in which the University Student Senate, supported by the administration, refused to provide funding to a student organization because they objected to the viewpoints being advanced. Again, the student plaintiffs finally prevailed before the U.S. Court of Appeals for the Eighth Circuit, in an elegant First Amendment opinion by Judge Richard S. Arnold.

The University of Arkansas, Fayetteville, was also the scene for the story told by Josh Bertaccini that raises an important question as to whether criticism of public employees might be suppressed by trademark or private contract provisions. Bertaccini tackles a very interesting event at the intersection of a citizen's right to comment on the performance of public employees with the university's assertion of trademark rights to squelch critical commercial expression, specifically a T-shirt with a caricature and message critical of Razorback football coach Houston Nutt. These issues have never been fully adjudicated by the courts, because the citizen capitulated to a threatened lawsuit by the university, but the conflict here illustrates the stance of the institution and its power exercised merely with the threat of litigation.

Cortney Smith provides an excellent review of two incidents involving the attempt to ban books in the Fayetteville Public Schools.

The first was an attempt in 1985 to restrict *The Chocolate Wars*, a book assigned in a high school English class that resulted from a complaint filed by a parent of one of the students. The second dealt with a challenge to more than seventy books in the school libraries of the Fayetteville School District in 2005, filed by Laurie Taylor based on a list of titles identified as objectionable by an organization of which Taylor was a member. Both of these controversies were attended by large public meetings and finally adjudicated by the school board members.

The repeated censorship of programming at the Arkansas Educational Television Network, carried out by staff at their own discretion without an official policy, was the subject of the study by Allie Taylor. She examines the concept of state action that would be absent in commercial broadcasting decisions and documents both political pressure and staff assumptions that led to unusual programming decisions. Numerous citizens complained about censorship and eventually led the commission to adopt new standards.

Off-campus speech by high school students and whether it is subject to disciplinary actions by school officials were addressed by Andrew Long in a case involving two students at Greenwood High School and another at Valley View High School who had created parody websites that school officials found inappropriate or offensive. Both cases were heard in federal district court, and the students essentially prevailed.

Jamie Kern, in a chapter from her longer master's thesis on anarchy prosecutions in Arkansas, looks at the local power structure's use of criminal anarchy statutes to suppress the speech of Ward Rodgers, who was attempting to organize black and white sharecroppers in Poinsett County. Rodgers was convicted in the local court and appealed to the circuit court. While the prosecuting attorney later *nolle prossed* the charge, the episode demonstrates yet another instance where those in power use the legal process to suppress dissent with impunity, knowing that the defendant's constitutional rights are in play.

Rebekah Huss Fox, in a similar approach, looks at the way in which local officials employed the Arkansas Flag Desecration Statute to charge a member of the Jehovah's Witnesses for words spoken in a public building. Coming after the U.S. Supreme Court's *Minersville v. Gobitis* decision in 1940 but before the court reversed its position

three years later in *West Virginia State Board of Education v. Barnette,*
local Arkansas authorities prosecuted and eventually convicted Joe
Johnson in Searcy County Circuit Court for expressing religious reservations when a local functionary demanded that he salute the flag
before receiving public assistance for his family. In the only such case
to reach the Arkansas Supreme Court, the conviction was upheld in
a 5–2 decision.

David R. Dewberry focuses on an incident near Lake Ouachita
when an environmental activist was distributing pamphlets critical
of an expanded lease agreement between the U.S. Army Corps of
Engineers and Mountain Harbor Resort. Chris Burch was arrested
for distributing the pamphlet in violation of regulations, although he
eventually prevailed in federal court when the policy was declared
unconstitutional. The story details the suppression of speech under
government regulations and private actions, but Dewberry also illu-
minates a perhaps larger conflict involved when government property
is leased to private individuals, unrestrained by the First Amendment.

Ryan Gliszinski tells a fascinating story that began when Wayne
Nichols raised a one-finger salute to Arkansas state trooper Jose Charon
in an oncoming vehicle. Charon issued a citation to Nichols for disorderly conduct, but Nichols was found not guilty because his exercise
of expressive conduct did not constitute "fighting words." Nichols then
filed a civil suit against Charon for deprivation of his First Amendment
rights under 42 U.S.C. § 1983. Gliszinski focuses on the legal storytelling
and the narrative of the federal trial in which Nichols prevailed.

The last three essays explicate stories grounded in the religion
clauses of the First Amendment. In an essay from his master's thesis
that takes a longer view of the theme regarding the public school curriculum, Matthew McNair traces the political and constitutional history of efforts in Arkansas from the banning of evolution in the 1920s
through later efforts to require the teaching of "creation science" and
"intelligent design." His recreation of the arguments through extensive interviews with key participants reveals the ongoing tendency by
public figures to breach the boundaries of the establishment clause.

Afsaneh N. Roe also examines an establishment clause case, one
involving the Gravette Public Schools and the longtime tradition of
offering Bible stories and religious instruction during school hours.

She recounts the arguments of the school officials and community leaders for continuing the practice and ignoring the constitutional rights voiced by a minority, making clear that the normative devotion to freedom of religion seldom considers the implications of subtle establishment. Even when the plaintiffs prevailed in federal court, the school and community continued to pursue a subterfuge to continue Bible story time.

The final essay by Kattrina Baldus Jones looks at a contemporary conflict between ministers arguing the protection of the free exercise clause of the First Amendment against the challenges to the nonprofit status of churches under the Internal Revenue Code. While neither of the two instances she examines have resulted in litigation, the public statements and interview comments make clear that the two Arkansas ministers believe the political messages from their pulpits should be considered protected speech.

These essays are essentially narratives with important characters contesting the basic premises of the First Amendment. In that sense, Judge Arnold once said, "The Constitution, grand as it was, was just a piece of paper. It had to be brought to life by practice in order to become a living plan of government."[5] These essays tell stories that bring the First Amendment to life and are important because they connect law to the human experience.

Stories give life to the First Amendment, and both students in the classroom and the larger audience can learn from and appreciate the lessons of the First Amendment in everyday life. As evidenced by the stories presented in this book, the First Amendment is not a self-executing document. The locus of power reveals a significant advantage for institutional actors who can and often do ignore the commands of the Constitution until called to account by an independent judiciary. Yet, as clearly shown in these stories, individuals must muster the resources to assert their First Amendment rights, and even if successful the financial and social cost is often great and vindication often comes after the opportunity for effective speech has passed. Those are stories that need to be told and lessons that need to be shared. This book does that and honors the legacy of Judge Richard Arnold, the essence of the First Amendment, and the efforts of the students who recorded and framed these important stories of contested First Amendment freedoms.

NOTES

1. Polly J. Price, *Judge Richard S. Arnold: A Legacy of Justice on the Federal Bench* (Amherst, NY: Prometheus Books, 2009), 225. Chapter 9 of this volume includes a review of Judge Arnold's First Amendment opinions, 225–50.

2. William J. Brennan Jr., "Preface: A Tribute to Chief Judge Richard S. Arnold," *Minnesota Law Review* 78 (1995): 1–2.

3. Richard S. Arnold, "Madison Lecture: How James Madison Interpreted the Constitution," *New York University Law Review* 72 (1997): 270.

4. Ibid., 269.

5. Ibid., 271.

CHAPTER 1

Pickings v. Bruce

Students United for Rights and Equality

PAULA KILLIAN AGEE

THE UNITED STATES came into a new world in the decade between 1960 and 1970. For the first time, television brought us history as it was being made. The presidential debates, Neil Armstrong's first step on the moon, Martin Luther King's I Have a Dream speech were made real for the average American. Tragedies like the assassinations of John F. Kennedy, Malcolm X, Martin Luther King Jr., and Robert F. Kennedy were covered by news media and explored in ways no newspapers could. The passing of the Civil Rights Act, integration of public schools and colleges, demonstrations, sit-ins, bombings, and marches were dissected on the nightly newscast. All this information left the public with a personal connection and relevance that was fresh, authentic, and troublesome.[1]

The late 1960s were a volatile time in the hearts of young men and women who struggled with a lack of social justice, a lack of rights and equality, and a lack of honor and respect for the draft and the Vietnam War. Just as the hearts of young men and women were torn so was America torn. Joe Neal was born into an all-American family who took their commitment to military service as seriously as their Christian faith.[2] For generations, their loyalty had been resolute. Joe was a churchgoing member of ROTC until one day when he realized that the reports out of Vietnam could not be true. The truth therefore the trust was hauntingly gone. The lies tore at Joe's heart, as it ripped at the fabric of many American families and hacked at the foundation of this country. There was uncertainty and fear, courage and strength, right and wrong.

Nowhere was the unrest more evident than on college campuses across the United States. Dissent was escalating into frightening demonstrations, riots, and bombings. College administrators were nervous. Students were disillusioned and frustrated. The United States was now the first society in the history of the world with more college students than farmers.[3] The social base of reform had shifted away from workers to students, blacks, and women. In large numbers these bright young minds organized an opposition movement to redefine the dominant culture, to change the world. Like so many movements before them, they became a family, bound for support while they worked to get their message out through underground newspapers, pamphlets, speakers, popular press, and the evening news. It is a hard sell when you voice against the patriarchal norm, when you challenge your father's world.

For many including Joe Neal the issues of the Vietnam War and the civil rights movement were undeniably intertwined. Young black men were dying daily in Vietnam, fighting a war for countrymen who still excluded them from common life in the States. Schools in the South were being integrated by federal mandate. Blacks were challenging rules and customs of the local lunch counter and public transportation. There were numerous organizations with goals of education and change. Joe Neal and his wife at the time, Barbara, founded a local chapter of the Southern Student Organizing Committee (SSOC). The Neals lived out of their car traveling primarily to college campuses across Arkansas, to share an alternative view of the American way. Their message through film, pamphlets, and voice was not always welcomed or appreciated by school administrations or local government officials. This was not a violent, radical group. It was a low-key approach from a soft-spoken, clean-cut young man and his new bride.

The Constitution of the United States guarantees the individual's right to free speech and freedom to assemble. Stephen A. Smith argues that it was the intent of our founding fathers to offer this true liberty as a noble freedom.[4] When these fundamental rights were violated, the students embraced the establishments' rules and structure and went to court to equalize the power and to claim their rights. Examination of such a case, *Pickings v. Bruce* will expose the heart of freedom of expression, the right to assemble, and academic freedom .[5] John W. Johnson argues in his book, *The Struggle for Students Rights*, that court cases in general and the Tinker case specifically offer a "convenient window through which to observe revealing moments in a nation's overall history."[6] The Tinker Supreme Court case set precedent for students' freedom of expression just months before the Pickings case went to court. We will peek through this little-known window that *Pickings v. Bruce* chiseled out and discover some remarkable findings about power, character, and virtue and their effect on communication.

At first glimpse it is a most unexpected setting for such a remarkable case. When Dr. Jordan E. Kurland, assistant general secretary for the Association of American University Professors (AAUP), mentioned to Senator J. William Fulbright at a dinner in Washington, DC, that he had been in contact with his constituent, Imon Bruce, president of Southern State College (SSC), Magnolia, Arkansas, Fulbright was surprised. "Why would the AAUP bother itself with someone as insignificant as Bruce?" Fulbright asked. There were certainly bigger issues at larger institutions around the country. Kurland responded with "If you let the likes of Imon Bruce get away with violations then the big boys will run with it. You have to tend the small fires to avoid the forest fires."[7]

Magnolia, a small town in southern Arkansas with a population of 12,500 in 1968, was home to Southern State College with approximately 125 faculty members and a student population of 2,200 of which about 200 were black. Southern State accepted its first black student in 1962; however, it had no black faculty.[8] Magnolia was beginning to experience the turmoil associated with the times. On campus everyone drank from the same water fountain but in the Columbia County Court House, fountains were still marked "White Only" and "Colored." Doctors' offices still had separate waiting rooms designated as "White" and "Negro."[9] Unmarried students twenty-two years of age and younger were required to live on campus; women in dorms had a

curfew while the men did not; the boys and girls club was still segregated.[10] In the summer of 1968, a white Magnolia police officer intentionally shot and killed a black man rumored to be having an affair
with a white woman. As acknowledgment, the local chapter of the
NAACP organized a funeral march in which several SSC faculty and
students participated. In the fall, there was an alleged rape of a white
woman by a black man, which sent the black male students into hiding
for days. Like a shift in the atmospheric pressure before a storm, one
could feel a similar pressure, a storm was brewing: change was coming
to Magnolia.[11]

According to an article in the *Lafayette County Democrat*,
"Approximately 90 members of SURE (Students United for Rights
and Equality) attended an organizational meeting on October 28,
1968."[12] Officers elected were Earnest Pickings as president; Talmadge
Davis, vice president; Carolyn Gaylord, secretary; and Brenda Morris,
treasurer.[13] There were seventeen faculty members including faculty
advisors Nik Hagler and Kenton Stellwagon. The article goes on to
state that it was the largest student group on campus. SURE adopted
five main purposes:

> To provide an organized program of leadership and par-
> ticipation among representatives of all races, nationalities, and
> religions;
> To provide service to the college to assist in realization of
> its goals;
> To stimulate closer relationships among members of all
> races, nationalities, and religions;
> To provide members an opportunity to develop philosophies
> regarding human relations; and,
> To provide recognition for members for contributions in
> assisting SURE to fulfill its purposes.

Earnest Pickings remembers a warm, supportive group of friends
that wanted to make the "university experience relevant to us." They
were searching to fill a void left by the student associations on campus. Pickings recalls, "Inclusion: we (SURE) were about including
everyone, whites, blacks, students from Massachusetts, New York,
other states, even other countries. We were about having fun and listening to other ideas like leaders in civil rights. We weren't looking

for trouble. The crisis was created from the administration."[14] While this appears to be an admirable objective, it was an offense to the administration of Southern State College. Integration on campus was mandated but socialization was not acceptable. Those who interacted with other races were considered as outsiders and treated as such. Yet, Don Baldridge, an SSC history professor, Donald Hays, a student, and others willingly helped establish a local grocery cooperative in the "negro-section" of town. Baldridge, who was an experienced electrician, spent his spare time wiring the building.[15] It was Magnolia's only black grocery store.

On Sunday, December 8, 1968, five black female students attempted to worship at College View Baptist Church where they had been previously welcomed. The church pastor, the Reverend James Schoenrock, as quoted in several newspaper articles, told them that his church was "unprepared for integration now" and offered them transportation to any other church they would like to attend.[16] The students worked in a college cafeteria and needed to be close to campus in order to walk back for work. The church's rejection was topic of discussion at the SURE meeting on December 12, 1968. One of SURE's primary purposes was the promotion of social understanding and human rights; therefore, SURE directed the public relations committee chair, Steven Bouley, to write a letter of inquiry.[17] Reverend Schoenrock did not respond to the letter but contacted President Bruce instead.[18]

Four days later, President Bruce summoned Mr. Bouley and faculty advisors Stellwagon and Hagler to his office and demanded they resign from SURE. Bruce followed up with a memorandum to the staff and faculty that was widely circulated on campus and became known as the "Black Face memorandum." The next day, the president of the local NAACP, Travis Tucker, requested that Governor Winthrop Rockefeller investigate the "grossly offensive" language of President Bruce and questioned Bruce's competence in dealing with race issues.[19] Bruce's memorandum in part said:

> I realize that there are people who have convinced some of our
> youth that a black face is a free admission ticket to any place or
> program and some think it is a license for uncouth behavior
> and even unlawful conduct. I hope that you who are members
> of this organization will use your influence to see that the group

limits its activities to this campus and serves the purposes of the
organization rather than building up racial unrest, suspicion, and
antagonism.[20]

Ozell Sutton, Governor Rockefeller's former butler and director
of the Arkansas Council on Human Relations who would later serve
as the regional director of the Community Relations Services of the
United States Department of Justice, approached his visit to SSC and
Dr. Bruce with resolve: "I have [seen] these kinds of situations my
whole life. It is with one of my assets and my problems for I have the
mind of Esther.'I will go and see the King. If I perish, I perish.'"[21] Mr.
Sutton recalls: "I got in my car and drove from Little Rock to Magnolia
and tried to do some mediation with the case. I didn't get very far with
the president of the college. This was not a big case and it was one of
so many cases, in so many places, and [there were] so many issues of
desegregation and discrimination that took priority. This was a minor
thing compared to what was going on in Arkansas at the time, like
the public school desegregation." Mr. Sutton's resources—his time, his
energy, his abilities—were the lump sum of the black community's
resource in the governor's mansion. "There were definitely limited
resources. As far as the governor's office, the only one who was concerned about it was me; the only one to spend any time on it was me;
and there was not too much public pressure on that case."

Mr. Tucker said he and the NAACP were disappointed but
acknowledged Sutton's visit yet feared nothing would be done. "A man
came down and talked," Tucker said to a reporter from the *Arkansas
Gazette*, "He said that it was politics and that he thought it would be
dealt with politically and not on whether it was right or wrong."[22] Mr.
Tucker was familiar with the bureaucracy and frustrations of dealing
with government. Don Baldridge remembers Tucker admirably, "He
had more guts than anyone I ever knew."[23] Baldridge and Tucker had
both received threatening phone calls concerning the grocery co-op.
When the mayor and city council offered no police protection, Tucker
looked them in the eye and reminded them that while the black community had but one grocery to burn, whites had several. Police protection followed.

Health, Education, and Welfare (HEW) planned an investigation into the SSC situation.[24] Bruce contended that HEW had planned to visit all colleges and universities to verify their compliance with the recent civil rights legislation. "Quite often, the colleges that are investigated first are the ones that have made the greatest effort and progress toward satisfactory integration," Bruce is quoted as saying to a reporter for the *Bray*.[25] After the investigation, Robert Finch, HEW secretary, sent a letter to Dr. Bruce stating: "I hope at the same time you will take the opportunity to review university policy and regulations with regard to student participation in campus affairs in order to guarantee that in maintaining order on the campus that the right of legitimate and responsible dissent is fully protected." The SSC Board of Trustees announced in late April 1969 that SSC would fully comply with the HEW Appropriation Act.[26]

Mary Towns, a student at SSC, wrote a letter to the editor of the *Bray* in which she pointed out that SSC did not have one black instructor on the faculty.[27] "We demand complete integration of this school system, not partial. We, the black students, see no reason why a Black instructor has to be super-qualified because he's Black—except maybe because of the Southern tradition—prejudice." Dr. Bruce objected to the use of the word "demand." According to Ms. Towns, Bruce threatened her with suspension unless she retracted the letter.[28] Her retraction was published in the *Bray* on December 20. She corrected that she only spoke for herself and not as a spokesperson for all black students. She cited Webster's definition for the word "demand": to claim as due, just or fit; or to call for as useful or necessary."[29] Towns also claims that Dr. Bruce deleted a portion of the letter before submitting it to the *Bray*, which read: "The choice to write this letter is not mine.[30] It was an alternative to being suspended from classes."[31] Under oath, Bruce admits to "editing" Ms. Towns's letter.[32] Baldridge remembers Towns as a "firebrand." "Not many were willing to stand up to Bruce. He had an overbearing, dictatorial attitude. She was really impressive. She couldn't have weighed eighty pounds."[33] There are many stories about black students being threatened with a loss of their work-study positions, which in effect would terminate their college career. Earnest Pickings, president of SURE, was denied a job as a dormitory counselor after he had previously been promised the job.[34]

When classes resumed in January, SURE proposed that President

Bruce deny the use of college facilities or equipment to any group on or off campus that failed to admit all students on a completely open and equitable basis. Bruce never acknowledged the proposal directly but responded in the SSC student newspaper, the *Bray*, with an accusation that "SURE had disrupted peaceful integration on campus."[35] President Bruce remarked that the members of SURE have not tried successfully to further good will between all students, regardless of race.

Professor James L. Meikle described himself to the investigating committee of the AAUP as "a non-militant integrationist, more in a pragmatic vein than in an idealistic one."[36] He had been active in the community, writing a letter to the national headquarters of the Boys and Girls Club inquiring about the Magnolia branch that continued to be segregated. Several months later, Meikle heard from an administrator in Dallas that national headquarters was aware of the situation but had no control over it. The next day, the college lost its contract with the Boys and Girls Club for internship work with students in the physical education department. President Bruce severely criticized Meikle and the other two professors who authored the letter for "embarrassing" the college.

Professor Kenton W. Stellwagon was hired as an instructor of organ. He was involved with the local chapter of the NAACP, lived in the "negro section" of Magnolia, and became openly and actively associated with the black community. Professor Stellwagon was one of the first faculty advisors to SURE.[37]

On January 11, 1969, Professor Stellwagon and Professor James L. Meikle traveled to Little Rock for a meeting with Otto Zinke, president of the AAUP Arkansas conference. The state AAUP investigation and subsequent letter to President Bruce criticizing the lack of due process in asking the two faculty advisors to resign from SURE and for his demanding Mary Towns retract her letter to the editor was not well received. On the seventeenth, Meikle and Stellwagon were notified their appointments would not be renewed. No grounds for non-reinstatement were ever given even when accompanied by his lawyer, Burl Rotenberry, to a board of trustees March 20 meeting.[38] Rotenberry, Baldridge, Hays, Pickings, and others who were involved as well as the investigation by AAUP suspect or are convinced that the primary reason for Meikle's and Stellwagon's lack of reinstatement stem from their involvement with SURE and the black community in Magnolia. The administration seemed to be on a mission. These were not the only instructors to lose their job during Bruce's tenure.

An extensive article in the *Arkansas Democrat* on February 9 titled "Academic Freedom Is in Dispute at SSC" reviews and criticizes the administration's handling of several issues: a church's rejection of integration; SURE; Mary Towns's letter; the Black Face memo; investigations by Rockefeller's staff, HEW, and AAUP; and Meikle's and Stellwagon's non-reinstatement. Dr. Bruce defends his actions in the closing three paragraphs. A few days later a letter to the editor of the *Democrat* signed only as an "SSC Student" criticized the accuracy and fairness of the previous article for giving "Southern State College a black-eye" and for devoting 35 inches of type to build a case against Dr. Bruce and the school and only 4 inches in its defense. Professors Baldridge and Calhoun defended SURE in a letter to the editor.[39] This letter was one of the administration's justifications for charges of unprofessional behavior and disloyalty against Dr. Bruce later in the spring. The letter confronts each charge the "student" had made and concluded with:

> Finally, as to the charge that 35 of the 39 inches of type in the *Democrat*'s article are used to build a case against Dr. Bruce, we can only say that Dr. Bruce had done 35 of the 39 inches of talking about the matter—without ever consulting the Negro students involved while we have not been granted a voice in either the campus paper or the President's newsletter. If this has given Southern State College a black eye, we suggest you look to a source other than SURE for the fist.

SURE's officers and faculty advisors wrote a letter to the editor of the *Bray* questioning the tenets of responsible, ethical journalism.[40] The letter went on to highlight SURE's varied pursuits including survey work conducted for the City of Magnolia, a dance, an educational documentary film, President Bruce's address on his conception of the role of responsibility of students, tutoring program preparation, and aiding a wheelchair-bound student up and down stairs in order to attend class. While not seeking commendation, they asked that SURE be treated equally and fairly. The letter ended with "How the program

outlined above supports the charge that SURE is responsible for dete-
rioration in racial progress, we leave for others to explain."

SURE invited Joe and Barbara Neal, representatives of the
Southern Student Organizing Committee (SSOC), to show a film,
Southern Political and Economic Structure and Its Relation to Racism,
on the SSC campus. The day before the event Dr. Bruce insisted that
Dr. Donald C. Baldridge and Professor John C. Calhoun, the new faculty advisors for SURE, cancel the invitation. Baldridge and Calhoun
carried the directive back to the officers of SURE but all agreed to
ignore the demand. As scheduled, March 20, 1968, the Neals came to
campus, showed their film, and delivered a soft-spoken message for
a few minutes without incident.[41] Bruce cited his concerns because
the Neals had been arrested for trespass on the Henderson College
campus in Arkadelphia, Arkansas, just up the road a few weeks prior.
The next morning, Dr. Bruce fired off a memo to the board of trustees recommending SURE should be barred. On March 24, 1969, SSC
banned SURE and revoked its charter[42] in spite of support from the
Student Senate.[43]

Professor Baldridge, a native of Idaho, had always been somewhat of an outsider in Magnolia but now some relationships were
awkward and strained. Don Hays suspects some were embarrassed
by their own inaction and some feared the commitment to stand with
him.[44] Although on February 17 President Bruce told the trustees that
despite Professor Baldridge's involvement with the controversy, he
intended to retain him on the faculty. Baldridge had been commended
the past two years for his excellence in the performance of his teaching
duties. Many shared Bruce's regard for Baldridge then and now. Burl
Rotenberry, Don Hays, Earnest Pickings, and James Willis continue to
speak very highly of Baldridge's intellect, character, and commitment.

Baldridge's wife, a secretary in the nursing school, was told she
would not be needed the following school year suspiciously without
cause.[45] The only difference this year, according to Baldridge, is his
position as student advisor to SURE after two other advisors had been
forced to resign by the administration.[46] On April 15, Professor William
C. Nolan, Baldridge's supervisor, sent a memo to L. A. Logan stating
three charges of unprofessional conduct: violating the president's
directive to cancel the Neals' appearance; his letter to the *Arkansas*

Democrat was misleading and discredited SSC; and insufficient progress toward completion of his dissertation in spite of $10,000 support
to do so.[47] Bruce received this memo on April 16 and proposed for
the matter to be considered by a faculty committee. Baldridge was
given a three-sentence notice that his contract would not be renewed
but did not specify when he was being dismissed. Students wore
black armbands to mourn the death of academic freedom.[48] Attorney
Burl Rotenberry and an AAUP representative were allowed to attend
the closed hearing granted Baldridge, not the public hearing he had
requested.[49] Rotenberry called this "an outright reprisal and retaliation for the lawsuit to which he (Baldridge) was a party and because
of his involvement and association with SURE."[50]

On April 3, 1969, Burl Rotenberry filed suit on behalf of SURE
against SSC in United States District Court, Western District of
Arkansas, El Dorado Division asking that "the court dissolve the suspension of its charter, to instruct the administration from imposing
sanctions on the organization, and to declare that its past actions had
been lawful and constitutionally permissible."[51] On May 26, the hearing began in Judge Oren Harris's court.[52] During a brilliant opening
statement delivered without a note, by W. Haywood Burns,[53] NAACP
Defense Fund, the courtroom was hushed and the judge mesmer-
ized. Burns was already an exceptional orator. Rotenberry and Burns
shared the floor until Burns returned to New York. The testimonies
continued for a total of five long days as Rotenberry remembers it.

Steven Bouley, who had written the letter to College View Baptist
Church, returned from New Bedford, Massachusetts, to testify as
one of the founding members of SURE. He said that SURE was not
associated with the SDS or the SSOC. Bouley said that he had been
threatened by Bruce with suspension his final semester at SSC if he did
not resign as chairman of the Public Relations Committee of SURE.[54]
Stellwagon testified Bruce directed him to resign from SURE because
he "didn't know how to deal with Southern Negroes."[55]

Earnest Pickings, described by the *Arkansas Gazette* as twenty-one,
Negro, and president of SURE, testified that he had been denied a
job at the college because he disagreed with official college policy on
campus speakers. Pickings continued that he had been told that SURE
lost its charter because of its off-campus activities; however, it had

been commended for its help with a survey of low-income areas of Magnolia.

Don Hays, a student and plaintiff in the case, testified that Bruce told him if SURE caused any trouble on campus, it would be the Negro students who would suffer and as a "responsible white student" to tell the Negroes that this would happen.[56] At the close of final arguments without taking a recess, Judge Harris gave an oral opinion dismissing the complaint without prejudice. He said that the group (SURE) did not have the same rights as individuals and that there was no evidence that the college practiced racial discrimination. Mr. Rotenberry asked for clarification, and Harris repeated that the case was dismissed.[57]

On the way out of the courtroom, Mr. Rotenberry was stopped by a radio reporter who asked for his reaction. He said he and his clients were, of course, disappointed. The reporter pursued with questions about appealing. Mr. Rotenberry confirmed that they would indeed appeal the judgment. The decision to appeal had been made when they began the trial, insinuating that they did not anticipate that the court would hear the case without prejudice. It was later repeated to Rotenberry that Judge Harris had heard the interview on the radio and had threatened to find him in contempt of court.[58]

At the end of the spring semester 1969, SSC reinstated SURE's charter.

In July 1969, the Arkansas Advisory Committee to the U.S. Commission on Civil Rights said that the SSC administration had been discriminatory in its treatment of SURE.[59] The committee found that Dr. Bruce had made unwarranted assumptions against SURE and recommended that HEW investigate further the policies and practices of SSC "as they affect students in a racial minority and those who choose to work and associate with them." Other recommendations included that the administration should provide written guidelines for formation of student organizations and give the students a voice in student-faculty committees and in discussions of the college curriculum.[60]

The Arkansas State Advisory Committee to the United States Commission on Civil Rights recommended that all state-supported colleges and universities require all campus-related organizations to adopt a broad antidiscrimination policy. The state committee urged

Governor Rockefeller to work with trustees to formulate a uniform state policy that would assure students the rights guaranteed citizens by the First Amendment to the Constitution.[61]

The United States Court of Appeals for the Eighth Circuit, St. Louis, heard the appeal of *Earnest Pickings et al., v. Imon E. Bruce et al.*, before Vogel, Heaney, and Bright, circuit judges.[62] On August 6, 1970, the appellate court reversed on First Amendment grounds. Interpretation of the court:

> Students and teachers retain their rights to freedom of speech, expression and association while attending or teaching at a college or university. They have the right to express their views individually or collectively with respect to matters of concern to a college or to a larger community. They are neither required to limit their expression of views to the campus or to confine their opinions to matters that affect the academic community only. It follows that here the administrators had no right to prohibit SURE from expressing these views. Such statement may well increase the tensions within the College and between the College and the community but this fact cannot serve to restrict freedom of expression.

This was one of the first cases to cite *Tinker v. Des Moines Independent Community School District* in which Judge Abe Fortas stated in his judgment that "It can hardly be argued that either students or teachers shed their constitutional right to freedom of speech or expression at the schoolhouse gate. While the Tinker case involved high school students, the precedent was effective." In the *Creighton Law Review*, the author highlights the Eighth Circuit's notation that students may "express their views individually or collectively with respect to matters of concern to a college or to a larger community." Support for the collective voice of students was what set the SURE case apart.

The administration claimed after the fact that its real concern with the Neals' appearance on campus was one of safety. Bruce began his defense of censorship shortly after the Neals' visit to campus.[63] He tried to link SURE to outside interests, namely the Students of a Democratic Society (SDS), described by the *Gazette* as a militant leftist group. The *Wall Street Journal* reports that Bruce "was upset because SDS literature appeared on campus last fall when SURE was organizing, along with strangers on campus 'whose appearance is what we'd call hippy.'"[64] No member of SURE admits to any association with the SDS or any other outside organization. The court states:

> The administrators could reasonably conclude no more than: that the Neals' appearance would expose the students and faculty to the militant views of a couple that was seeking substantial change in race relations and that these views would be apt to exacerbate the tensions between the College and the community; and that these views would be apt to provoke discussions between students and encourage them to action. These conclusions, however, do not justify an infringement of First Amendment rights.[65]

In addition, the court states that the fear of the administration was not based on any experience at SSC, because the campus remained completely peaceful, "free of incidents involving interference with the rights of students or faculty and that school officials made no showing that tensions could reasonably have been expected to explode into aggressive, disruptive action."[66]

The press gave little coverage to the SURE victory in the appellate court except to interview Dr. Bruce, who claimed that the court of appeals had erred but that SSC would not appeal because it had already made the changes the court ordered:[67] "SURE suspension and probation must be removed and any existing orders or directives prohibiting students or faculty from holding office or serving as an advisor of SURE must be rescinded."[68]

An editorial in the *Bray* observes that there are no clear winners and that while SURE won the case legally, "no changes have or are expected to occur as a result of the decision."[69] It goes on to question the expense of the trial: $8,000 for SSC plus twelve faculty members contributed forty hours each in answering questions and taking part in the hearings. They ask, "Was the case, then, worth the effort?" They conclude not.

That spring semester, SSC offered a new class in Literature by Blacks to its curriculum in "recognition of its failure in the past to include the contribution of black Americans to the building of America."[70] This

was the fifth course offered in black culture at SSC, and some consideration was being given to eventually offering a minor in the field.

In the 1970–1971 AAUP Investigative Report of Committee A, the
committee concluded that "a healthy climate of academic freedom, as
academic freedom is generally understood in American higher education, will not exist for faculty members at Southern State College until
there is basic recognition by the administration of the right to criticize
and to dissent." Every year between 1971 and 1994 the AAUP committee continued to report very little progress at SSC toward recommendations for revisions or redress that resulted in twenty-three years
of consecutive censure. Through President Bruce's tenure, little or no
progress was made in spite of a few gestures by President Bruce and
a stated willingness to cooperate with the AAUP. Associate General
Secretary Jordan E. Kurland traveled to Magnolia in August of 1972
to confer with President Bruce and with officers of the local AAUP
chapter. Dr. Kurland remembers much about the trip including Dr.
Bruce's patent stance and his white patent-leather shoes.[71]

Upon Dr. Bruce's retirement in 1979, there was hope at the AAUP
that there could be a more cooperative environment with the new
president, Harold T. Brinson. In the May 1980 Committee A report,
it is noted that the SSC Board of Trustees refused to pay any financial restitution. The AAUP continued to work with SSC in hopes of
persuading the board to modify its position and resolve the issue. In
1984, President Brinson reiterated that "the governing board is hostile
to any expenditure of funds on the matter." The AAUP continued to
communicate with President Brinson. Some years, he would return
the courtesy, some not.

The five members of the board of trustees at SSC were appointed
and often reappointed for decades by the governor with a great deal
of input from the president of the college.[72] Southern State had previously been a boarding high school. Many of the same patriarchal,
heavy-handed disciplines remained. Dr. John Wilson, chairman of the
board of trustees, stated that the "Board largely relied upon President
Bruce (whom he identified as his college classmate) and Professor
Childers (who taught him as a student at Southern State College)."[73] Of
the five board members, two were next-door neighbors of Dr. Bruce;
another had immediate access to former governor Orval Faubus and

was politically very powerful. These board members were privileged, "cut from the same cloth," and part of the good-ole-boy network that they represented well. One of the problems with a small board and lengthy tenure is that cohesiveness interferes with progress.

Conflict is "an expressed struggle between at least two independent parties who perceive incompatible goals, scarce resources, and interference from others in achieving their goals."[74] These parties were in conflict over power and control. Bruce and the board of trustees had it. Members of SURE wanted it: the power of academic freedom, freedom of speech, freedom to assemble. Don Hays wrote, "They were the enemy, the men who wore the suits and did their damnedest to hold the line for institutionalized racism."[75] The members of SURE attempted to bring balance with the strength of numbers: they were the largest student group on campus. They tried with the might of the press through letters to the editor and interviews with the few reporters willing to talk with them. Ultimately, they decided to equalize that imbalance of power by adding the weight and strength of the Constitution of the United States of America to their end of the rope in this tug-of-war battle.

SURE suffered casualties: at least three professors lost their jobs; members were ostracized; Oren Harris mislaid the blindfold of justice. In due course, they won their war at St. Louis, in the Eighth Circuit Court of Appeals. There are things worth the fight. One begins with, "We hold these truths to be self-evident, that all men are created equal . . ."[76] The brave souls of SURE took up their fight equipped with the armaments of the First and Fourteenth Amendments. They emerged better human beings with a bond forged by their shared experience.

Could they have won another way? I think they tried. It appears that the leader of the opposition was as hard-headed, cranky, and surly as reported. Imon Bruce, like many college presidents, considered this a personal attack on his authority. He felt betrayed. He hated the embarrassment for the institution and for himself. He clinched his dictatorial ways with self-righteousness. With the help of free or cheap legal defense, the NAACP Legal Defense Fund in this case subsidized Burl Rotenberry and flew Haywood Burns in for a few days during trial, there were victories. Federal judges granted students the right to hear controversial speakers, the right to demonstrate peaceably, and the right to due process.[77] Historically, institutions like SSC and men like Bruce won these battles. Some still do.

AAUP was encouraged in 1992 with the naming of a new president at what is now called Southern Arkansas University, Magnolia. Under Dr. Steven G. Gamble's leadership new regulations and policy of tenure and promotion were adopted and written in a new faculty handbook and discussion of a financial settlement occurred. In 1994, twenty-three years after the AAUP first censured SSC, Professor Donald C. Baldridge received redress for $9,000 and Professor James L. Meikle received $1,000. Baldridge said, "It was never about the money." Nevertheless, it must have been sweet to get retribution. No interest, no accounting for inflation, sweet just the same.

> I can't tell you it isn't thrilling to take center stage—not only to "put your body on the line," as the civil rights movement told us, but to watch the authorities react to you, to celebrate the almost sinful pleasure of being right, to see people surge into your ranks, to feel that your analysis penetrates to the heart of things. The lore isn't wrong: The sixties were thrilling. That's one reason why we grizzled types get a hazy look in our eyes when we reminisce. It's not that we're trying to remember, or to forget. Never mind all the ironical defenses we've fashioned to protect ourselves from the burning flares of hope that we once harbored in a past too far gone to retrieve but for little shards of memory. Look at the miserable state of the world! Why shouldn't we feel pained at the yawning gap between the grandest ideals of our youth and the bitter world we actually live in?[78]

Pickings v. Bruce, affectionately referred to as the "SURE case" by those who were involved, was a defining moment for people like Don Baldridge, Earnest Pickings, Buddy Rotenberry, and Don Hays. Dr. Baldridge compared it to "doing battle with the forces of evil."[79] Dr. Hays said it most succinctly, "We were all going through the same thing. We were under a lot of pressure. We all knew that we could be kicked out of school. Any violation was just so much fun. It was that clear. I don't know that it ever has been again for me. It absolutely, anything that mattered, absolutely, (he touched his chest), right was here and wrong was there (as he pointed across the room). It was just as clear as it could be."[80]

NOTES

1. For a history of media and the civil rights movement, see Todd Gitlin, *The Whole World Is Watching: Mass Media in the Making and Unmaking of the New Left* (Berkeley: University of California Press, 1980); Hunter James, *They Didn't Put That on the Huntley-Brinkley!* (Athens: University of Georgia Press, 1993); and Katharine Whittemore and Gerald Marzoratti, eds., *Voices in Black and White: Writings on Race in America from* Harper's Magazine (New York: Franklin Square Press, 1993).

2. Joe Neal, telephone interview with author, November 3, 2006.

3. Gitlin, *The Whole World Is Watching*, 1980.

4. Stephen A. Smith, "The Origins of the Free Speech Clause," *Free Speech Yearbook* 29 (1991): 48–84.

5. *Pickings v. Bruce*, 430 F.2d 595 (8th Cir. 1970). Brief for Appellees, National Archives and Records Administration, Central Plains Region, Kansas City, Missouri, Box 30, Book 83, Volume 13.

6. John W. Johnson, *The Struggle for Student Rights: Tinker v. Des Moines and the 1960s* (Lawrence: University Press of Kansas, 1997). *Tinker v. Des Moines School District*, 393 U.S. 503 (1969).

7. Dr. Jordan E. Kurland, assistant general secretary for the Association of American University Professors, telephone interview with author, November 21, 2006.

8. Leo Kanowitz, O. Lawrence Burnette Jr., and Bobby N. Corcoran, "Academic Freedom and Tenure: Southern State College (Arkansas)," *AAUP Bulletin* (Spring 1971): 40–49.

9. Donald Slaven Hays, associate professor of English, director of programs, Creative Writing, University of Arkansas, Fayetteville, interview by author, Fayetteville, Arkansas, November 14, 2006.

10. Kanowitz et al., "Academic Freedom and Tenure," 42–43.

11. Erma Hanson, Letter to the Editor, *Bray*, December 9, 1968: "request the appointment of a Black instructor. This will be a first on this campus, but it was also a first when the first Black student enrolled here; it was a first when the Civil Rights Bill of 1964 opened the doors of Southern educational facilities to Black students. The 'Old South' no longer exists, sectionalism is no longer the prominent issue, and the swinging banner of Dixie has been crushed. We are not speaking with the voices of militants, but with the concern that should be considered by all."

12. November 7, 1968.

13. *Lafayette County (AR) Democrat*, "Organizational Meet for SURE Held," November 7, 1968. Other sources state as many as two hundred members, one-third of which were black students.

14. Earnest Pickings, telephone interview by author, September 19, 2006.

15. Hays interview.

16. Magnolia, AR, SSC, *Bray*, "Black Students Turned Away by Local Church," and Delores Shepherd, Letter to the Editor, "Southern State Student Writes about Incident at Local Church," December 13, 1968, 1, 3; *Camden (AR) News*, "Our Church Is Not an Integrated Church and Our People Are Not Prepared for It," December 19, 1968; *Pine Bluff (AR) Commercial* (AP), "'Some' Unprepared, Pastor Says, Baptist Church Asks That Negros Leave," December 19, 1968.

17. Appendix.

18. *Arkansas Democrat*, "SURE Wins Court Ruling against SSC," August 13, 1969.

19. *Arkansas Gazette*, "NAACP Asks WR Probe in Southern State Protest," January 29, 1969; *Bray*, "Peaceful Integration Disrupted, Bruce Says," January 31, 1969.

20. Kanowitz et al., "Academic Freedom and Tenure," 44; *Camden News*, "Discrimination Charged: HEW to Investigate Southern State," January 29, 1969; *Arkansas Democrat*, "Academic Freedom Is in Dispute at SSC," February 9, 1969.

21. Ozell Sutton, telephone interview with author, November 30, 2006. In reference to the biblical figure Queen Esther is persuaded by Mordecai to intercede on behalf of the Jews who were being persecuted and to seek an audience with the king even at personal risk. Esther 4:16.

22. *Arkansas Democrat*, February 9, 1969; *Arkansas Gazette*, January 29, 1969; *Camden News*, January 29, 1969.

23. Donald Carl Baldridge, professor of history (retired), University of Idaho, Moscow, Idaho, telephone interview by author, October 26, 2006.

24. *Banner News*, Magnolia, Arkansas, "Investigation Possible on SSC Campus," January 29, 1969; *Arkansas Democrat*, February 9, 1969.

25. January 31, 1969.

26. Minutes of the Board of Trustees Meeting, Southern State College, April 22, 1969, including News Release, Letter from Robert Finch, Secretary of HEW, Washington, DC, March 22, 1969; *Smackover News* (AP), "Southern State College to Uphold HEW Rules," April 25, 1969; *Pine Bluff Commercial*, "HEW Requests Integration Increase," April 23, 1969; *Camden Democrat* (AP), "SSC to Follow HEW Rules," April 24, 1969; *Arkansas Gazette*, "Southern State to Comply with New HEW Regulations, April 23, 1969; *Banner News*, "Trustees Announce Intention to Comply with HEW Rulings," April 23, 1969.

27. December 9, 1968.

28. *Bray*, December 20, 1968; *Arkansas Democrat*, February 9, 1969.

29. Mike Bearden, *Bray*, "Dictionaries Prove Necessary to College Leaders," December 20, 1968.

30. *Arkansas Gazette*, "Motion to Kill SURE, SSC Suit Is Turned Down," May 27, 1969.

31. *Arkansas Democrat*, February 9, 1969.

32. *Arkansas Gazette*, "Motion to Kill SURE, SSC Suit Is Turned Down," May 27, 1969.

33. Baldridge interview.

34. *Pickings v. Bruce*, 430 F.2d 595 (8th Cir. 1970); *Camden News* (AP), "Dean Testified SURE Violated Its Charter," May 28, 1969; *Arkansas Gazette*, "Bruce Tells of Hearing about a Conversation concerning Plans to Disrupt the SSC Campus," May 28, 1969; Hays interview; Pickings interview.

35. January 21, 1969.

36. Kanowitz et al., "Academic Freedom and Tenure," 41.

37. Ibid., 43.

38. Minutes, Board of Trustees, SSC, March 20, 1969.

39. *Arkansas Democrat*, "Another View on SSC Disturbance," March 1, 1969.

40. Earnest Pickings, president; Carolyn R. Gaylord, secretary; Tal Davis, vice

president; Brenda Morris, treasurer; Donald C. Baldridge and John Calhoun, faculty advisors, February 28, 1969.

41. Hays interview.

42. *Arkansas Democrat* (AP), "SURE Charter Revoked by Southern State Dean," March 28, 1969; *Arkansas Gazette* (AP), "Charter of SURE Revoked by SSC," March 28, 1969; *Camden News* (AP), "Controversial Interracial Group: Southern State College Administration Suspends Charter of Student Group," March 28, 1969.

43. John Thurston, *Bray*, "SURE Receives Senate Backing," March 28, 1969.

44. Hays interview.

45. *Arkansas Gazette*, "Fired Teacher at SSC Asks Hearing, Cause," April 25, 1969; *Camden News* (AP), "Don Baldridge Plans to Resist: Southern State Professor Dismissed," April 24, 1969.

46. *Arkansas Democrat*, "Civil Rights Action Blamed: SSC Fires History Professor," April 24, 1969; *Arkansas Gazette* (UPI), "Faculty Adviser for SURE Fired by Southern State," April 24, 1969; *Camden News*, April 24, 1969.

47. Kanowitz et al., "Academic Freedom and Tenure," 44–48.

48. *Arkansas Gazette*, April 25, 1969.

49. *Banner News*, "Closed Hearing Held Tuesday," May 21, 1969; *Arkansas Gazette*, "Baldridge Gets Hearing on Dismissal; He's Told Not to Talk to Reporters," May 23, 1969.

50. Kanowitz et al., "Academic Freedom and Tenure," 44–48; *Arkansas Gazette* (UPI), "Letter, Suit Cited in Firing of Baldridge," May 14, 1969.

51. United States District Court, Western District of Arkansas, El Dorado Division, Civil No. ED-69-c-11, *Pickings v. Bruce*, Judge Oren Harris.

52. *Camden News* (AP), "Judge Harris to Hear Plea of SSC Professor," May 15, 1969.

53. Black civil rights activist (1941–1996), graduate of Harvard University and Yale Law School. Baldridge interview, Rotenberry interview, Hays interview.

54. *Arkansas Gazette*, May 27, 1969.

55. *Arkansas Gazette*, "Southern State Is Ordered to Reinstate SURE Chapter," August 14, 1970.

56. *Arkansas Gazette*, "Action on SURE by SSC Is Upheld," May 29, 1969.

57. Ibid.; *Banner News*, "Injunction Denied in SSC Case," May 29, 1969; *Banner News* (AP), "Judge Makes Decision in SURE Case," May 30, 1969; *Arkansas Gazette* (AP), "SURE Loses Bid for Order on Its Charter," May 30, 1969; *Smackover News*, "SURE Suit Is Dismissed," June 6, 1969.

58. Burl C. Rotenberry, attorney for SURE case, co-operating attorney with the NAACP Legal Defense and Education Fund, interviews with author, October 26, 2006, and November 2, 2006.

59. *Arkansas Gazette*, August 14, 1970.

60. Ibid.

61. *Arkansas Gazette*, "End Discrimination in Organizations, Colleges Are Urged," July 3, 1969.

62. *Pickings v. Bruce*, 430 F.2d 595 (8th Cir. 1970). Brief for Appellees, National Archives and Records Administration, Central Plains Region, Kansas City, Missouri, Box 30, Book 83, Volume 13.

63. *Arkansas Democrat* (AP), "Bruce Links SURE to Outside Interests," April 17,

1969; Sylvia Spencer, *Arkansas Gazette* (UPI), "College Officials Attempt to Link SURE with SDS," April 17, 1969; *Banner News*, "Bruce Says Students Being Used," April 18, 1969.

64. Herbert G. Lawson, "Courts & Campus: Some Students Find They Can Win Demands by Suing Their Schools," November 29, 1969.

65. *Pickings v. Bruce*, Court of Appeals. Kanowitz et al., "Academic Freedom and Tenure," 46.

66. *Creighton Law Review*, February 1999.

67. *Arkansas Gazette*, "Appeals Court Erred, Head of SSC Says," August 16, 1970; *Arkansas Democrat*, August 13, 1969; *Arkansas Gazette*, August 14, 1970; Janet Waters, *Bray*, "SSC Officials Not Surprised: Court of Appeals Reverses Decision in SURE Case," August 28, 1970.

68. *Pickings v. Bruce*, Court of Appeals.

69. "As We See It, SURE Case Sees Little Results," August 28, 1970.

70. *Arkansas Gazette*, "SSC to Offer New Class in Literature by Blacks for '70 Spring Semester," November 23, 1969.

71. Kurland interview.

72. James Willis, SSC historian, electronic mail received December 5, 2006.

73. Kanowitz et al., "Academic Freedom and Tenure," 48.

74. W. Wilmot and J. Hocker, *Interpersonal Conflict*, 6th ed. (Boston: McGraw Hill, 2001), 15.

75. Don Hays, electronic mail received November 30, 2006.

76. U.S. Constitution.

77. *Wall Street Journal*, November 25, 1969.

78. Todd Gitlin, *Letters to a Young Activist* (New York: Basic Books, 2003), 21.

79. Baldridge, telephone interview with author, November 30, 2006.

80. Hays interview.

CHAPTER 2

Neal v. Still

Unconstitutional Suppression
of Campus Speech

DAVID N. MORRIS

A major purpose of the First Amendment . . . is to pro-
tect the romantics—those who would break out of the
classical forms: the dissenters, the unorthodox, the out-
casts. The First Amendment's purpose and function in
the American polity is not merely to protect negative
liberty, but also affirmatively to sponsor the individu-
alism, the rebelliousness, the anti-authoritarianism,
the spirit of non-conformity within us all.

—STEVEN H. SHIFFRIN

JOE NEAL MIGHT seem an unlikely dissenter and champion of
the First Amendment. As an undergraduate student at the University
of Arkansas in 1967, he wore his Army ROTC uniform for his yearbook picture as a member of the Young Republicans Club.[1] His views,
and those of his generation, were shaped and altered by the military
adventure in Vietnam and its direct impact on the lives of young men

subject to being drafted to fight an unpopular war in a faraway land. By 1969, Neal became the state organizer for the Southern Student Organizing Committee (SSOC), an organization that promoted progressive positions on civil rights, union organizing, and opposition to the war in Vietnam.

The Vietnam Conflict era was a particularly interesting time for the exercise of First Amendment freedoms. There were innumerable protests against the war, and many of the participants in these protests were arrested by local authorities on a variety of charges. "On many predominantly white campuses, SSOC activists were the first outspoken proponents of such causes as university reform and desegregation, and they played the key role in popularizing these issues with the student body and pressuring administrators to institute reforms." For many white college students in the South, "becoming an activist was not a decision made lightly. Stepping 'outside the magic circle' and rejecting the dominant views of the white South required great courage, for these students knew that their activism could lead to the loss of friends, rejection by their families, and expulsion from school."[2]

One of these many arrests happened on February 21, 1969. Joe Neal and Barbara Wink Neal were arrested on the campus of Henderson State College in Arkadelphia, Arkansas. They were arrested, as the deputy prosecutor said, "on the 21 day of February, 1969, then and there did unlawfully and willfully create a disturbance in the Student Union Building of H. S. C. by the use of loud and offensive language and by distributing offensive literature designed to incite the emotions of the students of said campus, in violation of Ark. Statutes Section 41-1431 against the peace and dignity of the State of Arkansas."[3] Their arrest eventually lead to the Arkansas Supreme Court holding the statute under which they were arrested (Act 17 of 1958) to be unconstitutionally vague and violating the free-speech clause of the First Amendment.

In order to gain a better understanding of the importance of this ruling, it will be necessary to look at the details surrounding the Neals' arrest, their incarceration, and the legal proceedings that led up to their case's hearing before the Arkansas Supreme Court in addition to examining the history of Act 17 of 1958.

There has been much research on antiwar activity during the

Vietnam era; however, there has been little scholarly research regarding antiwar activism in the state of Arkansas, and this specific case has received mention only in a student essay based on newspaper accounts.[4] Consequently, this study is very important to the understanding of the Neals' case from an academic standpoint.

The purpose of this essay is to focus on the story of the arrest and subsequent trials as told by Joe Neal, Mort Gitelman, and Jim Guy Tucker. Neal was obviously a participant in the act that led to his arrest. Gitelman was the president of the Arkansas chapter of the American Civil Liberties Union at the time and helped the Neals obtain legal counsel via the ACLU, the first case taken by the state affiliate.[5] Tucker was the counsel retained for the Neals and represented them when the case went before the Arkansas Supreme Court.[6] Although attempts were made to obtain interviews with other participants and key players in these events, none of these interviews was possible.

Beginning with a brief overview of the history of the student antiwar movement during the Vietnam Conflict era, it then will take a brief look at the origins of Act 17 and the events leading up to its passage. After that, the focus is on three accounts of the story as told by Joe Neal, Mort Gitelman, and Jim Guy Tucker. This will provide a valuable first-hand perspective on these events as they transpired, but it also shows that oral history can provide varying accounts from the individual participants, so I have addressed them separately to emphasize the varying perspectives. Finally, the paper will analyze the aftermath of these events, employing the theories posited by Steven H. Shiffrin in *The First Amendment, Democracy, and Romance.*

During the Vietnam Conflict, there were many student groups both national and local on college campuses across the United States that organized to protest the war. Among these groups were the Students for a Democratic Society (SDS), the Weather Underground Organization (WUO), and the Southern Students Organizing Committee.

The exploits of the SDS and the WUO have been well documented in a number of scholarly texts.[7] The activities of the SSOC have been less documented but are covered extensively in the book *Struggling for a Better South: The Southern Student Organizing Committee, 1964–1969* by Gregg L. Michel.[8]

Although these texts highlight many of the important issues motivating the protests and their importance, none of them really draws
attention to the particular concerns about the rights of dissenters or
the other important First Amendment issues that the Neals' case does.

Act 17 of 1958

Ironically, Act 17 was the last of the laws enacted by the Arkansas
General Assembly in a special session in 1958 that was called by then
governor Orval E. Faubus to prevent desegregation of the Arkansas
schools and particularly at Little Rock Central High School.[9] Former
state senator Jerry J. Screeten of Hazen was the author of Act 17.

Act 17 made it a misdemeanor to enter school property "and while
therein or thereon . . . create a disturbance, or a breach of the peace, in
any way whatsoever, including, but not limited to, loud and offensive
talk, the making of threats or attempting to intimidate, or any other
conduct which causes a disturbance or breach of the peace or threatened breach of the peace."

Joe Neal

At the time of the incident, Joe Neal was a recent graduate of the
University of Arkansas, and he was active as a state traveler for the
Southern Students Organizing Committee, the Nashville-based civil
rights, antipoverty, and antiwar group. He traveled with Barbara Wink
Neal, corresponding secretary of the Arkansas SSOC, who was his
wife at the time. Barbara Neal, who was quoted extensively in the state
newspapers during the events, said that she and her husband were at
the campus at the invitation of a student, who had invited other interested students to talk with them, and they were talking quietly with a
group of white and black students when Dean Scifres arrived, accompanied by a police officer, and told them to leave, that "everything was
fine in Arkadelphia, that the Negroes there liked it and that the dean of
students had a complete open door policy to the students." However,
"we decided there was no reason we should sit there and talk to the
students about rights and then let ourselves be bullied out of town by
a threat." She said that the city policeman originally told them that

he was not arresting them but was going to escort them out of town. "So we told him that we were not ready to leave the Union until the students were ready to stop talking or until the Union closed. We were then told we were being arrested for 'refusing to obey an officer,' but we were later charged with 'creating a disturbance on school property.'"[10]

In an interview with the author in May 2006, thirty-seven years later, Neal remembered he was invited by a group of students to speak at the Henderson State College campus.[11] He was invited due to his involvement as a state traveler for the SSOC, which basically meant that he traveled to campuses to speak about the issues the SSOC advocated and to distribute literature promoting those views. Neal did not recall the specific individuals who invited him; he just remembered that they were loosely affiliated with the SSOC. As Neal recalls, the students that invited him to speak had requested beforehand to book a room for his presentation, but they had been denied by the Henderson administration. Because of this, the Neals and their audience met at the Student Union.

At the time of the incident the Neals had been showing an SSOC film about the bombing in North Vietnam in addition to distributing pamphlets and other literature. Neal recalls that there were approximately twenty students gathered on the evening in question, and, since the meeting had to occur in the Student Union, they weren't going to be able to show their film. As Neal recalls, they were just getting started with their meeting when Thomas Scifres, the dean of students, entered the Student Union and asked them to leave. At that time Neal told him that they weren't going to leave, because to his knowledge there was no law that prevented them from being on campus, and they weren't doing anything illegal. Scifres then told Neal that he was going to call the police. According to Neal he had known Scifres when he was an undergraduate at the University of Arkansas, because Scifres had worked as head resident in Yocum Hall when Neal was a resident of Yocum as a freshman. Neal said that he pointed this out to Scifres and that he responded that he didn't remember him.

According to the February 22, 1969, edition of the *Arkansas Democrat* some students had reported the meeting to the dean and consequently Patrolman David Hathcoat arrived on the scene and asked the Neals to leave, but that wasn't what Joe Neal recalled. He

stated that since the administration had denied the student request
for a room in which to meet that the administration obviously knew
they were coming and were concerned about their arrival.

Neal said that after he continually refused to leave the campus,
police were summoned. According to Neal, after he was asked to leave
he told the students that were present that if they could just be told
to shut up and go away they were wasting their time. The police told
Neal that they didn't have a right to be there because they were not
students. The police never cited Act 17 or any other specific law that
the Neals were in violation of but they simply said that they were
disturbing the peace.

Neal doesn't remember any other details beyond that and stated
that after they continually refused to leave the Student Union the police
placed him and Barbara under arrest and took them to the police station. Once he arrived at the jail, Neal states that he and Barbara were
separated, and he was taken to a room with five or six various police
officers, including a state trooper. He doesn't recall the names of any of
the officers but he said that the officers told him that he "might as well
admit that he was a member of the communist party." Neal denied this
accusation and could not believe that the officers were serious. He said
that the officers continually questioned him and accused him of being
a subversive. Neal said that he tried to remain as polite as possible
but that he was starting to get frightened and at that time one of the
officers said, "you know all we really have to do is open the door and
push you out the door and say you were trying to run away," implying
that the officers could have killed him and simply stated that he had
been shot while trying to escape custody.

While this was going on, Neal could hear Barbara screaming and
crying in another part of the police station. At the time he thought that
the police were attacking her, but it turned out that she was just being
questioned in the same way that he was and she was just screaming
and crying because she was frightened.

Eventually the police allowed Neal to make a phone call, at which
time he called Dr. Ben Drew Kimpel for help. Kimpel was a professor of
English at the University of Arkansas. Kimpel agreed to put up a property bond to secure the Neals' release and also contacted the Arkansas
chapter of the American Civil Liberties Union (ACLU) for assistance.
The president of the ACLU at the time was Mort Gitelman, who was a

professor of law at the University of Arkansas and whom Neal knew from his on-campus activism while attending the university.

Neal doesn't remember exactly how long he was in town, and I wasn't able to recover any documents that specified exactly how long he was in custody. Neal also doesn't really recall much after he was released. According to him, Jim Guy Tucker was brought in to represent him around the time of his hearing in municipal court, but he doesn't remember anything about it specifically. One thing that he does recall is his testimony in the municipal hearing. When the Neals were arrested, their pamphlets and literature were confiscated by the police. One of the pamphlets was entitled "The Student as Nigger," which was written by Jerry Farber and was very popular with antiwar activists at the time. Portions of this pamphlet were read to Neal and he was asked whether or not he agreed with the pamphlet. Neal responded that although he didn't agree with everything in the pamphlet that this situation sort of proved that some of the positions taken in the pamphlet were indeed true.

Neal also remembers that Judge J. E. Still, who heard their municipal case, was particularly hostile toward them. He didn't feel like there was any impartiality in the trial or that Judge Still really paid any attention to their actual testimony.

The Neals had previously made visits to other cities in the state such as Jonesboro, Conway, Little Rock, and Russellville for similar purposes and never had the trouble that they did in Arkadelphia. Neal believes that part of the reason he was greeted with such hostility is because the Henderson administration as well as the local law enforcement were concerned that radical extremists were trying to plant the seeds of sedition and communism in an attempt to overthrow the state of Arkansas and even the United States government. In reality, all the Neals were trying to do was to raise awareness and help bolster the antiwar sentiment among students. Police Chief Marvin Miller thought that was quite enough. "Mr. and Mrs. Neal were passing out leaflets at the HSC Student Union and their conversation was anti-ROTC (Reserve Officers Training Corps)," Miller said. "They were talking in terms of rebellion toward the faculty and this irritated some of the students, and they [the couple] were asked to leave by the Dean of Students."[12]

Neal also believes that if this particular incident hadn't happened that his trip to Arkadelphia wouldn't have had much of an impact, if any at all. He stated that if dissent isn't allowed to happen in the daylight then it happens in the darkness and it turns into a sort of explosion. He thinks that a few students might have organized and had an antiwar information network but beyond that nothing else would have really happened.

What actually did happen was a little more dramatic. After the incident, Joe Neal was very scared. Prior to these events he says that people had warned him of the dangers of going to smaller towns as an activist trying to raise awareness on issues that were not popular with the residents of these towns. He hadn't really seen any danger and wasn't concerned about it. After everything that happened during his detainment in Arkadelphia he came to believe that it *was* dangerous to go out to smaller towns as an activist. This was very discouraging for him and essentially ended his tenure as a state traveler for the SSOC. For a long time he didn't really feel safe leaving the city of Fayetteville.[13] He feels that if he hadn't had the connections that he had with Ben Kimpel and Mort Gitelman that his situation could have been much worse.

Yet, seemingly undeterred by the experience at Henderson State, Joe and Barbara Neal paid a campus visit to Southern State College in Magnolia in March 1969. Students United for Rights and Equality (SURE) invited them to attend the regular monthly meeting of SURE, to show an AFL-CIO-produced film, *The Face of the South*, and to discuss the film after it had been shown. President Imon Bruce learned of the invitation to the Neals on March 19, 1969, the day before the Neals were scheduled to speak. He decided that the Neals' appearance would substantially disrupt the educational functions of the college. President Bruce requested SURE's president and its two new faculty advisors to cancel the invitation, because "he had been told by the president of Henderson State College that they had 'created a disturbance' on that campus following an engagement there about two weeks earlier." They refused. On the following day, the Neals made their scheduled appearance, and there were no incidents related to their campus visit.[14] Later, Southern State College revoked SURE's status as a campus organization and dismissed its two faculty advisors, in part because the group had hosted the Neals. Donald Haefner, dean of students, later said that Southern State objected to the campus talk because the SSOC "advocates confrontation on a variety of issues, and suggests that students should take exception to official school policies." President Bruce also testified that "he feared there would be violence and property damage at the school."[15]

Neal wasn't really concerned about what happened after his municipal trial with regard to the appeal of his case to the Arkansas Supreme Court. He trusted Mort Gitelman and the people involved in the ACLU to do what was right but it wasn't a big concern. He wanted to see Act 17 overturned but that was definitely not his primary goal. He really had no major involvement in the appeal and subsequent overturning of his case. Even though the municipal ruling was over-turned, Neal didn't feel like he had accomplished anything and he felt numb about the whole situation. He was glad that the situation in his opinion had sort of been corrected, but he feels like the powers that be had really won because his speech was suppressed and he was basically intimidated out of doing the activism that he had previously been involved in.

Mort Gitelman

At the time of the incident, Mort Gitelman was the president of the Arkansas chapter of the ACLU and was a professor of law at the University of Arkansas.[16]

As Gitelman recalls, he received a phone call from Joe Neal on February 21, 1969, around 9:00 P.M. Neal informed him that he and his wife, Barbara, were arrested at the Henderson State College Student Union for passing out SSOC literature. Gitelman thought that this was a clear-cut ACLU-type free-speech issue so he agreed to try to find an attorney for Neal that was closer to Arkadelphia at the time. The following day he called Jim Guy Tucker, a former student of Gitelman's who had recently graduated and who was interested in the ACLU. At the time Tucker was working for the Rose Law Firm in Little Rock.

According to Gitelman, Tucker agreed to represent the Neals and a trial date had been set. Tucker called Gitelman shortly thereafter and said that he had a scheduling conflict with the trial date so he was going to contact W. H. "Dub" Arnold,[17] who was the prosecuting attorney, to see about changing the date. Arnold agreed but reneged on the agreement without informing Tucker and brought the Neals to court anyway. The case was heard by Judge J. E. Still,[18] who ruled against the Neals and fined them the maximum of $500 each and sentenced them to six months in jail. The imposition of the sentence was suspended on the condition that they not return to Arkadelphia.

Gitelman states that Tucker and his partners at the Rose firm were upset with Arnold for breaking his promise and that sort of galvanized Tucker to pursue the case. At the time there was no court of appeals so the case went directly to the Arkansas Supreme Court. Gitelman had no official involvement in the case after this point, although Tucker did run his brief by him before submitting it to the Arkansas Supreme Court. The ACLU did offer to pay for Tucker's legal services. However, the Rose Law Firm decided that the case should be handled *pro bono*.

The Arkansas chapter of the ACLU had been founded only a few months before this incident, and this was one of the first cases it was involved in. This case was the first ACLU case that ever received a decision from an Arkansas court. Although the ACLU wasn't targeting Act 17 nor was the ACLU even aware that the Neals were being charged under this act initially, according to Gitelman this case dealt with one of the issues at the very core of ACLU policy. The ACLU was designed to deal with First Amendment issues, and Gitelman felt that this was a prime example of a situation that the ACLU was designed to help people in. The climate at the time was not very favorable to the Neals or anyone else in this type of situation. Most individuals would not have the resources to retain legal counsel without the assistance of a group like the ACLU.

This issue was highlighted in the ACLU newsletter, and the ACLU used it as a means of publicity for the organization and for First Amendment rights.

Jim Guy Tucker

Jim Guy Tucker was an attorney at the Rose Law Firm in Little Rock. He was a recent graduate of the University of Arkansas and had been involved in the ACLU through this relationship with Mort Gitelman.[19]

Tucker doesn't recall who first contacted him regarding this case, but to his memory he was not involved until after the Neals had been tried and sentenced in municipal court. He says that it was clear to him from the beginning that this was not a proper legal adjudication or sentence. Tucker doesn't recall the agreement that Gitelman states he had with W. H. Arnold, and he believes that he wasn't contacted until after the municipal hearing.

Aside from a few visits and phone conversations with the Neals, Tucker states that he didn't have much involvement with the Neals and the situation was primarily handled as a set of legal matters. Normally a case that was appealed from municipal court would be appealed to circuit court, but there was a dispute on the record as to whether or not a notice of appeal had been filed out of municipal court. Because of this, Tucker filed a *Writ of Coram Nobis* in the Arkansas Supreme Court, and as he recalls that was the basis of jurisdiction for the Arkansas Supreme Court. The *Coram Nobis* allowed movement directly to the constitutional issues of law in the case without reference to the facts involved other than the sentence that involved banishment, which is prohibited. A *Writ of Coram Nobis* comes from English common law, and it allows citizens to have an unjust or unlawful action taken to a higher court.

According to Tucker the climate of the Arkansas Supreme Court reflected much of the judicial temperament of the time since it was an elected court and 1969 was a difficult time for issues of freedom of speech. Tucker notes that although the plaintiffs prevailed in this instance he understands Neal's feelings that he lost out in this matter as a dissenter because his dissent had still been stifled and his rights had still been violated. Tucker doesn't recall any specific details of his arguments before the Arkansas Supreme Court in this matter.

After the court's ruling, Tucker was quoted in the June 24, 1970, edition of the *Arkansas Democrat* as saying that college campus disturbances would not increase because of this ruling. In the fall of 1970 Tucker was elected prosecuting attorney, and in 1974 he was elected as attorney general. He doesn't recall dealing with any cases involving college students and free-speech issues during this time, and he would have necessarily dealt with them if there had been any on appeal.

Newspapers and Court Documents

According to the case file from the Arkansas Supreme Court, there was a hearing in this matter before Judge W. H. Arnold III in Clark County Circuit Court on April 14, 1969.[20] The circuit court declined to hear testimony as to the facts surrounding the arrest of the Neals. The circuit court did consider argument of counsel and on October 14, 1969, entered on the docket an order modifying the portion of the sentence banishing the Neals from Clark County imposed by the Clark County Municipal Court and substituting therefore the condition of good behavior. All other relief was denied. A separate written "order" entered the same day modifies the sentence imposed by the Clark County Municipal Court "to the extent the portion imposing a jail sentence and its suspension" was vacated but the "portion of the sentence imposing a fine of $500.00 upon each" of the Neals was affirmed.

The crux of the arguments made on behalf of the Neals before the Arkansas Supreme Court is that "the statute under which the petitioners were convicted (Act 17, or Arkansas Statutes 41-1431) is unconstitutional because it is so vague as to deprive petitioners of due process of law under the Fourteenth Amendment to the Constitution of the United States and Article II, Section 8, of the Constitution of the State of Arkansas."

The circuit court record indicates that "at the time of sentencing, attorney for petitioners, James Guy Tucker, Jr. gave the Court oral notice of appeal and requested the Court to set amount of appeal bond for petitioners." This would seem to indicate that, contrary to the recollections by Neal, Gitelman, and Tucker, the Neals did indeed have representation from Tucker at the time of their municipal trial and that this case also went before circuit court.

According to a letter from James Guy Tucker to the Honorable Judge J. E. Still dated March 15, 1969, Ben Drew Kimpel signed a property bond in the amount of $4,000.00 to secure the appearance of the Neals before the circuit court. Still responded with a letter dated March 21, 1969, stating that he could not accept Kimpel's surety bond because there was not one for each individual defendant. However, documents were recovered that indicate that the Clark County Circuit Court on April 14, 1969, "heard arguments of counsel for both petitioners and respondent in support of and against the petition filed herein wherein a Writ of Certiorari, Writ for Coram Nobis, and Writ of Prohibition are prayed by petitioners as the result of convictions entered against both petitioners by the Clark County Municipal Court at a trial conduct on February 21, 1969." This is when the modifications previously mentioned were made.

The Arkansas Supreme Court ruled 5–2 that the Neals' conviction under Act 17 was unconstitutional. The majority opinion was written by Associate Justice Lyle Brown,[21] who said,

> It is difficult to conceive of language more vague than that which declares one a law violator when he "creates" a disturbance or breach of the peace "in any way whatsoever." The same is true of language which makes it a misdemeanor to use "offensive talk." Then we find a prohibition against "attempting to intimidate," which is about as vague as one can imagine. Finally, we find in the forbidden category "any other conduct which causes a . . . threatened breach of the peace." We have no hesitancy in concluding that men of common intelligence would have to guess as to what conduct is proscribed by those phrases.
>
> . . . The entire section consists of one sentence. In fact, when the impermissive words and phrases are deleted there remains hardly a skeletal sketch of a section with which to deal. We are further persuaded in that view because any permissible portions of the section are duplicated in misdemeanor statutes of long standing.
>
> It is our conclusion that § 41-1431 HN4 should be, and is hereby, declared unconstitutional in its entirety.[22]

Conclusion

As previously stated, Shiffrin argued that a major purpose of the First Amendment was to protect dissenters. In this instance the Neals were clearly dissenting on both a macro and micro level. The Vietnam Conflict had been going on for many years by 1969, and it was clearly an entrenched policy in the United States government at the time. Because the Neals' activism called for action that was contrary to the conflict and the ideology of the powers that were at the time it can logically be classified as dissent against the federal government.

The climate in Arkadelphia at this time was less than friendly to those opposed to the war. The students of Henderson State College were denied the reservation of a room, because they were having representatives from the SSOC on campus to speak. The Neals were arrested, jailed, and intimidated because they were simply suspected of being communists and troublemakers.

The circumstances of the situation brought editorial derision from the *Arkansas Gazette*:

> Across town in Arkadelphia, at a time when Henderson State College still was trying to get the Legislature to declare it a "university"—and in spite of the fact that the first definition of a university is that it is a place of free inquiry—college administrators and city police combined to run out of town (rather in the fashion that labor unions were run out of town in Eastern Arkansas not so many years ago) a husband-wife team from Fayetteville. . . . they were fined $500 each—the maximum— on a disturbance charge. Six-month jail sentences—also the maximum—were suspended on condition that the two stay out of Arkadelphia. "The Law West of the Pecos;" or, "Vigilantism Rides Again."[23]

Shiffrin contends that the dissenter should be the symbol of the First Amendment because dissent enables change. Romantics and others that defy convention are the ones that force people to question assumptions and think about issues differently. Without this crucial process, change would not occur. If people don't think of doing things differently, how can they change?

The Neals defied convention in a few ways. First, they obviously challenged the idea of the war itself, of whether or not it was right and just, and whether or not it should continue to take place. The criticism of government for reasons such as this is part of the reason the First Amendment exists in the first place. It was also, Joe Neal contended, why the SSOC existed—"to organize dissent" and to help students "legally and peacefully protest what they think is wrong."[24]

Second, the Neals defied the community norms of Henderson State College and Arkadelphia at the time. As part of the SSOC, they went to help the students on campus who were concerned about or opposed to the war organize and presumably to protest. This had not happened on that campus or in that town previously, and while it is impossible to speculate if it would have actually happened or if it would have had any effect, the act itself was inherently progressive and in defiance of the prevailing community standard. This qualifies it as a dissent and according to Shiffrin and according to First Amendment case law it affords it constitutional protection.

The content of the Neals' speech in this case is largely irrelevant regarding whether or not it should be protected. In this instance the Neals had a right to speak, and the vagueness of Act 17 should not have been a barrier for them to do so. The only importance that the actual content of their speech has in this particular instance is to prove that it was political dissent, which links it to the ideas offered by Shiffrin.

Ultimately, the dissent of the Neals led to the overturning of an unjust and unconstitutional law. Although the dissenters didn't prevail in this instance, because their speech was initially suppressed, the idea of dissent was protected in the end because the law suffocating it was eventually overturned.

NOTES

1. Epigraph. Steven H. Shiffrin, *The First Amendment, Democracy, and Romance* (Cambridge, MA: Harvard University Press, 1990), 5.
Razorback (Fayetteville: University of Arkansas, 1967), 351.

2. Gregg L. Michel, "Building the New South: The Southern Student Organizing Committee," in *The New Left Revisited*, ed. John MacMillian and Paul Buhle (Philadelphia: Temple University Press, 2003), 49.

3. Joe Neal et ux v. The Honorable J. E. Still, Municipal Judge, 248 Ark. 1132 at 1136 (1970).

4. Lisa Huang, "History of Integration of Black Students at Henderson State University: 1955–1975," *Academic Forum* 20 (Arkadelphia: Henderson State University, 2003). http://www.hsu.edu/academicforum/2002-2003/2002-3AF History of Integration.pdf.

5. Ernest Dumas, "American Civil Liberties Union of Arkansas," *The Encyclopedia of Arkansas History and Culture,* updated 2014. http://www. encyclopediaofarkansas.net/encyclopedia/entry-detail.aspx?entryID=3796.

6. Jim Guy Tucker received his A.B. from Harvard College and his J.D. from the University of Arkansas, Fayetteville. He was subsequently elected prosecuting attorney, Arkansas attorney general, U.S. congressman, lieutenant governor, and governor of Arkansas.

7. See Robbie Lieberman, Praise Power: Voices of 1960s Midwest Student Protest (Columbia: University of Missouri Press, 2004); David Gilbert, SDS/WUO: Students for a Democratic Society and the Weather Underground Organization (Montreal, Quebec: Abraham Guillen Press, 2002); Robert Pardum, Prairie Radical:

A Journey through the Sixties (Santa Cruz, CA: Shire Press, 2001); Melvin Small, Covering Dissent: The Media and the Anti-Vietnam War Movement (New Brunswick, NJ: Rutgers University Press, 1994); and Robert Buzzanco, Masters of War: Military Dissent and Politics in the Vietnam Era (New York: Cambridge University Press, 1997).

8. Gregg L. Michel, Struggling for a Better South: The Southern Student Organizing Committee, 1964–1969 (New York: Palgrave Macmillan, 2004).

9. The arrest of the Neals at Henderson State College was placed in context of the ongoing struggle to integrate that institution. See Huang, "History of Integration of Black Students at Henderson State University."

10. "Doing Nothing Wrong, Say Couple Arrested at HSC," *Arkansas Democrat*, February 22, 1969, 3A; "They Caused No Trouble at Henderson, Couple Says," *Arkansas Gazette*, February 22, 1969, 2A.

11. The following recollections, unless otherwise noted, are from author interview with Joe Neal, May 1, 2006.

12. "They Caused No Trouble at Henderson, Couple Says," *Arkansas Gazette*, February 22, 1969, 2A.

13. Joe Neal was arrested the following year for obstructing traffic while leading a sit-down demonstration outside the Selective Service Office on Center Street in Fayetteville. See Tom Keith, "57 Members of Splinter Group Arrested as Peace Marchers Parade through Town; Nixon Burned in Effigy on Campus," *Northwest Arkansas Times*, May 9, 1970, 1.

14. Earnest Pickings et al., Appellants, v. Imon E. Bruce et al., Appellees, 430 F.2d 595 at 597 (8th Cir., 1970).

15. "Witnesses for Bi-Racial Group, SSC Official Heard in Court," *El Dorado Times*, May 28, 1969, 6; "Injunction Is Denied in SSC Complaint," *Northwest Arkansas Times*, May 30, 1969, 9.

16. The following recollections, unless otherwise noted, are from author interview with Mort Gitelman, May 6, 2006.

17. William H. "Dub" Arnold was a 1957 graduate of Henderson State Teachers College, the newly elected prosecuting attorney in 1969, having served two years as a deputy prosecutor. He would later serve as Clark County municipal judge, again as prosecuting attorney, then as circuit-chancery judge, and chief justice of the Arkansas Supreme Court (1997–2004).

18. Jefferson Ernest Still (1909–1973) was a graduate of Arkadelphia High School, received a B.A. degree from Henderson State Teachers College, did graduate work at the University of Texas, and earned his law degree from the University of Arkansas. Still served as city attorney for Arkadelphia from 1936 to 1944 and served as Clark County clerk from 1944 to 1950. He held the office of municipal judge from 1962 until his death in 1973.

19. The following recollections, unless otherwise noted, are from author interview with Jim Guy Tucker, May 7, 2006.

20. Judge William H. Arnold III of Texarkana received his undergraduate degree from Rice University and a law degree from the University of Texas, Austin. He was a distant cousin of the prosecuting attorney, W. H. "Dub" Arnold.

21. Associate Justice Lyle Brown (1908–1984) was a 1931 graduate of Henderson State Teachers College, where he was student body president and a member of the

debate team. He received his M.A. at Southern Methodist University and did doctoral studies at Louisiana State University, then returned to Henderson as a history instructor and dean of men. He represented Arkadelphia and Clark County for two terms in the Arkansas House of Representatives, before moving to Hope in 1942. He served as mayor of Hope, prosecuting attorney, and circuit judge, before being elected associate justice of the Supreme Court (1967–1975).

22. Joe Neal et ux v. The Honorable J. E. Still, Municipal Judge, 248 Ark. 1132 at 1134–35 (1970).

23. Editorial, "Lesson in Intolerance," *Arkansas Gazette*, March 2, 1969, 2E.

24. Bill Simmons (AP), "Two Types of Student Protest Seen on Campuses in Arkansas," *Northwest Arkansas Times,* May 6, 1969, 6.

CHAPTER 3

Gay and Lesbian Students Association v. Gohn

Content Discrimination in Funding

CAROLINE M. HEINTZMAN

Judge Richard Arnold, writing for the United States Court of Appeals in *Gay and Lesbian Students Association v. Gohn* 850 F.2d 361 (8th Cir., 1988), offered a meticulous recitation of the facts and a clear articulation of the law, then said, "In brief, we hold that a public body that chooses to fund speech or expression must do so even-handedly, without discriminating among recipients on the basis of their ideology. The University need not supply funds to student organizations; but once having decided to do so, it is bound by the First Amendment to act without regard to the content of the ideas being expressed."

This chapter examines the stories behind the events leading up to the decision in *Gay and Lesbian Students Association (GLSA) v. Dr. Lyle Gohn*. In this case the GLSA brought suit for declaratory and injunctive relief under 42 U.S.C. § 1983 and 28 U.S.C. §§ 2201 and 2202, contending that the denial of university funding constituted a "content based" discrimination against GLSA for its exercise of its rights of association and free speech under the First and Fourteenth Amendments and violation of its right to equal protection under the Fourteenth Amendment. Named defendants were Dr. Lyle Gohn, vice-chancellor for Student Service at the University of Arkansas, Fayetteville, and the University of Arkansas Board of Trustees.

In this chapter, I reconstruct the story from personal interviews, newspaper articles, related archive and microfilm documents, pamphlets, letters, newsletters, flyers, the *GLSA Report*, a letter from the GLSA to Chancellor Willard Gatewood, a book coauthored by Dr. Lyle Gohn, a master's thesis, a student thesis, law review articles, and court cases.

Prior research has examined University of Arkansas, Fayetteville, student, staff, or teacher attitudes and experiences related to homosexuality. Jacqueline Froelich's thesis, "The Gay and Lesbian Movement in Arkansas: An Investigative Study," informs of attitudes about and treatment of people in the gay and lesbian community before the late 1990s.[1] Froelich reveals that it was a time of ignorance and discrimination by otherwise reasonable people, as well as by elected officials and administrators. Shehan Welihindha's thesis, "From Razordykes to PRIDE and Everything in Between: A History of LGBT Student Organizations at the University of Arkansas," examines the history of the lesbian, gay, bisexual, and transgender (LGBT) community at the University of Arkansas.[2] Both studies provide an excellent overview of the research and a broader view of the issues in Arkansas, while this chapter provides a pointed analysis and review of *GLSA v. Gohn*. The history of the case provides an excellent case study for the examination of the state of inclusiveness for gays and lesbians at the University of Arkansas during the late twentieth century and its contribution to cultural advances on campus and the slowly changing attitudes across Arkansas.

Homophobic environments are, discouragingly, not rare on college campuses. They are also not rare in most other environments, particularly prior to the twenty-first century. It was the twenty-first century that brought on a time when the gay rights movement increasingly became more known, accepted, joined, and successful in arguing and receiving citizenship rights.[3] It is also when more money entered the sexual orientation equality debate and action, which, in turn, resulted in more and stronger organizations fighting for equality of lesbian, gay, bisexual, transgender, and queer (LGBTQ) rights and interests. Important to this study is the influence of authority figures pre- and

post-1982 in the defining of cultural acceptance or rejection of someone or some group on account of sexual orientation. At the end of the
twentieth century and through the existing twenty-first century, there
was a gradual groundswell of public figures demonstrating acceptance
of the equal treatment and allowance of rights to individuals despite
their sexual orientation. Such was not the case with 1980s University
of Arkansas authorities. University culture during this time regarding
sexual orientation and LGBTQ acceptance can be seen in a study of
Gay and Lesbian Students Association v. Dr. Lyle Gohn.

Events prior to the *GLSA v. Gohn* case are instructive as to the
culture of the time and elements of the case. In 1976 Fayetteville,
Arkansas, a group of lesbian students formed the University of
Arkansas Associated Lesbians under the umbrella of the Women's
Center.[4] It is not clearly stated why this group decided to form during
this time, but it did occur in the years when women were discover-
ing their political voices when protesting gender discrimination, and
war protests were occurring across country on college and university
grounds. In 1977, the group unofficially took on the name "Razordykes."
The administration and many students were not pleased by this development. The group soon fell victim to discrimination, name-calling,
and interrogation.[5]

On October 5, 1978, a reporter at a Student Services forum raised
a question about where the Razordykes got their funding.[6] An investigation by the administration revealed that the group was being funded
indirectly through student fees because it was under the umbrella of
the Women's Center. The *Traveler* reported that the Razodykes had
been funded $730 as part of the $6,265 allocated to the Women's
Center, which did not sit nicely with some students. Student senators
claimed they were unaware of having funded the organization and
alleged that the Razordykes had received illegal third-party funding.
The vice president of Student Services at the time, Merlin Augustine,
pressured the Razordykes to change their name and to become separate from the Women's Center. A few weeks later, the Student Senate
passed a resolution saying that the Razordykes were of low merit and
should be the Women's Center's lowest priority.[7] The Student Senate
requested that the Razordykes change their name and suggested
that the Women's Center should gradually faze the group out. The

administration agreed with the Student Senate. The Women's Center went on undeterred. On November 7, the Women's Center responded with a statement saying that they would support and stand behind the Razordykes and that they would not give in to the Student Senate and the administration's suggestion to force them out.[8]

In 1979, the Women's Center was relocated to the basement of the Arkansas Union. The administration told them to accept members of conservative student groups (two antiabortion groups and Family, Life, America and God—FLAG) as viable women's interests groups that required the center's umbrella funding. The student government was already funding the organizations the administration wanted joined so the center denied them access.

In February 1981, another group, Problem Pregnancy, was denied funding by the Student Senate. Like the Razordykes, Problem Pregnancy was a controversial group. This group assisted students in unwanted pregnancies. The group filed a complaint in student court, and a Student Senate justice was appointed to investigate the case.[9] The vice president of Student Affairs, Dr. Gordon Beasley, cited bias in the investigation. Because of this, he was accused of supporting a lesbian group on campus and was asked to resign by Dr. James Martin, then president of the University of Arkansas system.[10]

A year after Dr. Beasley was asked to resign (claiming he had been "drummed out of my job by a local fringe group" for funding a campus lesbian group), a group of students formed the Gay and Lesbian Student Association (GLSA). These students were worried about the possibility of rising discrimination against lesbians and gay students on campus. The GLSA's purpose was to educate the community on campus about gay and lesbian issues, and advocate for their protection at the University of Arkansas. Also, the GLSA wanted to provide emotional support for gay and lesbian students and wanted to educate the university community in order to encourage more humane and compassionate treatment of the campus minority group. There was no evidence to show that GLSA was not a helpful support group for a significant number of students. As Anne Vaccaro pointed out in her chapter in *Understanding College Student Subpopulations: A Guide for Student Affairs Professionals*, there is a reality that gay and lesbian individuals make a decision to come out to three distinct entities: themselves, other gays and lesbians, and heterosexuals. A student organization like the GLSA could ease this process by providing a safe place for this process to happen. But, that requires funding. The GLSA was a student organization; therefore, the group was eligible to request funds directly from the Associated Student Government (ASG), and it met all the existing qualifications and requirements for funding consideration and award.

In January 1983, the GLSA submitted a budget for $136 to the University of Arkansas ASG, which was denied.[11] The GLSA then contacted the American Civil Liberties Union (ACLU), who agreed to represent them if they required it.[12] The GLSA held a rally to raise awareness of the Student Senate's decision and its organization. The rally drew extensive media attention and a negative reaction from some state legislators. In response to the rally, state representative Travis Dowd of Texarkana submitted HR16, a resolution to "contain the spread of homosexuality on the Fayetteville campus," requiring the university administration to monitor the activities of gay and lesbian students, and soon after a bill to extend that provision to the entire state.[13]

Gohn remarked that "when the GLSA group formed, there were those who questioned if such should be allowed, but we supported their right as a student organization." He added, however, "There is no question, it was a time of change, a time of misrepresentation of information and lack of understanding, a time of hostility.... And, yes, we were greatly concerned with safety at the time and took a number of measures to address such concerns."[14]

In the book *Understanding College Student Subpopulations: A Guide for Student Affairs Professionals,* Dr. Lyle Gohn and Ginger Albin authored the introduction and second chapter.[15] The book reviews who college students are, how they have changed, and how they will be different in the future. It also analyzes the unique qualifications of various subpopulations found on college and university campuses nationwide, and examines how these factors affect student success. The rest of the introduction breaks down student characteristics from the 1920s to the 1990s and addresses how generations are shaped. The authors also discuss Cass's Model of Homosexual Identity Formation. According to the authors, Student Affairs professionals should have a

working knowledge of psychological and identity development theories because these theories address developmental issues occurring
in the lives of students. Cass's model proclaims that individuals move
from "minimal awareness and acceptance of homosexual identity to
a final stage in which homosexual identity is integrated with others
as aspects of the self."

In chapter 16 of the same book, titled "Gay, Lesbian, Bisexual and
Transgender Students" and authored by Anne Vaccaro, Cass's model is
shown to have six stages through which people recognize and adapt to
a nonheterosexual identity.[16] In all the stages, it is evident that people
coming into their homosexual identity need support, as provided by
organizations like the GLSA. Such theory serves as good justification for such an organization receiving funding on a college campus.
Evans and Brodio suggested that gay and lesbian individuals should
make decisions to come out to three distinct entities; themselves, GLB
people, and to heterosexuals. A homosexual student organization
could ease this process by providing a safe place for this to happen,
another good justification for funding.

In January 1983, the GLSA submitted a budget for $136 to the ASG,
which was denied. On January 28, Annette Frazier wrote an article in
the *Arkansas Traveler* titled "Senate Cites Law in Denying Funds to
Homosexual Group."[17] The student senators voted 35–17 to deny the
thirty-member organization money because of a state sodomy law.
"Although an Arkansas law states that it is not illegal to be a homosexual, it prohibits citizens from engaging in homosexual acts." A representative from the GLSA said that the group was devoted to educating
the public and did not advocate homosexuality. Senator Dick Davis
said, "This is a group that supports gay and lesbian homosexuality.
We cannot use state money to support a homosexual group." He then
compares funding the GLSA to funding an arsonists club. Ultimately,
the final decision was up to Dr. Lyle Gohn.

According to an *Arkansas Traveler* article written by Sherri Ward
on March 29, the GLSA is denied $136 in "B" funds in January.[18] The
co-chairwoman of the GLSA, Sarah Humble, said that Dr. Gohn indicated that he would not overrule the Student Senate and grant funds to
the organization. The GLSA said that they were willing to settle out of
court, which in hindsight was a financially better option for the univer-

sity. It is clear that ACLU executive director Sandra Kurjiaka believed that the denial had to do with their message and nothing more when she argued, "Gay and lesbian student groups must be recognized and receive all the privileges that other student groups receive."

In response to the university denying them funds, the GLSA set "Blue Jean Day" on March 30, which was an effort to increase awareness of the stigma attached to homosexuals. The idea was for homosexuals and their friends to wear something as superficial as blue jeans and to be judged. In response to "Blue Jean Day," an unidentified writer at the *Arkansas Traveler* felt it was necessary to write a disclaimer article soon after.[19] The article says that the newspaper does "not support the cheap gimmicky of 'Blue Jean Day,'" and gives a scenario of how a straight person may be ridiculed by his friends if he were to forget the meaning of "Blue Jean Day" and wear blue jeans. According to the article, this would cause the person to say, "it's those faggots' fault that my friends are laughing at me." This is more evidence to support the conclusion that the GLSA's First and Fourteenth Amendments rights were violated.

To raise awareness of the organization and the Student Senate's decision to deny them funds, the GLSA held a rally, which received extensive media attention. News of the rally traveled to Little Rock, and state representative Travis Dowd of Texarkana made his opinion about homosexuality known. He submitted HR16, a resolution to "contain the spread of homosexuality on the Fayetteville campus." This resolution required the administration to monitor the activities of homosexual students, not too different than if they were presumed to be criminals.[20] Dowd later withdrew his resolution so he could create House Bill 25, which would expand monitoring of homosexuality to the entire state.[21] HB25 would have required school administrators and campus police to report any homosexual activities on their campuses to the state.[22] This proposed legislation caught the attention of the ACLU of Arkansas, and with help from the Arkansas chapter of the National Organization for Women, the Arkansas Women's Political Caucus, and Arkansas Gay Rights, House Committee support was gained, and the bill was blocked.[23]

Unfortunately, while gay rights activists were able to gain support of the House Committee, they did not have the support of many students at the University of Arkansas. Things worsened for gay and lesbian students on campus. In the fall, a new group called Angels of War emerged. According to the founder, the purpose of the group was "to be a helping organization for people who are being pressured by homosexuals."[24] In an *Arkansas Traveler* article, the founder called homosexual individuals "emotionally sick" and claimed that there is no such thing as homophobia.[25]

In the fall semester of 1985, several members of the ASG introduced a bill to deny money to any group "whose primary function is the promotion of sexual preference or any education thereof." The bill aimed at GLSA passed but was vetoed by ASG president Sarah Hicks. The student senators petitioned to override the veto, but they were reluctant for fear of a lawsuit by the ACLU. Dr. Lyle Gohn stated, "In 1984 when Student Government funded GLSA, and then a bill was introduced to then deny the funding which Sara Hicks vetoed, there were those who wanted the administration to overrule the funding and her veto, but that did not happen. This was the same position that was taken when funding was denied by Student Government a couple years later."[26]

Members of the GLSA were victim to harassment for the rest of the year, including an incident where several masked men fired bottle rockets into the room where the group was meeting. There were children in the room. Some required therapy.[27] From that meeting forward, the GLSA had to meet with a university police guard to protect them. On another occasion, a GLSA member was "outed" to his parents. Vaccaro commented, "Some families welcome their children with open arms, yet research has shown that [some] families are less than positive in their reaction."[28] In December, the ASG gave the GLSA $70 for a movie and lecturer. The discussion preceding the ASG's decision was heated and lasted almost one hour.[29]

In February 1985 the *Arkansas Traveler* article talks about Senate Bill 32 and says the bill was dropped and allowed to die. Clint Beutelschies introduced the bill and said he thought the bill was "without malicious intent" when he brought it before the senate.[30] He said that he was not challenging the Gay and Lesbian Student Association's right to exist, but said he felt groups promoting a religious or sexual preference should not be funded. Beutelschies remarked that it had been suggested he incorporate the bill as a constitutional amendment and let the students decide the issue.[31]

In March, the GLSA wrote a letter to Chancellor Willard Gatewood. The letter begins by telling the chancellor what it is like to be homosexual on the University of Arkansas campus. It was stated that the environment is repressive for gay and lesbian faculty, staff, and students. "Gay faculty and staff worry about the possible loss of their jobs; gay students are subjected to degrading and oppressive treatment in the classroom when instructors make derogatory remarks or jokes about homosexuality. Few gay members of the University community feel able to speak out or complain against their own oppression because they fear recrimination."[32]

The letter also referenced a new student organization called the United Students' Association (USA). This group announced a campaign to call for a halt to the funding of GLSA. The group accused six university officials of "leading a homosexual takeover of the U of A," by embezzling "thousands of taxpayers' money and have given secretly to the Gay and Lesbian Society."[33] The leader of the group announced plans to go to the state legislature to speak about homosexuality on the Fayetteville campus. A flyer the USA posted around campus about a press conference said that the president was invited by one of the state legislators to go to Little Rock to tell the Arkansas General Assembly about the homosexual activities happening on campus. The flyer had bold letters saying, "Help stop your tuition money from funding GLSA." The letter says that the leader gave false and inflammatory information about the goals of homosexuals and of gay rights groups. "It is clear to gays on campus that this USA group, while not yet advocating violence, has the dangerous potential for arousing the mob instincts of antigay students. Gay faculty, staff, and students have every reason to believe that they are in physical danger. In addition, gay faculty and staff fear that the activities of the USA group will lead to a 'witchhunt,' a purge in which homosexual faculty and staff will be fired from their jobs, or forced to resign because of harassment," the letter stated.

Even though the gay community on campus was afraid of this group, the GLSA was not advocating for censorship of the USA group or of anyone else with antihomosexual opinions. The GLSA believed that the silence of the university administration on the issue indicated a lack of concern for the welfare of gay staff, faculty, and students. "We believe that it is the duty and the responsibility of the University administration to try to circumvent violence, and to publicly offer assurance of basic rights to the University's gay popularity."[34]

The GLSA also attached documents to the letter, one being a list of words or phrases used in the *Arkansas Traveler* when referencing homosexuals or homosexuality. The words and phrases were quoted from articles and letters to the editor from February 1, 1985, to March 15, 1985. The list includes "fascists," "degenerates," "violation of biological law," "send homosexuals to China," "perverted," "unnatural," "prostitutes," "misguided individuals," "social leprosy," "illegal," "corrupt," and "cut off from light and spirituality." Another document attached is a list of forty-seven schools around the country that had progressive policies regarding homosexual faculty, staff, and students.

The university administration heeded the call from the GLSA. After this letter and a meeting between Chancellor Gatewood and the GLSA, it was recommended that a directive be sent to all university supervising personnel providing the university's policy to prohibit discrimination on the basis of sexual orientation and to create a safe learning environment. There is no evidence that Chancellor Gatewood followed through on these recommendations.[35]

On November 19, the university's Student Senate refused to fund the GLSA.[36] The GLSA appealed the senate's vote to Dr. Lyle Gohn on November 21 and on December 9, Dr. Gohn upheld the senate's decision. "Gohn wrote that, although the GLSA had been made to adhere strictly to ASG Code Guidelines for funding, while other groups which were funded had violated the Code, the strict appliance of the Code to GLSA had been done in order to 'help' the GLSA."[37] It is important to note that three groups that failed to meet code guidelines were funded over $400 each—the GLSA was asking for $164.36.

In April 1986, the GLSA filed a lawsuit against Dr. Gohn and the Board of Trustees of the University of Arkansas in the district court alleging violations of their First Amendment and Fourteenth Amendment rights because they were denied funding.[38] A month later, the university's representatives filed documents requesting dismissal of the case. They asserted that Dr. Gohn and the board of trustees had nothing to do with the ASG's decision. The motion to dismiss was denied and a court date was set for January 20, 1987.[39]

According to the June issue of the *GLSA Report*, the GLSA's sign displayed on Garland Avenue for Gay and Lesbian Culture Week was defaced, but the GLSA requested that it stay up because (1) the sign provided tangible evidence that homophobia is a serious problem on the UA campus and (2) those who defaced the sign probably believed it would be removed.[40] The university police received a large number of phone calls from concerned university community members who complained on behalf of the GLSA organization. However, the sign was ordered removed by Dr. Lyle Gohn on April 17. It was taken down by university staff.

Around this time, on September 9, although unrelated to this case but important for this cultural analysis, a gay bar in Fayetteville called St. John's burned to the ground. A local media outlet reported the burning, but the story was given minimal coverage despite it being a story of high public interest due to its location, and the story described it as a bar, but not a gay bar. The mass media business conversation avoided the homosexual question; however, a student wrote a letter to the editor and remarked that he/she thought it was intentionally burned down because it was a gay bar.[41] In October, the GLSA requested to amend the lawsuit by including the University of Arkansas system president Ray Thornton and thirty-five members of the ASG.[42] Judge Waters denied this request because it was past the ninety-day period in which additional parties could be added to the case.

On January 21, Peggy Treiber of the *Arkansas Gazette* interviewed Betsey Crow, chair of the Student Senate Finance Committee.[43] She testified that her committee recommended funding the GLSA although several members said they would vote against it when the full senate convened. Crow said the senators told her voting for the request would be lending support to homosexuality, which they believed was immoral and illegal. Nearly twenty-seven years later, Crow still remembers this incident and the overall opinion about homosexuality on campus. She remarked, "Back then I was very concerned with fairness. Actual fairness, not lip service. The rules were the rules, and it wasn't fair that the GLSA followed all the rules but wasn't funded. So that's what I said, to the consternation of my fellow ASG members."[44] When asked if she was bullied because of her stance, she said, "Was I bullied? Hm. There WERE some passionate 'discussions.' I didn't shy away from speaking my mind and neither did the guys who were against voting to fund the GLSA's pitifully small request. I told them (the B fund committee and the ASG) that it was wrong to deny the funding request and that it was discrimination." On February 25, Chris Osher wrote an article saying that "although the University could not justify denying a homosexual group the right to be recognized and the privileges that go with that, the courts haven't said the University has to give funding to such organizations."[45] In March 1987, the district court ruled that while the case was not moot and that state action was present, the GLSA's First Amendment right of free speech was not violated by the senate's action, concluding that "the denial of funding had an impact, but did not prevent the organization from advocating its views."[46]

Shortly before the decision had been announced, a newspaper article announced antihomosexual advocate Dr. Paul Cameron's upcoming speech at the University of Arkansas.[47] Dr. Cameron was the chairman of the Family Research Institute in Lincoln, Nebraska. According to the Americans Informing Americans organization on campus, Dr. Cameron "has been called the most dangerous anti-homosexual zealot in the United States." Cameron had previously spoken at the university in April 1985 (just a few months after Chancellor Gatewood's meeting with the GLSA) on "The Medical Consequences of Homosexuality." Cameron also argued that the existence of humanity and society depends on suppressing homosexuality.

After Dr. Cameron's speech, the GLSA sent out a press packet that included a set of grievances that GLAD (Gay and Lesbian Action Delegation) and the GLSA wanted to present to the university.[48] The excerpt said: "The failure of the University administration to make a responsible statement on Dr. Paul Cameron's call for total quarantine of all gay males and for the extermination of all gay males and lesbians in the United States as an acceptable option has contributed to the community's misinformation about AIDS and has helped to create a climate of hysteria, bigotry, and the discrimination against gays and lesbians in Fayetteville. The University administration has allowed exploitation of the University and its facilities by a special interest group. The University has failed to provide intellectual leadership for the city of Fayetteville and for the state of Arkansas."

The United Students' Association (USA) distributed Dr. Cameron's literature to the student body. The literature said that AIDS is transmissible through shaking hands, food handling, saliva, and casual contact with gays and lesbians. The GLSA and GLAD said that this literature is a direct source for "the growing climate of misinformed hysteria surrounding AIDS in the city of Fayetteville." The document also mentions that Dr. Cameron was expelled from membership in the American Psychological Association in December 1983 for ethical reasons. It stated, "The failure of the University to make a responsible statement on this issue makes the University culpable for the climate of hysteria which is now evident in the city of Fayetteville." Vice Chancellor Gohn contended otherwise, when he recalled, "We supported the formation of USA, although we despised their purposes. We were totally opposed to Cameron's speech, but because he was being brought in by a registered student organization, he was allowed to speak."[49]

Likely coincidence, but definitely providing a view during the time, there was an advertisement in the same newspaper for a booklet called "Homosexuality is not inherent."[50] The booklet was about how students can change if they are gay. "Written by Colin Cook, a former homosexual for 35 years, is available to help those seeking a new lifestyle." In the April 1 issue of the *Arkansas Traveler,* Heidi Stambuck reports on Dr. Cameron's presentation.[51] This article is indicative of the view of those who denied them rights. "Homosexuality is a crime against humanity and should be treated and dealt with as such," said Cameron. Cameron said that homosexuality must be made illegal and eradicated. He advocated mass screening of the population to determine carriers of AIDS, wanted to close gay bars and baths, to eliminate all gay organizations and other promotional tools funded by the public, and to institute a mass antihomosexuality campaign in schools. During his presentation, women advocating gay rights were removed from his discussion by campus police officers.

On July 6, the GLSA appealed the court's decision to the Eighth Circuit Court of Appeals in St. Louis. The GLSA was represented by Nan D. Hunter of the ACLU foundation in New York and Clay R. Blackstock of Little Rock.[52] A month later, the university appealed Judge Waters's ruling that the university was responsible for the action of the ASG.

On August 18, 1988, the Eighth Circuit Court of Appeals decided to reverse the district court's holding that the Student Senate's denial of funding to GLSA did not violate the First Amendment.[53] The court opined that the First Amendment violation is apparent. "When the original two premises are applied to the facts in this case, the First Amendment violation is apparent. The GLSA met all objective criteria for funding and received the Finance Committee's recommendation, yet was denied funds twice. The one time the GLSA received funds, an unusual procedure was followed in presenting requests before the Senate. And, immediately after the granting of funds, the Senate voted never to fund the GLSA again." Ray Minor wrote in an August issue of the *Traveler* that the university appealed the decision but was denied a review by the court of appeals. All of the university officials refused to comment in this article.[54]

After the GLSA's victory, Jennifer Fulford of the *Northwest Arkansas Times* wrote an article about how someone stole and threw away 4,500 copes of the *Grapevine*, a local, semimonthly newspaper.[55] The newspapers were distributed on campus on September 3, and were stolen by midday. The managing editor said this was the first time this had ever happened since publication began in 1969. The newspapers were stolen because the front-page story was about the GLSA victory over the university at the Eighth Circuit Court of Appeals in St. Louis.

Even though the Eighth Circuit Court of Appeals ultimately decided that the GLSA's First Amendment rights were violated, it's interesting to examine what convinced so many authorities to conclude the opposite. In some cases, things like this happen from ignorance or by accident. But, it can be said that antihomosexual views were the norm in many cultural hamlets of Fayetteville, Arkansas, during the 1980s and 1990s.

In a 2014 interview with Dr. Lyle Gohn, he describes his mentoring and why he decided to not overturn the ASG's decision to deny the GLSA funding. According to Gohn, his mentor stressed the importance of student leadership without interference from the administration. Gohn said that he did not overturn the decision because it was the right of the student government to make decisions, even if the administration knew it was wrong. He also said that there was "subtle pressure" from the Arkansas legislature, specifically the bill Travis Dowd was trying to pass. He said that the trial was embarrassing, but deep down he was glad the judge ruled in favor of the GLSA. Gohn said that there was no hostility before or after the trial between him and the members of the GLSA. He said that they understood why he did not overturn the Student Senate's vote. When asked if he would have done it differently, he said that he probably should have, but he really did not want to destroy student leadership responsibility.

In 2006, Dr. Gohn and Ginger R. Albin, a doctoral academy fellow in the Higher Education Leadership program at the University of Arkansas, edited *Understanding College Student Subpopulations: A Guide for Student Affairs Professionals*. It is important because Gohn's views completely contradict his perceived views in the 1980s. Gohn admits that during this time, he was still growing as a person and probably would not have purposely hired a gay or lesbian person. He said that the campus during that time was not a friendly, open environment. However, he added, "My statement was reflecting on the time, but in reality, as I mentioned also, several of my staff were alleged to be gay, some of whom I hired or promoted."[56]

In the introduction, Gohn and Albin say, "With such a blend of students on college campuses, perhaps there is no simple way to describe today's students other than to think of them as a mixture of several generations, several subcultures, several subgroups, all with different agendas, different goals and ambitions, different attitudes, and different experiences that have shaped and are shaping their future." The student population in 2006 and 1983 may have been very similar, but being part of a subgroup was much more acceptable in 2006 than in 1983. Because of homosexual hostility on college campuses, these "blend of students" were unable to be themselves. Homosexual students, faculty, and staff were scared for their lives and physical well-being. They were unable to fully express themselves and possibly were obstructed in reaching their full potential during their higher education.

Also in the introduction is a section on student stereotypes. According to Gohn and Albin, "Stereotyping is generally viewed as unhealthy and often derogatory in regard to a particular subgroup." Later in the section, they say that stereotypes are always inappropriate. They could not be more right. Basic human decency and having an open, loving heart isn't something that came to American college campuses in the late twentieth century. People have always had it, like Sarah Hicks, Betsey Crow, Sandra Kurjiaka, and all the people that supported the homosexual community during the hard times. Our society still has a long way to go, but hopefully soon no group or individual will have to feel what the gay community had to feel. When the federal courts hold for equal rights and equal treatment, as did Judge Arnold in the decision in *Gay and Lesbian Students Association v. Gohn*, public attitudes and private actions hopefully will tell a different story in the years ahead.

NOTES

1. Jacqueline A. Froelich, "The Gay and Lesbian Movement in Arkansas: An Investigative Study" (M.A. thesis, University of Arkansas, 1995).

2. Shehan Welihindha, "From Razordykes to PRIDE and Everything in Between: A History of LGBT Student Organizations at the University of Arkansas" (M.A. thesis, University of Arkansas, 2010).

3. The 1977 Arkansas criminal sodomy statute was ruled unconstitutional by the Arkansas Supreme Court in *Jegley v. Picado*, 349 Ark. 600 (2002). The 1997 Arkansas statute and 2004 Arkansas Constitutional Amendment prohibiting same-sex marriages were declared unconstitutional by both state and federal courts in 2014. "Final Order, *Wright v. Arkansas*, No. 60CV-13-2662," Circuit Court of Arkansas, Pulaski County (May 15, 2014); *Jernigan v. Crane*, 64 F. Supp. 3d 1261 (E.D. Ark., 2014).

4. "Razordykes Continue, Despite Flack," *Arkansas Traveler,* February 15, 1979.

5. Froelich, "The Gay and Lesbian Movement in Arkansas."

6. Welihindha, "From Razordykes to PRIDE and Everything in Between."

7. "Women's Center Controversy: Questions Raised on Razordyke Funding," *Grapevine* (Fayetteville), November 15, 1978.

8. "Women's Center: We Won't Tolerate UA Forcing Razordykes Out of WC," *Arkansas Traveler* (Fayetteville), November 7, 1978.

9. Welihindha, "From Razordykes to PRIDE and Everything in Between."

10. Froelich, "The Gay and Lesbian Movement in Arkansas."

11. Annette Frazier, "Senate Cites Law in Denying Funds to Homosexual Group," *Arkansas Traveler,* January 28, 1983.

12. Sherri Ward, "GLSA, ACLU Threaten to File Suit to Acquire Funds," *Arkansas Traveler* (Fayetteville), March 29, 1983.

13. "Dowd Plans Resolution on Homosexuality at UA," *Springdale News,* February 1, 1983; "Newest Resolution Mandates Reports on Homosexuality," *Arkansas Democrat* (Little Rock), February 16, 1983; "Panel Defeats Homosexual Resolution," *Springdale News,* February 27, 1983.

14. Email from Lyle A. Gohn to the author, May 8, 2014.

15. Lyle A. Gohn and Ginger R. Albin, eds., "Introduction to College Students: Generations, Stereotypes, and Subpopulations," in *Understanding College Student*

Subpopulations: A Guide for Student Affairs Professionals (Washington, DC: National Association of Student Personnel Administrators, 2006), 1–23.

16. Anne Vaccaro, "Gay, Lesbian, Bisexual and Transgender Students," in *Understanding College Student Subpopulations: A Guide for Student Affairs Professionals*, ed. Lyle A. Gohn and Ginger R. Albin, 349–86. (Washington, DC: National Association of Student Personnel Administrators, 2006), 349–86.

17. Frazier, "Senate Cites Law in Denying Funds to Homosexual Group."

18. Ward, "GLSA, ACLU Threaten to File Suit to Acquire Funds."

19. "Blue Jean Day," *Arkansas Traveler* (Fayetteville), March 29, 1983.

20. Associated Press, "Dowd Plans Resolution on Homosexuality at UA," *Springdale News*, February 1, 1983.

21. Welihindha, "From Razordykes to PRIDE and Everything in Between."

22. O. Greene, "Newest Resolution Mandates Reports on Homosexuality," *Arkansas Democrat* (Little Rock), February 16, 1983.

23. Associated Press, "Panel Defeats Homosexual Resolution," *Springdale News*, February 27, 1983.

24. Welihindha, "From Razordykes to PRIDE and Everything in Between."

25. S. Crockett and D. Beeber, "UA Student Forms Anti-Gay Group," *Arkansas Traveler* (Fayetteville), March 6, 1984.

26. Interview with Dr. Lyle A. Gohn by Caroline Heintzman, April 22, 2014; Email from Lyle A. Gohn to the author, May 8, 2014.

27. Froelich, "The Gay and Lesbian Movement in Arkansas."

28. Vaccaro, "Gay, Lesbian, Bisexual and Transgender Students," 349–86.

29. Trinita Tracz, "GLSA Bill Override Attempt Fails; Hicks 'Scares Away' Petitioners," *Arkansas Traveler* (Fayetteville), February 22, 1985.

30. Ibid.

31. Ibid.

32. GLSA to Chancellor Willard Gatewood, March 21, 1985. University of Arkansas, Fayetteville.

33. Welihindha, "From Razordykes to PRIDE and Everything in Between."

34. GLSA to Chancellor Willard Gatewood, March 21, 1985, University of Arkansas, Fayetteville.

35. Welihindha, "From Razordykes to PRIDE and Everything in Between."

36. "*GLSA vs. GOHN, et al.*" *GLSA Report* (Fayetteville), June 1986.

37. Ibid.

38. Welihindha, "From Razordykes to PRIDE and Everything in Between."

39. S. Morris, "GLSA Files Suit Alleging Rights Violation," *Arkansas Traveler* (Fayetteville), April 23, 1986.

40. "*GLSA vs. GOHN, et al,*" *GLSA Report* (Fayetteville), June 1986.

41. "Club Burns," *Arkansas Traveler* (Fayetteville), September 24, 1986.

42. Chris Osher, "Waters Denies GLSA Lawsuit," *Arkansas Traveler* (Fayetteville), October 22, 1986.

43. Peggy Treiber, "Judge Hints UA Suit May Turn on Why Gay Group Not Funded," *Arkansas Gazette* (Fayetteville), January 21, 1987.

44. Betsey Crow Mowery, interview with Caroline Heintzman, April 15, 2014.

45. Chris Osher, "GLSA Loses Lawsuit, Will Appeal Decision," *Arkansas Traveler* (Fayetteville), February 25, 1987.

46. Gay and Lesbian Students Association v. Gohn, 656 F. Supp. 1045 (W.D. Ark. 1987).

47. Ed Schimberg, "Cameron to Speak Monday," *Arkansas Traveler* (Fayetteville), February 25, 1987.

48. GLSA. 1987. *Grievances*. [press release].

49. Email from Lyle A. Gohn to the author, May 8, 2014.

50. "Homosexuality Is Not Inherent," *Arkansas Traveler* (Fayetteville), February 25, 1987.

51. Heidi Stambuck, "Homosexuality Crime against Society," *Arkansas Traveler* (Fayetteville), April 1, 1987.

52. Chris Osher, "GLSA Appeals Ruling in Discrimination Case," *Arkansas Traveler* (Fayetteville), September 23, 1987.

53. *Gay and Lesbian Students Ass'n v. Gohn*, 850 F.2d 361, 362 (8th Cir. 1988).

54. Ray Minor, "GLSA Wins Appeal: University Remains Silent," *Arkansas Traveler* (Fayetteville), August 1988.

55. Jennifer Fulford, "Grapevine, GLSA Story Thrown Out," *Northwest Arkansas Times*, September 9, 1988.

56. Email from Lyle A. Gohn to the author, May 8, 2014.

CHAPTER 4

Curtailing Criticism of Public Figures through Trademark and Branding

JOSH BERTACCINI

The concept of freedom of speech has long been one of the most famed components of the Bill of Rights. Americans have always had the protected ability to express themselves—politically, artistically, religiously, and commercially. This has led to a degree of responsibility and accountability for individual actions and behaviors. However, in the modern age, as economics and labor organizations have evolved, giving up some of these freedoms has often become a contingent piece of garnering employment for some people. It is now in fact common for many universities to exert their influence over employees as parts of their larger product. This is perhaps most glaring when institutions frequently require merchandising contracts with those coaches and broadcasters working in the highly lucrative realm of collegiate athletics. However, in some cases, these encroaching agreements have led to blurry grounds in the debate of freedom of expression versus trademark and branding rights. Which is to say, do universities operating in such a fashion maintain absolute trademark, copyright, and control over all publicity involving consenting employees? Or does the freedom of expression of the private citizen supersede such

agreements in a court of law? Over the following pages, I will attempt
to assess some of the most relevant current literature pertaining to the
subject of freedom of speech in the public domain versus trademark
and brand infringement, specifically as it pertains to institutions of
higher learning and athletic competition. I will summarize some existing views and relevant court decisions on both local and federal levels,
continuing up to the present day's discussion in periodical literature.
I will then proceed to the study of a particularly relevant recent case
involving the University of Arkansas, the Razorback athletic brand,
and freedom of expression of the individual. I will share firsthand
interviews with some of the key subjects involved in a specific case
to paint a fuller picture of the elements at play. In closing the paper, I
will propose the direction of future study and research on some of the
subject material at hand.

From the very beginning, the notions of branding and trademarking have been fraught with a plague of vagueness. Given that the
exchange of ideas and information is inherently a critical part of democratic society, there has always been a gray middle when it comes to
who establishes control and domain over what idea first. Undoubtedly,
first to the punch is usually the one who wins out, but even then,
brand confusion still remains a concern for those it pertains to. As
Daniel Howard, Roger Kerin, and Charles Gengler describe in their
piece of analysis for the *Journal of Public Policy and Marketing*, "Under
high-involvement conditions, brand names with shared meaning
cause consumers to infer that both brands are likely made by the
same company. Under low-involvement conditions, brand names that
sound alike result in common source inferences."[1] This means that it
is harder for consumers who care about brand names to distinguish
between two brands with similar products than those who do not care
about brand names. Clearly third-party efforts to mix product lines
and trademarks in with the original copyright owner's materials and
merchandising has rendered the source of content almost impossible
for consumers to determine. As it relates to larger brands, it can be
assumed that some citizens believe them to be part of the already
existing public domain.

In a 2003 article for the *Rutgers Computer and Technology Law
Journal*, Alayne Manas writes about the issue of trademark and brand-

ing as it relates to website names, institutional images, and school logos being used in the public domain. Harvard University has proactively sought to obtain and control a number of websites that were created without the school's authorization or approval in recent years. By proactively obtaining these sites in advance, the school largely avoided significant legal action as it corresponds to brand management and merchandising. The Trademark Act of 1946, which was amended in 1988 and is called the Lanham Act, is the law that currently governs trademark law federally. The United States Patent and Trademark Office actually lists a symbol as a trademark if the owner can prove the mark's capacity to "distinguish a product or service which emanates from one source, from products or services emanating from other sources."[2] In other words, Harvard University would probably have been able to judicially shut down these websites through appropriate legal channels if it had needed to, but by showing foresight and being proactive, saved itself a lot of legal nuisance.

Two additional landmark cases from more than a half century ago have helped further set the precedent for trademark infringement on university brands. In 1930, *Trustees of Columbia Univ. v. Axenfeld* was a case in which the New York Supreme Court found in favor of Columbia University in regards to its branding rights. The defendants called their educational service "Columbia Educational Institute" with the intention to lead the public to believe that they were in fact affiliated with Columbia University when they were not.[3] They were forced to give up the moniker immediately. *Cornell Univ. v. Messing Bakeries* was the second of these precedent setting cases on the university level, taking place in 1956. In that instance, a baker who relied on a bread recipe developed by a Cornell University professor marketed the bread as Cornell Recipe Bread. The court ruled that the baker could not use the name "Cornell" without express written permission from Cornell University.[4]

Another highly relevant periodical piece for the topic at hand appeared in the *Journal of Legal Aspects*, written by J. D. McMillen, L. M. Benedict, and R. S. McMillen. This article discussed the roles of the artist and freedom of speech as they relate to the depiction of university-owned trademarks. As the article reveals, determining where in this gray area to draw lines of jurisdiction for current and future cases is hazy at best. Essentially, Harvard University had to go to court to get Eschool to stop using the word Harvard in their domain names. The university claimed that by allowing them to do so, the brand name Harvard was being diluted and consumers were mistakenly being taken to the wrong place. Though Eschool argued that "notharvard.com" did not break trademark laws, they did settle out of court, ultimately agreeing that they had "diluted and infringed the Harvard mark."[5] They also turned over any domain names that included the term "Harvard." As we will later learn in our study of the Razorback brand, averting an ongoing legal battle is often incentive enough for many individuals or companies to cease and desist their commercial efforts.

In a 2008 article for the *Tulsa World* entitled "OSU Objects to Bud Light Cans," Shannon Muchmore described another example of intent versus profit. The article focuses on the proposed advertising campaign of Bud Light beer and its use of Oklahoma State colors and logos on beer cans in the greater Stillwater, Oklahoma, area.[6] As the writer illustrates, not all opportunities to profit from brand rights are necessarily worth the investment and publicity that is inherently attached. Anheuser-Busch's advertising campaign used the colors of several universities on Bud Light beer being sold in campus vicinities; the campaign garnered public outrage, with some university officials claiming copyright infringement. Oklahoma State University spokesman Gary Shutt stated that "color matters when it comes to marketing and packaging. People in Oklahoma connect OSU with orange."[7] Therefore, in their opinion, using the team's colors or logo without university consent constitutes trademark infringement as well. According to a letter sent to Anheuser-Busch from OSU's governing board, "References to OSU cannot appear on promotional material without the university's consent."[8] That includes using team colors. The beer company in question was forced to pull the cans from markets where colleges complained and objected to their sale.

These issues apply to almost all levels of athletics. As Randy Sharer found in his piece for *Pantagraph*, there is a loosely managed world of high school athletic emblems and logos as it pertains to merchandising as well. With so many team nicknames overlapping these days, the distribution and flow of brand-name merchandise can be hard to monitor and track. According to the court decision described in the article, "Federal law requires trademark holders to police their own trademarks. If too many entities use a logo, a college could lose its trademark."[9] Though the ruling finds on behalf of the athletic brands in question, it also places the emphasis for keeping them secure on the schools themselves. For this reason, colleges and professional teams are sometimes forced to bring legal action against high schools for sports logos that look too similar to their own. But some colleges actually like the extra attention it brings, as in the case of the Kansas State University Wildcats. A high school in Illinois actually pays the Manhattan-based university one dollar per year to continue using the Wildcat logo. Few other collegiate or professional teams embrace the publicity in this kind of situation the way Kansas State University does.[10] It is hard to argue against the practicality of such an arrangement.

An additional timely article on the unauthorized use of trade-marks by the individual was written by Matthew Fischer and Jia-Ming Shang for *Intellectual Property and Technology Law Journal* in 2011. They discuss a circuit court's determination that any use of the name or likeness of a previously trademarked brand without the expressly dictated consent of the brand owner itself is a violation of copyright law.[11] Generally speaking, nonspecific inference of a trademark was acceptable to certain courts prior to 2010. "Nominative use involves the use of a trademark to describe the trademark owner's own prod-uct,"[12] often used in comparative advertising or criticism of a mark where trademark disputes arise. "The Federal Trade Commission gen-erally encourages comparative advertising,"[13] as long as it is not done deceptively. However, the Lanham Act prohibits the unauthorized use of a trademark in advertising where the use is likely to cause consumer confusion about the origin of goods or to perhaps even suggest an affiliation with the trademark. Prior to the 2010 decision by the Ninth Circuit Court, trademark infringement cases based on nominative use were upheld, even when the complaint did not demonstrate consumer confusion. After the 2010 decision, courts could dismiss trademark infringement cases before they even proceeded to trial based on fail-ure to demonstrate confusion. This means that nominative use of a trademark, especially in comparative advertising, is acceptable as long as no consumer confusion can be proved.[14]

It is important to remember that a school's actual name is clearly a significant part of its brand as well, particularly as it can relate to the geographic specificity of a certain city, state, or area. In a 2012 article for the *Augusta Chronicle*, Sandy Hodson wrote about just this issue. Her article discussed the relevance of such locational ties and how already existing athletic institutions sometimes try to block the creation of newer schools with similar area-related names, citing prior consent.[15] As Hodson described, that year the name for the consolidated schools of Augusta State and Georgia Health Sciences universities was brought to court by a Virginia school. The proposed name for the new school, Georgia Regents University, was opposed by Regent University in Virginia, claiming "trademark infringement and unfair competition."[16] According to the article, Regents University has been trademarked since at least 1990. Though citizens of the city wanted to see "Augusta" as part of the name, it was not incorporated. The decision to include "Augusta" in the new university name did not settle the matter as far as Regents University in Virginia was concerned as a lawsuit is still pending as of 2013.

The dollars at stake here are a huge determinant of branding protection policy in play as well. Richard Miller and Kelli Washington recently wrote of this effect in an article for *Sports Marketing*. They describe at length the extremely high numbers and dollars in play when it comes to big business athletics and advertising. This piece contains informative and descriptive charts and details on the annual contracts of highly renowned athletes, organizations, and universities.[17] The data included is a valuable tool for dissecting which brands, sports, and athletes carry the most economic weight. On the same grounds, *IEG Sponsorship Report* writes that sports sponsorship spending has increased from $6.5 billion in 2002 to $13.2 billion in 2012. The more than double growth in spending was derived from data accumulated from the four major professional team sports in America: baseball, basketball, football, and hockey.[18] With this idea in mind, one gets a much better gauge of why the protection of such highly valuable brands remains an ongoing priority for their keepers. Looking at soccer's English Premier League, three of their teams each receive $32.6 million per year for sponsorships on the front of their players' jerseys. In 2006, the United States' Major League Soccer also adopted the trend, with top companies paying millions of dollars annually to advertise on the players' uniforms. Women's Professional Soccer and the Women's National Basketball Association also permit sponsorships on their jerseys.[19] So far, the four major professional sports leagues of the United States have only considered such advertising but have yet to incorporate the practice. The NBA, NFL, MLB, and NHL must first weigh cost versus benefit. Among the top questions raised is "how [a] jersey logo deal would affect league broadcast and marketing revenue."[20] Though the figure would likely skyrocket, one can speculate that the negative impression on longtime fans might cancel out the financial gain.

Playing loosely with brand names and infringing on trademarks can have dire consequences for those involved, even on individual scales. In an article for the *Virginian-Pilot* by Scott Daugherty, the case of an entrepreneur attempting to profit off of professional and collegiate brands without prior authorization or consent is discussed at length. The man in question argued that his company was simply trying to counter already outrageous existing prices for team apparel and merchandise. Despite this common-man-type defense, Keith Carter was found guilty of a felony count of trademark infringement and ordered to pay $10,000 in restitution. He was deemed to have counterfeit sports jerseys in his store, selling them for far less than his competitors. Carter claimed he did not know they were counterfeit, though the jerseys in his store numbered more than 1,200. The Coalition to Advance the Protection of Sports Logos, an alliance formed in 1992 by several professional sports leagues, initiated prosecution of the case. The coalition's aim is to "address common trademark protection and enforcement matters of its members."[21] It is to this coalition that the court assigning judgment determined that Carter's restitution must be paid.

In summation of the previously discussed literature, one can determine that various courts are liable to reach different determinations on similar subject matter in different places at different times. Good lawyers can help their clients to decent resolutions in many cases, but as we described initially, those infringing upon trademark and branding rights run the risk of serious litigation on both criminal and civil levels. Even without proof of malicious intent, those who infringe upon branding rights put themselves in vulnerable positions. Historically, most courts have tended to find on behalf of those who first patented the brand or trademark in question. While some courts have previously sided with those individuals utilizing artistic and creative expression for noncommercial gain, the burden of proving and defending such a motivation will likely fall on the defendant. Generally, if someone intends to use or inference an already existing brand, it most behooves them to proceed along the appropriate trademark channels in regards to seeking express written permission and consent. As discussed earlier, even if a brand holder is not the motivating presence behind such usages, there is a good possibility that it will license the brand out to those interested in its use for a percentage or fee. In many cases this can benefit both the brand holder and those intending to use it, though that is not always the case.

Case Analysis

An informative long-form magazine feature by Jim Harris and Max Brantley appeared in the *Arkansas Times* in October 2006, describing the distribution and dissemination of images and names of university employees as it relates to merchandising.[22] The article discusses the gray area between freedom of speech and the right of institutions to protect their brands, particularly as it pertains to the University of Arkansas and former football coach Houston Nutt.

When, in 2006, Arkansas resident and lifelong Razorback fan Caleb Larru decided he was sick of then head football coach Houston Nutt, he decided to make a T-shirt that represented Nutt's perceived shortcomings as a joke among friends. The front of the T-shirt (which, per Larru's request and settlement with the University of Arkansas, is not depicted herein) showed a caricatured image of Nutt wearing his game-day headset, with the phrase "Moral National Championship" written above it. This was a reference to the sports cliché of "moral victories," where a team comes close but fails to win. The shirt did not have Houston Nutt's name on it, nor did it have the words Arkansas or Razorbacks anywhere on it either. The back of the shirt listed all of the coach's failures, in Larru's eyes. Among them were a bunch of bullet points led off by the numeral "0," as in 0 ten win seasons; 0 SEC championships; 0 top 10 recruiting classes; 0 wins for the month of October in four out of eight seasons of SEC play; 0 SEC wins against teams with winning records since 2002; it also listed a 1–11 win/loss record against the Universities of Georgia, Florida, and Tennessee; just 2 wins in 6 bowl game appearances; a 7-24 mark against SEC teams with winning records; and a 31-34 overall SEC record, with 12 of the 31 wins against lowly respected football programs Ole Miss and Mississippi State.

Larru originally printed only a few of the shirts for his friends, selling them at cost and making no profit. Then, the T-shirts became popular with some of his similarly disheartened fellow Hog fans, so he decided to have more printed. However, before he could distribute them, the University of Arkansas intervened and demanded the shirts be turned over to the school, claiming that "by common law, the University owns the name, likeness and image of its employees and additionally that it was written into its employment contract with Houston Nutt at the time of his hiring."[23]

The counterargument here is that Nutt was a public figure, just like a senator, governor, or president, and therefore anyone can cite freedom of speech and use his image without infringement if it is for the expression of a personal opinion. Still, this leaves room for extensive debate, being that the only major problem the university actually complained of was the sale of the T-shirts on their campus without express written permission, which is the cited university policy in question. Though the shirt merely depicted Nutt's image, not his name, nor any of the Razorback logos, anyone who wishes to distribute merchandise of any kind on public university grounds must go through the appropriate approval process first, beginning by contacting the university's marketing department itself. Larru readily admits that he failed to do this, likely because he felt that his request would be denied. Ultimately, threatened with a lawsuit and the removal of his season ticket privileges, Larru agreed to hand over the shirts, and his designated printing company immediately destroyed the existing screen images of the shirts in question. University officials claim they would have taken action even if the shirt had been positive, stating that the shirt maker was not on a list of "approved vendors." But surely the negative spin on their football program is what set off the reaction from the University of Arkansas in the case in question. It must be noted, though, that the federal courts were on Larru's side here, if precedent is any kind of an indicator. Hustler publisher Larry Flynt went right after this very point in his satires of the Reverend Jerry Falwell in the 1970s. Despite Falwell's assertions of slander and libel, Flynt was able to win his case on the grounds of freedom of speech and creative artistic expression. As described in an article for the *New York Times* by Shipp, the Supreme Court found on behalf of the publisher Flynt, saying: "The freedom to speak one's mind is not only an aspect of individual liberty—and thus a good unto itself—but also is essential to the common quest for truth and the vitality of society as a whole. We have therefore been particularly vigilant to ensure that individual expressions of ideas remain free from governmentally imposed sanctions."[24]

The Personal Account of Caleb Larru/ University of Arkansas

It was a matter of pride.

Most college football fans would agree with the sentiment echoed by Fort Smith native and diehard Razorback fan Caleb Larru. The thirty-two-year-old resident of Fort Smith, Arkansas, was born into his fanhood, as are many fans of one program or another in the world of college athletics. In the state of Arkansas, the passion and commitment of the fan base hits a whole different level, as there are no other professional teams in the area, let alone any other significant in-state Division I athletic programs. Very few universities can lay claim to such a special prestige and Larru is well aware of the fact.

"When you grow up here, calling the Hogs as a kid, going to the games, and being around the passion of the fans, there's not another team you even really care about," says Larru, with a confidence in his voice that underscores the seriousness of the sentiment he offers. "My dad is a diehard Razorback fan. His dad was a diehard Razorback fan. The torch gets passed from generation to generation . . . It's in your blood."[25]

Clearly that makes a lot of sense to anyone familiar with the culture and passion of college athletics, and so one might expect all kinds of excited displays of such emotion from various fan bases on a daily basis. Brian Pracht is the director of marketing for the University of Arkansas, and says it is both an ongoing asset and an issue for those in charge of such an inherently accepted piece of local culture. "The fan base here is phenomenal, there's no understating that fact. The support we receive everyday makes it a fun job for me, and at times it can make a lot of what we do, from a promotional standpoint, a whole lot easier. There's not of lot of stuff we do that is isn't well received by most of the fans." But Pracht offers a disclaimer too. "Unfortunately, the protection of the brand becomes an issue for us when fans decide to take the Razorback logo into their own hands. We always have to stay vigilant when it comes to merchandising and infringement, because some of the same fans who love the program also fall into the category of feeling like they own it as well . . . And that's just not the case."[26]

The University of Arkansas officially put in for a trademark of the brand name "Razorbacks" in the early 1980s, but that didn't preclude those who already held businesses or companies with the moniker from continuing to use it. In fact, university attorney Scott Varady believes the university has been gracious with the use of its brand ever since. "If you were a movie theater, a restaurant or whatever business that already had the Razorback name in your business name, you were grandfathered in," he says. "The idea behind officially trademarking the brand was to prevent others in the future from continuing to incorporate its use, and yet we have cases emerging all the time where people try to take advantage of that. The situation with Mr. Larru derived from exactly that kind of an independent infringement. And then you have the whole element of his selling the shirts on university grounds without permission, which by our interpretation is unacceptable."[27]

As described earlier, the previously mentioned Caleb Larru was involved in a legal dispute with the University of Arkansas in 2006. Larru arranged for a printmaker friend of his to create a first batch of fifty T-shirts and took them to the following weekend's home football game with him. They proved to be highly sought after by similarly disenchanted fans. Larru relates: "It was just me saying what all of my friends were saying, and that was that Houston Nutt had to go. I wasn't trying to make any money, I wasn't trying to insult the school, I was just trying to state the facts of where we were at as a team."[28] Indeed, according to Larru, the T-shirts were sold at the game for cost only, though he did have plans to have more made. The University of Arkansas didn't view the situation in nearly such innocent terms. They filed a cease and desist order against him and proceeded with legal action to make him stop with the shirts' production, proliferation, and distribution. But with no representation of the Razorback emblem, no mention of the coach's name, and no specific use of the word Razorbacks, on what grounds was the school even proceeding?

"We felt that we were justified to get him to stop on the grounds that Houston Nutt was a commercial employee of the University of Arkansas," Varady stated. "With that precedent in place, Mr. Nutt's likeness was, at the time, a property of the University as well. We have contractual agreements with certain employees that while they are employed by the school, any use of their name or likeness must be authorized by the University first, in writing, and Mr. Larru never proceeded down that avenue."[29]

Surely doing so would have meant getting the university's consent for negative publicity, and it is highly unlikely that the school was going to agree to that, but Varady's assertion of employee agreements taking precedent over freedom of speech is an interesting one with a fair amount of legal value. By nature, the United States of America grants its citizens the right to express themselves and to speak freely, so long as they are not violating laws or committing illegal acts in doing so. But a situation such as Larru and his T-shirts put this gray trademark area of the American legal system into the crosshairs. Just how far is too far? And at what point do personal expressions of freedom of speech infringe upon branding and trademark rights? As discussed in the opening passages of this article, the precedent for this realm of the commercial domain is still obscure in this country. It mostly seems to depend upon the court that is determining its decision, not to mention the judges in place at the time. But without an actual coach's name, and despite overt references to statistics compiled at a school under his watch, did Larru violate anything? Or was he just expressing his dissatisfaction with the team that he loved in a purely American fashion? Larru offers his own response.

"I knew Houston Nutt was the wrong guy for the job right away. I told my dad and my friends that right at the time and they didn't want to hear it. Ten years later they knew I was right and finally admitted it. All I was trying to do was get the word out that we the fans knew the team could be better with a better coach. I wasn't looking to make any money out of it. I just wanted to force the issue with the people in charge at the school. I guess, at the end of the day, I was able to do that."[30]

Marketing director Brian Pracht vehemently disagrees. "There are situations like this all the time that we have to be vigilant about. From what I gather, Larru already had plans to make and distribute more T-Shirts, and if we let him do that for profit on our campus, we run the risk of losing certain endowment privileges that we get from being an institution of higher learning first and foremost. It's not like we are looking to hold back fans and their passion, but we can't let everyone step all over our brand and our rules just because they want to. Every year we put together an independent vendor festival where Razorback fans can share their creations with others without the risk of legal intervention. But if we operated like that on a daily basis, we would run the risk of losing the value of the brand that everyone cherishes in the first place."[31]

University attorney Scott Varady agrees with Pracht, citing the process in place to create such items, if people so choose. "It's not like we have a system where there is no room for people to be creative. If someone wants to make a Razorback guitar, or a clothing line, or an automobile, with the logo or the school name or an employee's image on it, all we require is that they contact our marketing department first and in what we believe is the right and fair way. Mr. Larru never did that, and so he gave us no choice but counter legally like we did."[32]

Conclusion

Threatened with the possibility of losing his season tickets, Mr. Larru turned over his anti-Houston Nutt merchandise and agreed to not make any more. Larru claims he still got requests for the shirts for the remainder of Nutt's tenure at the University of Arkansas (he resigned two years later in 2008) but says ultimately it wasn't worth the trouble. At the end of the day, he remains a Razorback fan first and foremost. "I love this program and I love this state, so I didn't want to burn up my bridges. I just wanted the school to know that the fans weren't happy, and I think, in looking back, that I probably made my point. You can't hold people back when they have something to say. Especially when they're right." Larru points out that the final agreement left him free to express his opinion, albeit without the T-shirts in question. "I still have my season tickets to the football games in Fayetteville, and I'm actually a season ticket holder to the basketball and baseball games now too. So in the end I really don't get what kind of a message they thought they were sending."[33]

There's little doubting it would have been interesting to watch the case unfold in a court of law if it had come to that, as the University of Arkansas would have stood its ground on the notion of employee licensing agreements, while Larru and his attorney were prepared to proceed with the freedom of speech defense. However, the threat of losing season tickets along with the likely possibility of prolonged and highly expensive legal action was enough to dissuade Caleb Larru from proceeding.[34] But it does not answer the question of whether or not the issue was going to be settled definitively in a court of law. Referencing the cases earlier described in this article, it seems like freedom of speech likely would have won out in this specific situation, although employment agreement contracts carry weight as well. Indeed, if a court of law deemed the depiction of Houston Nutt to be an actual representation of his likeness, the University of Arkansas would have had valid legal grounds to cite its employment contracts as a controlling interest in the case. However, since the image used on Caleb Larru's T-shirts was not an actual photograph, but a caricature of the former football coach, with no specific mention of his name, nor the institution for which he worked, it is realistic to assume that a judge would have deemed the shirts and their distribution legally protected expressions of freedom of speech.

Future Research

As it pertains to future research on the subjects at hand, I would recommend studies focusing on the public's general knowledge of such trademark laws. I am assuming that a high number of sports fans feel similarly to Caleb Larru, and believe that they are within their rights to express themselves about the teams they care so passionately about, whether it is positive or negative in nature. The accumulation of statistics and data along these lines, obtainable through interviews and questionnaires, could prove to be very useful in better gauging just what the public knows and understands on the subject.

I also think it would be helpful if more researchers analyzed the legal weight of employee licensing contracts. In the previously discussed situation, it was just this kind of agreement that gave the University of Arkansas its grounds for stopping the distribution of Larru's T-shirts. But very little previously existing research is available on the full legal weight of these agreements and how much say courts actually give them. I find it likely that other universities and professional sports teams force their employees to agree to similar deals prior to obtaining employment. The legality of such arrangements needs to be further examined and clarified, as they currently seem to exist in the gray area that we discussed at the very outset of this paper. Until such research is conducted and published, it will be left up to plaintiffs to initiate and defendants to defend themselves on a case-by-case and court-by-court basis, with little concrete legal precedent to draw upon.

NOTES

1. Daniel Howard, Roger Kerin, and Charles Gengler, "The Effects of Brand Name Similarity on Brand Source Confusion: Implications for Trademark Infringement," *Journal of Public Policy and Marketing* 19, no. 2 (2000): 254.

2. Alayne Manas, "Harvard as a Model in Trademark and Domain Name Protection," *Rutgers Computer and Technology Law Journal* 29 (2003): 485.

3. Sandy Hodson, "Legal Challenge to Consolidated College New Name Narrowed by Regents University," *Augusta Chronicle* (GA), November 26, 2012.

4. Manas, "Harvard as a Model in Trademark and Domain Name Protection," 487.

5. J. D. McMillen, L. M. Benedict, and R. S. McMillen, "Control of University Sponsored Sporting Events: The Conflict between Sport Artist's Freedom of Expression and University Owned Trademarks," *Journal of Legal Aspects of Sport* 17, no. 2 (2007): 145.

6. Shannon Muchmore, "OSU Objects to Bud Light Cans," *Tulsa World* (OK), September 1, 2009.

7. Ibid.

8. Ibid.

9. Randy Sharer, "High School Athletics Logos Can Look Familiar," *Pantagraph* (Bloomington, IL), October 20, 2010.

10. Ibid.

11. Matthew Fischer and Jia-Ming Shang, "Trademark Infringement Claims Based on Nominative Use Get Boost from Circuit Court Ruling," *Intellectual Property and Technology Law Journal* 23, no. 8 (2011): 8–13.

12. Ibid.

13. Ibid.

14. Ibid.

15. Sandy Hodson, "Legal Challenge to Consolidated College New Name Narrowed by Regents University," *Augusta Chronicle* (GA), November 26, 2012.

16. Ibid.

17. Richard K. Miller and Kelli Washington, "Advertising and Sponsorships," in *Sports Marketing 2013*, 45.

18. Ibid.

19. Ibid.

20. Ibid.

21. Ibid.

22. Jim Harris and Max Brantley, "The Polarizing of Razorback Nation: What Houston Nutt Once Brought Together Is Torn Asunder as the Coach Struggles to Survive," *Arkansas Times* (Little Rock, AR), October 5, 2006.

23. Ibid.

24. E. R. Shipp, "The Right to Be Disgusting: Jerry Falwell v. Larry Flynt; The First Amendment on Trial," *New York Times*, March 5, 1989.

25. Caleb Larru, interviewed by Josh Bertaccini, April 9, 2013, via telephone.

26. Brian Pracht, interviewed by Josh Bertaccini, March 29, 2013, at the University of Arkansas.

27. Scott Varady, interviewed by Josh Bertaccini, March 29, 2013, at the University of Arkansas.

28. Larru interview.

29. Varady interview.

30. Larru interview.

31. Pracht interview.

32. Varady interview.

33. Larru interview.

34. Ibid.

CHAPTER 5

Book Censorship in Fayetteville Public Schools

"The Chocolate Wars" and the "Battle of the Books"

CORTNEY SMITH

There is more than one way to burn a book. And the world is full of people running about with lit matches. Every minority, be it Baptist/Unitarian, Irish/Italian/ Octogenarian/Zan Buddhist, Zionist/Seventh-day Adventist, Women's Lib/ Republican, Mattachine/ FourSquareGospel feels it has the will, the right, the duty to douse the kerosene, light the fuse. Every dimwit editor who sees himself as the source of all dreary blanc-mange plain porridge unleavened literature, licks his guillotine and eyes the neck of any author who dares to speak above a whisper or write above a nursery rhyme.

—RAY BRADBURY

The nature of this study is to analyze book censorship in America, especially focusing on book censorship in the past fifty years in American public school systems. In the literature review, the author will establish why certain works are actually censored or have been considered for censoring and the arguments used to debate the censoring. Court cases will be reviewed that involve not only book censorship in public schools, but First Amendment cases involving students in public schools. The particular cases that will be evaluated in this study will be two highly publicized book debates from Fayetteville, Arkansas. "The Chocolate Wars" (1985) and the "Battle of the Books" (2005) will be compared and contrasted in order to recognize and analyze argument patterns. Many individuals involved in both censorship cases will give their opinions—often quite differing opinions—about the debates and the details of the stories. The study will conclude with an analysis of the arguments made by both groups of objectors—their similarities and differences and their effectiveness or lack thereof. A study of this nature is important in helping to understand why certain books are repeatedly objected upon, and to develop a deeper understanding of why people choose to support censorship.

Literature Review

Since the invention of the Guttenberg Press, the written word has been challenged and debated. In the past fifty years there has been a consistent increase in the number of challenged books in school libraries and classroom curriculums. From 1963 to 1985 there were over 900 challenged book titles in the United States public school library system. These titles varied from *The Abortion: A Historical Romance* to J. D. Salinger's *Catcher in the Rye*.[1] A 1992 study done by People for the American Way (PAW) found 348 demands of library material removal in forty-four states. The success rate of book removal was 41 percent for the 1991–1992 school year.[2]

The first questions researchers try to answer when analyzing book censorship is why objectors wish to remove books from school library shelves and classroom curriculum. According to the PAW study, libraries involved with the study identified the three most common reasons for book challenges. The first complaint surrounded the idea that materials were "anti-Christian," "Satanic," "New Age," or generally contrary to the challengers' religious views. Of the 348 documented censorship attempts, 140 of them were based on this view. *Of Mice and Men* and *Catcher in the Rye* are two examples of books commonly linked with this challenge. The second most common challenge stated that the materials in question contained profane or otherwise objectionable language. Almost one-third of the challenged books in the PAW study found this as their objection. Books often associated with this complaint include Robert Cormier's *The Chocolate War* and Judy Blume's *Blubber*. The third reason for challenge was the materials' treatment of sexuality. The content and context of the sexuality was deemed offensive by the objectors. One-fifth of the books in the study were challenged using this rationale. The book titles that fell under this reasoning included *Grapes of Wrath* and *Slaughterhouse Five*.[3]

Along with establishing why certain books are often challenged, there is a desire to identify who wants works censored. Protests for certain books originate from many different places and groups of people. Women's groups often object to books that exploit women or works that establish traditional roles for women and restrict them to those roles. Civil rights groups often complain about books with racist language. This often includes Mark Twain's *The Adventures of Huckleberry Finn*, a literary work known for its use of racial slurs.[4] A large portion of challenges come from conservative political groups, who feel students should not have access to books the political groups find unsuitable.[5] In the PAW study, one-fifth of the challenges came from conservative political groups. Organizations that are known for their previous work in trying to remove books from school libraries include Citizens for Excellence in Education, the Blackstone Society, the Western Center for Law and Religious Freedom, and the American Family Association.[6] Today's immediate sources of censorship pressures on teachers and librarians are the parents of students in the schools.[7] J. D. Salinger's *Catcher in the Rye* is the single most censored work in the United States' school library systems.[8] Since it was published in 1951, the title has been challenged from Wisconsin to Missouri. The objectors have been parents, superintendents, school board members, ministers, and teachers. The list of specific reasons for its challenge varies from vulgarity and inappropriate language to blasphemy and objectionable references to homosexuality. The results of the challenges have also been vastly different among cases. The requests for removal have been denied and complied. In some cases the book was placed on a closed shelf, or the student was given an alternative book to read.[9]

There have been several court cases that have dictated standards and set precedent on book censorship in the United States. In *Tinker v. Des Moines Independent Community School District* (1969) students who opposed the Vietnam War wore black armbands. This was thought to be inappropriate, and the principal told the students to remove the armbands. Any students who refused to remove the armbands would be subject to suspension. The case went to the Supreme Court and the justices ruled in favor of the plaintiff. The court found "students may not be regarded as closed-circuit recipients of only that which the State chooses to communicate. They may not be confined to the expression of those sentiments that are officially approved."[10] In *Board of Education, Island Trees Union Free School District v. Pico* (1982) a school board in New York had received a list of objectionable books by parents associated with Parents of New York—United organization. The school board removed eleven books from the school district's libraries. Pico was a seventeen-year-old student who said the removal of the books violated his First Amendment rights. The Supreme Court agreed with Pico.[11] The court stated that "the right to receive ideas is a necessary predicate to the recipient's meaningful exercise of his own rights of speech, press, and political freedom."[12] This decision set forth the standard on that any removal of an entire genre of books, books with a particular subject matter, or books by a single author would be immediately suspect as unconstitutionally motivated.[13] In the Pico case, the Supreme Court recognized that a school library is an "environment especially appropriate for the recognition of the First Amendment rights of students."[14] The courts established the right of teachers, principals, and school boards to take action "within the school's educational mission that might otherwise be unconstitutional" in the 1988 case of *Hazelwood School District v. Kuhlmeier*. The court saw no constitutional restraint on a Missouri school principal who removed portions of a student newspaper.[15] The following year in Florida, the Eleventh Circuit ruled in favor of a school board that had removed a textbook from the curriculum of a humanities course in *Virgil v. School Board of Columbia County*. The circuit panel held that school officials could remove books from the curriculum if they believed the works are too vulgar for students and there is a legitimate educational reason for the removal.[16] In *Billy Ray Counts and Mary Nell Counts v. Cedarville School District* (2003), the court found that Dakota Counts's (child of Billy Ray and Mary Nell) First Amendment rights were being infringed upon by the defendants' decision to restrict access to the Harry Potter books to those students whose parents signed a permission slip allowing them to check the books out of the school library.[17] The purpose of this study is to compare and contrast "The Chocolate Wars" (1985) and the "Battle of the Books" (2005), and to determine what arguments (or lack of arguments) did those supporting restrictions on the novels fail to make.

Narrative

In the past twenty-one years, the state of Arkansas, and in particular the city of Fayetteville, has become a mecca for the debate on book censorship in public schools. In the fall of 1985, Ms. Cassandra Stone, a Fayetteville High School English teacher, assigned *The Chocolate War* by Robert Cormier to her Expository Writing Class, a junior-level, elective course. The novel tells the story of Jerry Renault, a student at a Catholic high school, who tries to stand up to a secret society, which manipulates and intimidates students, by refusing to sell chocolates—a school fundraiser supported by the headmasters of the school. The novel follows the pressures to conform and how the struggle against conformity sometimes has unfortunate consequences.[18] The novel was chosen for the class in order for the students conduct a character analysis. The novel had been used in the school system in past years without complaint, but instead with a multitude of praises. According to Judy Schwab (at the time Judy Gregson), a high school English teacher and the language arts coordinator for Fayetteville Public Schools in 1985, a number of parents asked for a reading list after their student read *The Chocolate War*. "This book turned their child on to reading like no other book had." Teachers had become aware of the novel through a well-known teachers' journal,

The English Journal. The journal raved about the novel and how it could impact students.[19] The novel had been named on the *New York Times* "Outstanding Book of the Year for Young Adults" in 1974. That same year it was named "Best Book for Young Adults" by the American Library Association (ALA).[20]

The book was handed out to the class by a substitute teacher without any special instructions in the fall semester of 1985. This was an extraordinary situation. In previous years, teachers had attached a warning note to the novel. The teacher would tell the class that if they found anything offensive in the book they were to let the teacher know and an alternative book would be assigned. According to Schwab, this was a known non-policy act teachers performed to help students who felt offended by the novel. It gave students a way to express concerns and read another book in order to fulfill the character analysis assignment. Schwab had informed Stone about this accepted non-policy; however, the new teacher did not incorporate it at any time during the initial process of dispersing the book and did not instruct the substitute to do so.[21]

On November 1, 1985, Robert Gross, a third-year law student at the University of Arkansas-Fayetteville Law School, submitted a formal request to the Fayetteville School Administration to have *The Chocolate War* removed from the curriculum of the English writing courses. The official complaint was known as a Patron Request for Reconsideration of a Work. Gross found several portions of the novel to be inappropriate and not beneficial to his eleventh-grade daughter. These reservations included the use of profanity and vulgarity. Gross detailed those incidents in his six-page complaint. Gross said his daughter was "embarrassed by the vulgarity and crudeness of language and was emotionally disturbed by the profanity, she was afraid to mention it to her parents for fear of academic reprisals from the teacher."[22] Don Deweese, the administrative assistant for Information Services for the Fayetteville School District, said Gross's request was the "most detailed and thoughtful response" he had ever seen to that point in his tenure, which was ten years at the time of the debate.[23] Gross had first become aware of the questionable material when his wife had dropped in on their daughter as she prayed. Mrs. Gross asked her daughter what she had been praying about. The daughter informed her mother that "she was actually praying that God would forgive her for having to read the book, since reading it so greatly violated her conscience and her spirit that she considered it a sin to do so."[24] Gross also felt the novel could lead to "an unwanted effect in students who are already unsuccessfully dealing with depression and lack of self worth" due to the "depressing and hopeless feeling that pervades the novel."[25] According to Gross, the family mutually agreed the girl should ask for an alternative reading assignment; however, Stone denied her request. Gross believed the entire situation could have been avoided if Stone would have warned the students about the content and provided them with an alternative assignment.[26] This belief is in contrast with Schwab, who believes there was a certain political climate during this time in Fayetteville. There were those looking for a case of "indecency" in the school system, and Stone provided it with her failure to provide a warning of the book's content. The situation could not have been avoided.[27]

Within a week of the complaint being filed, Deweese began work with two assistant superintendents, one elementary librarian, and one secondary education librarian to appoint a review committee to make a decision on Gross's complaint. Deweese followed a policy that had already been put in place since he obtained his position. The procedure included the following: a formal complaint was filed then the Library Council (Deweese and his peers) would appoint a four-member committee to review the complaint. After reaching a decision, the committee's recommendation would then become the standard for the book in question within the school system. Deweese and his colleagues tried to bring together a well-balanced committee, without bias, that could look at the situation and reach an appropriate and acceptable decision. The committee was composed of a representative from central administration staff, a representative from building level administrative, a materials specialist, and two classroom teachers familiar with the subject matter of the materials involved, two parents, and a student.[28] These members were chosen based on their qualifications. Each was from a Fayetteville junior high school (except for the student) instead of Fayetteville High to avoid biasing and to keep the representatives away from the school in question. Each committee member was asked to read the book and look over the complaint, and each was given copies of reviews of the material from several recognized sources, including the ALA.[29] On November 15, 1985, the Evaluation Committee concluded to keep the book in the curriculum; however, they did recommend that a standard practice be put forth that each teacher should preface the book with a disclaimer that if at any point a student felt the book contained objectionable material they would have the opportunity to read an alternative book.[30] Gross found the committee's decision inadequate and appealed the decision. At that point, the complaint went to the Fayetteville School Board.

From mid-November to the December 17 school board meeting, the debate continued with editorials in the local newspaper and the formation of groups that opposed and supported the use of the novel in the curriculum. The first group to form was the Citizens for Excellence in Education (CEE) with Gross serving as its president. This group was not a chapter of the national CEE, but its own separate entity. CEE felt the novel should be taken out of the curriculum. A few days prior to the December 17 school board meeting, Fayetteville High School parents received a thirteen-page packet from CEE. The packet included a summarization of the issue, names of school board members and their phone numbers, copies of Gross's complaint, the Evaluation Committee's report, and a statement from Stone and Schwab to the school board. The packet asked parents "if after reviewing the enclosed materials you have an opinion about whether the book entitled *The Chocolate War* should be used in the Fayetteville Public Schools, please contact the School Board members with your comments. Then attend the December 17 meeting to support your comments."[31] CEE had its counterpart in the Students for Enlightened Education (SEE). SEE was a group of high school students who formed not only in response to CEE, but also because they believed in the importance of *The Chocolate War* as a novel. The students believed the book provided "valuable thematic material in the form of a warning about conforming behavior and its consequences and a view of the dark side of human nature."[32]

The December school board meeting would end up being a hot ticket in town. Over 150 Fayetteville citizens attended the meeting. The school board listened to both sides of the debate. In the end they came to the decision to leave the book in the curriculum, but to make it policy that students be given a "warning" of the novel's content and inform students that an alternative assignment would be available.[33] The school board's decision remained a hot topic throughout the beginning of 1986 and became a vital issue in the school board election held in March.

Professor Howard Brill, a law professor and active member of the community, decided to run for one of the two open spots on the board. When Brill decided to run he believed the issue of *The Chocolate War* had been decided, but instead he discovered there was lingering resentment and controversy surrounding the issue.[34] When publicly asked about the issue, Brill responded, "I would have voted on Dec. 17th to remove *The Chocolate War* from the list of approved reading materials."[35] Brill and a fellow candidate in the second race were supported by the CEE. The CEE would place an ad in the *Northwest Arkansas Times*, a Fayetteville newspaper, March 7, 1986. The ad contained quotes from each candidate regarding their stance on *The Chocolate War* issue and excerpts from the book CEE deemed inappropriate. There were many who felt the ad was inaccurate and unethical to be published during the race. These objectors included Feriba McNair, school board president at the time, who had voted to keep *The Chocolate War* as part of the curriculum. McNair stated, "No student in the Fayetteville schools is or ever has been required to read *The Chocolate War*, and it is very disappointing when people attempt to influence the democratic process by misrepresenting the facts of a situation. This sets a very bad example for our youth when adults are not honest in resolving their political differences."[36] McNair would later recount this statement and state that some teachers had indeed assigned *The Chocolate War* as required reading. A group of English teachers also placed an ad in the same paper expressing their rationale for choosing the book. Some in the community felt that the English teachers wanted to establish their authority as instructors and in making decisions about their curriculums. Brill stated that the English teachers "took the position that it was improper interference with their professional judgment what book should be read." Brill felt citizens and parents should be entitled to have an influence on the books their children read, and that the burden of asking for an alternative assignment should not be placed upon the student and parent but the teacher. He never felt the novel should be removed from the school library, and instead felt the novel could be placed on an alternative reading list. In the end, Brill would lose the election in a close race to Sue Gohn. When asked about the book issue and its impact on the race, Brill believed the teachers' organization's support of his opponent (Gohn had agreed with the teachers' standpoint on *The Chocolate War*) had a great impact on his loss.[37] "The Chocolate Wars" battle was over, but it was not the end of book censorship debating in Fayetteville.

Twenty years later a book debate would again consume the Fayetteville community, albeit a very different debate. Instead of the debate concerning the use of a certain book in the classroom curriculum, the 2005 "Battle of the Books" (as it would become known) revolved around the access of certain books in the Fayetteville Public Schools Library. In early 2005, Laurie Taylor, a mother of two girls, ages ten and twelve, received a letter from a large conservative organization she financially supported. The letter informed Taylor of Robie Harris's novel, *It's Perfectly Normal*, a book considered by the organization to contain inappropriate material.[38] *It's Perfectly Normal* is a novel about sexual discovery, and the book contains explicit drawings. The drawings show the stages of sexual development in boys and girls, the many various kinds of bodies people have, drawings of genitalia and the reproductive organs, different forms of contraception, tampons and pads, and people engaged in talking about sex and even having sex.[39] Taylor bought and read the book. She was flabbergasted by the work's content and its availability to her children. "I was grieved and so incredibly saddened that this type of book was available to my children without my knowledge."[40]

On February 16, 2005, Taylor filed a Patron's Request for Reconsideration of Work form. In her complaint, Taylor stated she felt the purpose of the work was "to perpetuate sexual immorality, to entice young children to experiment both heterosexually and homosexually." On the request form, there were three options as to what the patron wanted to happen to the work. The three options included (1) do not assign or recommend it to my child, (2) withdraw it back from all students, or (3) send it back to the proper department for reevaluation. Taylor marked that she wished the novel to be withdrawn from all students.[41] According to Taylor, if there would have been a different option that was more feasible to the situation she would have marked it, but not feeling any of the other options were adequate she requested the removal of the book.[42] The policy that had been used during "The Chocolate Wars" was essentially the same except for the actual membership of the Materials Evaluation Committee. The committee would again be comprised of a representative from central administration staff, a representative from building-level administrative, a materials specialist, and two classroom teachers familiar with the subject matter of the materials involved, two parents, and a student. Within two weeks, the committee was organized and established to evaluate the request and come to a decision as to what would happen with the book. This decision would then be implemented throughout the school system. On March 2, 2005, the committee came to the decision to leave the book in the libraries without any restrictions. The committee felt "a decision of access (or not) does constitute one parent (or group of parents) deciding what the children of other parents are allowed (or not allowed) to see/read."[43]

Before the committee had come to a decision on *It's Perfectly Normal*, Taylor filed two more complaints about two other novels on February 25, 2005, and had once again asked for the books' withdrawal from the school libraries. The two books were Robie Harris's *It's So Amazing*, a novel about sexual development, love, reproduction, adoption, and sexually transmitted diseases, and Jeremy Daldry's *The Teenage Guy's Survival Guide*, a novel described as a humorous guide for boys ages ten to fourteen, offering advice on dating, sex, body changes, and social life.[44] Taylor stated in her complaint for each book that if a student read either book that he/she would be "compelled to sexual titillation and exploration" and that it would "desensitize children to sexual immorality both heterosexually and homosexually."[45] The same evaluation committee was once again used to review Taylor's new complaints, and once again on March 15 they came to the same conclusion to leave the books in the libraries' circulations. Again the committee based their decision on the idea that the right of a parent to exclude what his/her child can read cannot be applied to all parents in the school system and circumvents their authority.[46]

Taylor did not feel the committee had come to an appropriate decision and felt that by allowing her children to have access to these books she was losing her right to parent as she saw fit. According to Taylor she did not want to ban the books, although she did mark that they be withdrawn from the libraries. Instead she wanted a way in which books with "questionable" material would be identified, so she could inform her children they were not allowed to check out such books.[47] Taylor appealed the committee's decision on the three works and the issue was brought to the school board in their May meeting. On May 26, 2005, Dr. Bob New, superintendent of Fayetteville Public Schools, made a series of recommendations to the board on the appeal of the Materials Evaluation Committee's decision. These recommendations included putting the books on parental shelves in the libraries and to require a documented effort be made to contact the student's parents for approval before the book *It's So Amazing* is made available to a student. The board voted 4–3 to approve Dr. New's recommendations. The three books, *It's So Amazing, It's Perfectly Normal,* and *The Teenage Guy's Survival Guide,* would remain available on the parent shelves in school libraries and would be unavailable for checkout by students.[48]

However, New's decision to change the Materials Evaluation Committee's recommendation disturbed many citizens in the community. To these citizens any sort of restriction was a form of censorship and censorship of any sort was unacceptable. Included in those who felt the changes were not only inappropriate but also not legal was the school system's own attorney, Judge Rudy Moore, who had been at the May meeting. "I got concerned because I felt like the restrictions were more than what I anticipated."[49] Many in the community became disillusioned and shocked by the school board decision. This included two practicing physicians in the community, Dr. Janet Titus and Dr. Kat Paulson. Titus and Paulson both had children in the public school system. In June 2005, Paulson and Titus began organizing a group of like-minded people to counteract Taylor, who by this time had created a list of fifty-four novels she felt were inappropriate and wanted out of the reach of her children. Among these novels were several award winners. These awards included two Nobel Prize winners, one Pulitzer, two Parent's Choice, three National Book Critics Circle Awards, and the list goes on.[50] Titus and Paulson's group, Don't Ban Books (DBB), contacted school board members and other school officials, organized meetings, and created an email listerv that kept the group up-to-date and in contact with one another.[51] During the summer months, no books could be requested for removal because of the summer break—essentially everything was put on hold. The Evaluation Committee could not be formed and the vast number of books on Taylor's list would take a substantial amount of time to review. In fact, it had taken the committee eighteen hours to come to their decisions on Taylor's first three complaints.[52] However, during this time the American Civil Liberties Union (ACLU) became more actively involved via Titus and Paulson's group. The organization had been keeping an eye on the situation and once some of the books were restricted became actively involved. Titus and Paulson's group maintained contact not only with the local ACLU representative, but also the state in Little Rock. Both attorneys informed Titus and Paulson that the law was on their side, and that precedent for this type of case had already been set with a case in Arkansas, *Counts v. Cedarville*. They assured the group that if the school board did not reevaluate its decision there could, and would, be repercussions.

In the end, DBB would count upward of eighty members. To counteract Taylor's claims about the fifty-four newly questionable books, the group divided up the works among themselves to see if they could find objectionable material within the novels. According to Paulson, "We felt Bobby New had tried to appease Taylor with the parental library restriction, but instead he made the situation worse. We wanted the school system to honor its policy." The DBB group wanted each novel to be looked at on an individual basis, and for the decisions of the Materials Evaluation Committee to be honored and not "tweaked" by school officials.

After successfully reading all fifty-four of the new books and the initial three books, members of DBB found no reason any of the books should be restricted and/or removed. In fact, the majority felt the books were very beneficial. Paulson found no dishonesty or inaccuracy in *The Teenage Guy's Survival Guide* and decided to read it together with her then twelve-year-old son. In fact, Paulson was so impressed with the book she gave it to friends who had children and put it along with *It's So Amazing* and *It's Perfectly Normal* in her practice's office.[53]

Titus and Paulson weren't the only ones with support in the community. Taylor formed the organization Parents Protecting the Minds of Children (PPMC) in August. The organization had about sixty members who met and discussed the books' objectionable content, which included, in their opinion, promotion of homosexuality and pornography.[54]

In August, the issue was formally requested to be put on the school board's September agenda by Superintendent New. Steve Percival, school board president, decided in August to hold a town meeting in order to give both sides of the debate a chance to speak their mind. The town meeting was set for September 13, 2005, in the high school gym. Percival informed both Titus and Paulson's group, along with Taylor's group, about the meeting and rules on how it would be conducted. Each group would be given an allotted amount of time for speakers. The town meeting was limited to the three-hundred-seat capacity of the Fayetteville High School auditorium.[55] DBB decided they wanted to have a variety of speakers, each talking about one specific issue and how if restrictions were enacted on the books this would affect the community. The speakers included parents, students, professionals, and professors. One of the main speakers for DBB was Professor Tim deNoble, an architecture professor who at the time had two children in the Fayetteville School System. deNoble had gotten involved with DBB because the situation had "ruffled my feathers that someone was trying to assert my role as a parent." Due to the groups desire to have a wide variety of speakers and not appear to represent just one part of the community, but instead represent the entire community, deNoble was chosen because as he admits to, he is a "plain-speaking, good ol' male."[56] The main point of deNoble's speech was the comparison of the book restrictions in Fayetteville to the integration debacle of 1954 at Central High School in Little Rock. deNoble had graduated from Central in 1977 and, even after fifty years, anytime he mentioned where he graduated high school, others would not recognize the first-rate secondary education he had received but would associate the school's name with the 1954 integration. deNoble could not imagine what kind of "stain" restricting these books would put on the Fayetteville community, and the ammunition it would give others to label Arkansas as a backward state.[57]

The opposing view was represented by Taylor, PPMC, and fellow concerned citizens. Taylor spoke about her disillusionment with the novels in question and her inability to restrict her children from accessing them. Anna Hanna, a grandmother of five grandchildren in the school system, spoke of her beliefs. "It's very important for us to have guidelines to teach our children and grandchildren—my generation has failed to stand for righteousness and purity."[58] The town meeting ended with both sides speaking their minds, but without the school board giving their decision. Instead that would come two days later at the September 15 official monthly meeting. Before the board made their decision, they heard from the school system's librarians and the school's attorney, Moore. "I made my recommendation that they abandon the restrictions." Moore relied heavily on the *Counts v. Cedarville* case in his testimony to the board. "The Counts case was not only on point, but it was right down the street (referring to the fact that Cedarville is 60 miles from Fayetteville)."[59] Moore felt the board had overstepped their bounds and told them such. "When you say that you are going to set the books aside in a restricted place, that's going to be a problem legally. A parent library without student checkout sounds to me that the student can't access that book. I know it's hindsight, but it is my job to try to keep us out of litigation."[60] In the end it would be Moore's testimony that would appear to have the largest impact on the board's decision. The board voted 4–3 to remove the restrictions on the books and rescind its earlier decision. "The Chocolate Wars" and the "Battle of the Books" would shape the Fayetteville community. But why had two such public cases happened there? Was there a reason these debates occurred in Fayetteville? And what arguments did those opposing the books fail to make?

Conclusion

To answer the question as to what were the arguments of the book objectors and why they were not a success a comparison between the arguments needs to be made. These argument comparisons and their effectiveness will be illustrated through the use of Stephen Toulmin's argument model. In Toulmin's model a *claim* is made, *data* is offered in support of the claim, a *warrant* for connecting the grounds to the claim is conveyed, a *backing* is shown to lay down theoretical foundations for the warrant, appropriate *qualifiers* temper the claim, and possible *rebuttals* are considered.[61] The data given in both cases was that the works in question contained inappropriate material for children; however, the exact data given was different because the content of the novels were different. In the case of "The Chocolate Wars," Gross objected not only to the "profane and vulgar" words, but also to the novel's "disrespect for parental and educational authority" and to its possibility of angering students and leading to self-destructive behaviors.[62] Twenty years later, Taylor and her supporters would object to the sexual nature in the objected works and their use, talk, and explanation of sex and sexuality. The warrant in both arguments revolved around the idea that children are impressionable and highly influenced by others. The backing for this belief was that children who viewed these works could be enticed to act out, behave in manners that were inappropriate and/or detrimental to their health.

Why were the objectors unable to restrict/censor the books? There are several reasons why their arguments did not work. Neither objector group was able to respond to the several rebuttals those who opposed them made. First of all, neither group could provide adequate information or support as to why exposure or access to the work would lead to inappropriate and/or self-destructive behavior in children. "Being exposed to obscenity results in violence and harm to children has powerful rhetorical appeal but lacks data."[63] It would be difficult for the school board to have removed or restricted any of the objected works when there was no evidence to support the objectors' claims. In the years since the works had been in place, no parent or student had ever come forth and told of how reading the works in question had damaged the child in some way. In fact, there had not even been any prior complaints of any kind for any of the works. This lack of evidence is crucial to the objectors' loss. In the *Counts v. Cedarville School District* decision, Judge Jimm Hendren discussed how there was a lack of evidence on how reading *Harry Potter* would lead to disobedience in a child—the claim made by the Cedarville School Board as to why it had placed the restrictions. "There is no evidence that any of the three Board members was aware of any actual disobedience or disrespect that had flowed from a reading of the *Harry Potter* books. Their concerns are, therefore, speculative. Such speculative apprehensions of possible disturbance are not sufficient to justify the extreme sanction of restricting the free exercise of First Amendment rights in a public school library."[64] It would have been pure speculation on the part of the school board if they would have restricted the books in either case.

Second, neither *The Chocolate War* nor the novels Taylor objected to were in any way required reading for students. In *Virgil v. School Board of Columbia County*, the book that was removed from the curriculum was a required textbook for a required humanities course, and it was removed on the basis of legitimate educational reasoning, something that was not present in "The Chocolate Wars" or the "Battle of the Books."[65] Finally, the decision to remove or restrict works in a public school system will always have repercussions due to the fact that these decisions do not only affect the objector's child but the children of many other public school parents. As much as the objectors had felt their parental control boundaries had been stepped on by teachers and librarians, the parents who opposed them also felt like their parental control had been stepped on by the objectors. In the Battle of the Books, many parents felt placing restrictions on novels infringed upon their child's First Amendment rights. This was a problem addressed by Hendren in the Counts case. "It finds that the stigmatizing effect of having to have parental permission to check out a book constitutes a restriction on access. Further the fact that Dakota cannot simply go in the library, take the books off the shelf and thumb through them without going through the permission and check-out process is a restriction on her access. Thus, unless it is shown that such restrictions are justified, they amount to impermissible infringements of First Amendment rights."[66]

A method of persuasion used by both objector groups was one based on setting a moral standard in the community in order to protect the children of the community. This type of argument approach is not a new one. One of the first well-known censors in American history was a man named Anthony Comstock, who also used such a method. Comstock was a devout Christian who felt children who were exposed to obscenity would be drawn to evil. In a forty-year span (1872–1912), Comstock would see many persons, including children, placed in jail for their connection to publishment of obscenity—at least what Comstock thought was obscenity. Comstock believed his work to be inspired and directed by God and looked forward to a time "when there shall be in all the world not one object to awaken sensuous thoughts in the minds of young people."[67]

Obscenity was a key complaint during the "Battle of the Books." How does one define obscenity and what type of persons become involved with censoring as it pertains to obscenity? Zurcher and Kirkpatrick in *Citizens for Decency: Antipornography Crusades as Status Defense* state that those who censor make a judgment of what obscenity means, and this judgment will reflect their value systems, socialization patterns, and self-concepts.[68] With obscenity censors, the point at which most converge and agree is their value systems and a belief that children must be protected from such material. "To justify censorship, one theme remains constant: children are to be protected from obscene messages and images."[69] This is a belief surrounded by the idea that "children emerge as vulnerable, malleable, and of primary concern to those endeavoring to act as the moral conscience of society."[70] In Taylor's case it seems evident that she was shocked by the images she saw in these works and felt they were inappropriate by her standards of morals. At the same time, even though "The Chocolate Wars" did not involve obscenity, the Gross family's values had been violated when the daughter read the novel. Objectors were offended and upset that works of such a nature were in some way available or assigned to their children and felt others in the community would also be upset. When the issues became public cases, both groups (even though twenty years apart) tried to appeal to the moral standard in the community by using a "shock and awe" approach. Gross and Taylor did this by giving excerpts of the novels in public forums—excerpts with the most colorful language. Often these excerpts were not accompanied by a synopsis of the novel or the context in which these excerpts derived from. In the end this technique would shock some in the community, but at the same time these excerpts did not show any real evidence that the novels would harm or influence children in an inappropriate manner. The objectors put forth their beliefs and values instead of conceptualizing a true basis for censorship. It was their belief that the community would be shocked by such materials and would exercise their ability to censor within the public school system.

The objectors would discover that a moral standard would not suffice as an argument in censorship of the works.

It has been made apparent through court cases that the First Amendment rights of students do appear to have some boundaries in the public school system—in order to protect the children according to those who make and uphold censoring rulings. In the Hazelwood case, the Supreme Court ruled in favor of the school administrators. This set forth the constitutional understanding that students could have their freedom of speech restricted by school officials.[71] There also is a mentality that the school board is more in tune with students; therefore, their rulings are often supported by the courts. In *Virgil v. School Board of Columbia County*, Judge R. Lanier gave the majority opinion, "Like the district court, we seriously question how young persons just below the age of majority can be harmed by these masterpieces of Western literature. However, having concluded that there is no constitutional violation, our role is not to second-guess the wisdom of the Board's action."[72] This case shows it is possible to put forth restrictions and censor books in the public schools based on the belief that some material is unsuitable for children. It has been established through court cases that students do not have all the same First Amendment rights as their parents for their own protection. Even with this censorship possibility, objectors during "The Chocolate Wars" and the "Battle of Books" did not put forth a sound argument as to how or why these works would harm their children, and how this harm outweighed any educational benefits that could be received. In the interview with Moore, he said he did believe it would be possible to restrict access to books if the right debate came along with the right book and with an objector who had a sound, rational reason behind his/her objections.[73] In their efforts to protect their children, it would be most beneficial for objectors to look at previous cases and make sure they have established a sound argument with evidence as to why a work should be restricted or removed.

A limitation to this study would be a lack of interviews with all of those involved in these two debates. It would have been beneficial to speak with several more participants in both debates: in "The Chocolate Wars": Cassandra Stone, the English teacher who assigned the novel, and the Gross's daughter; in the "Battle of the Books":

Howard Hamilton, a school board member who voted to place restrictions; Mike Masterson, a local journalist who sided with Taylor; and Janet Titus, the co-creator of the Don't Ban Books organization. All of these interviews would have added more to the story, and perhaps provided viewpoints not presented. An interesting future study would be to attempt to understand why book debates happen in certain parts of the country more so than others and if there are particular characteristics of a city or area that provide the ideal breeding ground for the debates.

NOTES

1. Lee Burress, *Battle of the Books* (Metuchen, NJ: Scarecrow Press, 1989), 40.

2. Herbert Foerstel, *Banned in the U.S.A.* (Westport, CT: Greenwood Press, 1994), xvii.

3. Ibid., xviii.

4. Gregg Phifer, "School Libraries in Peril," *Communication Law Review* 2, no. (1984): 3.

5. Foerstel, *Banned in the U.S.A.*, xix.

6. Ibid., xvii.

7. Burress, Battle of the Books, 31.

8. Phifer, "School Libraries in Peril," 4.

9. Burress, *Battle of the Books,* 229–36.

10. Tinker v. Des Moines School District, 393 U.S. 503 (1969).

11. Foerstel, *Banned in the U.S.A.*, 63–65.

12. Theresa Chmara to Judith Krug, March 27, 2006. Letter in possession of Judith Krug, 1.

13. Ibid., 2.

14. Billy Ray Counts and Mary Nell Counts, both as parents of Dakota Counts v. Cedarville School District, 295 F. Supp. 2d 996 (2003), 4.

15. Foerstel, *Banned in the U.S.A.*, 65–66.

16. Virgil v. School Board of Columbia County, 862 F. 2nd 1517 (11th Cir. 1989).

17. Billy Ray Counts and Mary Nell Counts, both as parents of Dakota Counts v. Cedarville School District, 295 F. Supp. 2d 996 (2003), 18–19.

18. Forestel, *Banned in the U.S.A.*, 154–57.

19. Judy Schwab, interview by author, November 12, 2006, Fayetteville, Arkansas. Tape recording.

20. Don Eggert, "Round One of the Chocolate Wars," *Grapevine*, January 15, 1986.

21. Schwab interview.

22. Robert Gross, "Patron's Request for Reconsideration of a Work," November 1, 1985.

23. Don Deweese, interview by author, September 23, 2006, Fayetteville, Arkansas. Tape recording.

24. Robert Gross, interview by author via phone, November 29, 2006. Tape recording.

25. Gross, "Patron's Request for Reconsideration of a Work," 5.

26. Gross interview.

27. Schwab interview.

28. Chris Osher, "Waters Denies GLSA Lawsuit," *Arkansas Traveler* (Fayetteville), October 22, 1986.

29. Deweese interview.

30. Fayetteville Public Schools, Committee Recommendation of *The Chocolate War,* 1985.

31. Citizens for Excellence in Education, "Patron of the Fayetteville Schools," 1985. From the packet sent forth to all parents of Fayetteville school students.

32. Students for Enlightened Education, "Book Censorship Must Not Be Allowed," *Northwest Arkansas Times*, December 16, 1985.

33. Patricia May, "The Chocolate Wars Continue," *Northwest Arkansas Times*, December 18, 1985.

34. Howard Brill, interview by author, November 15, 2006, Fayetteville, Arkansas. Tape recording.

35. Citizens for Excellence in Education, Advertisement placed in *Northwest Arkansas Times*, March 7, 1986.

36. Patricia May, "County to Vote on School Races," *Northwest Arkansas Times*, March 9, 1986.

37. Brill interview.

38. Laurie Taylor, interview by author, October 10, 2006, Fayetteville, Arkansas. Tape recording.

39. Candlewick Press, Review of *It's Perfectly Normal*, 2004. Retrieved November 17, 2006. www.candlewick.com/cat.asp?mode=book&isbn=0763626104.

40. Taylor interview.

41. Laurie Taylor, "Patron's Request for Reconsideration of a Work," February 16, 2005.

42. Taylor interview.

43. Fayetteville Public Schools, Committee Recommendation of *It's Perfectly Normal,* 2005.

44. Candlewick Press, Review of *It's So Amazing* and *The Teenage Guy's Survival Guide*, 2004. Retrieved November 17, 2006. www.candlewick.com/cat.asp?mode=book&isbn=0763626104.

45. Laurie Taylor, "Patron's Request for Reconsideration of a Work," February 16, 2005.

46. Fayetteville Public Schools, Committee Recommendation of *It's So Amazing* and *The Teenage Guy's Survival Guide,* 2005.

47. Taylor interview.

48. Fayetteville School Board Minutes from May 26, 2005, General meeting.

49. Rudy Moore, interview by author, October 1, 2006, Fayetteville, Arkansas. Tape recording.

50. Associated Press, "Fayetteville Woman Takes Aim at More Books in School Libraries," *Arkansas Democratic-Gazette*, July 19, 2005.

51. Kat Paulson, interview by author, October 12, 2006, Fayetteville, Arkansas. Tape recording.

52. Associated Press, "Fayetteville Woman Takes Aim at More Books in School Libraries," *Arkansas Democratic-Gazette*, July 19, 2005.

53. Paulson interview.

54. Associated Press, "Woman Objecting to Books in Fayetteville Adds to Numbers," *Arkansas Democratic-Gazette*, August 19, 2005.

55. Associated Press, "Board to Meet Again Thursday as Censorship Debate Continues," *Arkansas Democrat-Gazette*, September 14, 2005.

56. Tim deNoble, interview by author, November 5, 2006, Fayetteville, Arkansas. Tape recording.

57. DeNoble interview.

58. Associated Press, "Board to Meet Again Thursday as Censorship Debate Continues," *Arkansas Democrat-Gazette*, September 14, 2005.

59. Moore interview.

60. Chris Branam, "Fayetteville Students Given Access to 3 Books, School Board Votes 4–3 to Rescind Order Restricting Library List," *Arkansas Democrat-Gazette*, September 16, 2005.

61. Stephen Toulmin, *Uses of Argument* (New York: Cambridge University Press, 1958), 15–30.

62. Gross, "Patron's Request for Reconsideration of a Work," 2.

63. Bernadette Mink, "From Comstock to Clinton: Children, Communication, and the Community of Censorship" (M.A. thesis, University of Arkansas, 1998), 168.

64. Billy Ray Counts and Mary Nell Counts, both as parents of Dakota Counts v. Cedarville School District, 295 F. Supp. 2d 996 (2003), 7.

65. Virgil v. School Board of Columbia County, 862 F. 2nd 1517 (11th Cir., 1989).

66. Billy Ray Counts and Mary Nell Counts, both as parents of Dakota Counts v. Cedarville School District, 295 F. Supp. 2d 996 (2003), 15.

67. Mink, "From Comstock to Clinton," 55.

68. Ibid., 2.

69. Ibid., 171.

70. Ibid., 172.

71. Foerstel, *Banned in the U.S.A.*, 65–66.

72. Virgil, *Virgil v. School Board of Columbia County*, 862 F. 2nd 1517 (11th Cir., 1989), 18.

73. Moore interview.

CHAPTER 6

An Inquiry into Control of Content by the Arkansas Educational Television Network

ALLIE TAYLOR

Most censorship in the United States occurs when private actors decide what content will be presented in private media such as commercial newspapers and television, a process the owners would label editorial judgment protected by the First Amendment. When the government acts as speaker, however, the editorial decision to censor content raises unique First Amendment concerns. *Voice of America* and *Stars and Stripes*, for example, are publicly funded media where "editorial decisions" arguably become "state action." So, too, are programming decisions by state-supported television such as the Arkansas Public Television Network, the focus of this study.

In some legally, ambiguously defined way, public service broadcast is obligated to the citizenry and should aim at providing a service to the entire population. With broad parameters set up for such a system, public broadcasting falls on a spectrum ranging from democratic to bureaucratic. A lack of definition for what falls under "public interest" and what constitutes "public service" exists a fatal, core problem for public broadcasting to coexist with a capitalist political economy. By coincidence perhaps, the United States is the most commercially saturated, money-motivated system in the world. As stated by Dr. Robert McChesney, "Genuine public service broadcasting, unlike commercial media, will always be in conflict with the political culture preferred by the neoliberal order."[1]

Public broadcasting hence was once conceived as our "cultural truth teller," potentially our cultures' "lie detector" to oppose its counterpart of commercial broadcasting. In reference to John Kennedy, "The greatest enemy of truth is very often not the lie, deliberate, continued, and dishonest—but the myth—present, persuasive, and unrealistic."[2]

A major issue situated around the regulation of broadcasting in America is the congressional vagueness of the term "public interest." In 1912 broadcasters were mandated by the government to work in the public's "interest, convenience, and necessity."[3] James Baughman gives a brief description of "public interest" as being "decisions [that] were to be made with a maximum regard for both the general welfare and popular opinion."[4] This definition still lacks boundaries. What does maximum regard look like? What constitutes the "general welfare" of the public? Some scholars believe this term is an idyllic phrase. It has obvious importance as a rhetorical feature in American broadcast policy, but possesses an unclear meaning that is vulnerable to politics.[5]

It is important to note that the term "public" is a social concept. As such a concept exists, it needs social space to thrive, to learn about the public interest, and to have the ability to act or not act upon this interest.[6] Jürgen Habermas proposes that the public sphere is an entity separate from state and private domains. This classical bourgeoisie view of the public sphere comes into crisis as the capitalistic drive of the economy contradicts to reflect social problems.[7] Even our Founding Fathers recognized that to represent, meaningfully, citizens must have strong public voices and an active role; but that all begins with access to information. As Dick Bennett states as his underlying principle, "Politics is public property. It ought to be grounded in the concerns of the citizens, not the machinations of professionals."[8]

Public television works as an independent participant in the free and independent press system in America. Public Broadcasting Service (PBS) states that it guards tightly the trust issued to them by the public and that citizens can "feel secure" that judgments on programming control are being held accountable.[9] The Federal Communication Commission's authority is constrained by the First Amendment principles that the government may not censor broadcasters and may not regulate content except in the most general fashion. For broadcasters to represent the public interest in this regard would then mean to present a wide diversity of perspectives within programming.[10] An interview conducted with Clifford Durr, a former FCC member, and James Fly, a former chairmen of the FCC, it was concluded, as Durr states, "At the time of the First Amendment the press, crude as it was, was in the reach of most people economically. Now by its nature it is a very costly thing that few control." The issue at hand is that we have both a problem of the right for people to hear and the issue of how to get more people to speak instead of limiting that number to the elite professionals.[11]

The term "diversity" is central to democracy. It allows for individuals to involve themselves in a wide range of topical discussion and to help shape the decision-making process in politics.[12] Diversity is listed as one of the six rationales for why the federal government began regulating television. The authorizing legislation defines the term as "Diversity—it is in the public's interest to have public, educational, and governmental access to promote diversity."[13] If we viewed diversity in the way Congress was viewed in its enactment, then we might make headway in understanding its importance to upkeep diversity in programming.

In an analysis of the censorship allegations regarding the Arkansas Educational Television Network (AETN), I argue that since its inception AETN has lacked definite policies with regard to program selection, beginning and especially during the administration of Lee Reaves and Fred Schmutz. Through a rhetorical lens, I will explicate how working in the "public interest" becomes a muddy debauchery in light of political pressure and lack of audience analysis.

Critical Discourse Analysis

As Michel Foucault believed, "our experience of the world is not limited to the web of language; rather, discourses themselves are like the symptoms of social forces colliding."[14] Critical discourse analysis

(CDA) is a study of discourse that views language as a social practice, focusing on social and political power that is reproduced in text and talk. Three major principles of CDA that Gulnaz Begum lists are (1) constructions and reflection of social and political issue in discourse in text or talk, (2) exerting and negotiating of powers relations through discourse, and (3) production and reflection of ideologies by using language.[15] An important focus within Foucault's work is the concern of power-knowledge. Power is recognized as central to all of discourse. Power produces knowledge, and in turn they imply each other. Power relationships within discourse bring to light questions of inclusion and exclusion. Foucault's interests, along with mine, include the criteria used to evaluate which views are considered legitimate and which individuals are allowed or not allowed to participate.[16]

Arkansas Educational Television Network

From its origin, AETN has been deeply rooted in politics despite its drive to be a separate entity. Arkansas Act 359 of 1959 created a committee to study the viability of education television in the state of Arkansas. Governor Orval Faubus appointed the committee members, whose responsibility was to conduct a comprehensive study of the feasibility of integrating and maintaining a program of primary and secondary education.[17] Soon afterward, Arkansas Act 198 of 1961 created the Arkansas Educational Television Commission, whose purpose was to make educational television available to residents of Arkansas. Section 9 of this act states:

> It has been found and is declared by the General Assembly that public education has suffered severely from numerous disruptive influences in the past half decade; that dangerous propaganda inimical to the American way of life is rampant on all sides; that the young people of the State, future citizens and leaders, are the chief objects of brainwashing operations engineered by the minions of totalitarianism; that countermeasures to such subversive influences are necessary to continued existence of constitutional democracy.[18]

So by this very definition, and AETN stating on their website, educational television in Arkansas was created in part to stop

Communism in the state in conjunction with major political unrest related to the Little Rock High Crisis.[19]

Early on in its foundation, AETN started receiving allegations of censorship. The first was on December 10, 1966, when Fred Schmutz, program director until 1983, canceled the Tennessee Williams play, *Ten Blocks on the Camino Real*. He stated that the program was "profane and lewd" and that he "could no more air it than [he] could fly." Schmutz considered the program unsuitable for broadcast despite stating that the program was beautifully produced and well acted. This program was the second time in the few short weeks of the facility being open that programming had been scheduled and then pulled due to content. A film interview with Hugh Hefner was set to be shown at 8:00 P.M. on a Wednesday but was replaced with a discussion on the Vietnam War.[20]

Schmutz was immediately accused of censoring KETS programming, which he denied publicly on a Little Rock radio station. He asserted that his job was "to govern what goes out (on KETS) to a certain extent." He was charged with censoring for canceling Williams's play as well as the Hefner interview. An interview on "Open Line," a program of KARK and Tom Longfellow, revealed that Schmutz did not make his decision to cancel the programs because of whether they were good or bad but based on the content. According to Schmutz, it was "language and situations you do not discuss in polite mixed society." He also went on to defend his decision by grounding his argument that KETS's primary objective was for children, not to entertain adults. There were some mixed reviews on his decision. During his first radio discussion on the matter, seven of thirteen callers criticized his decision, while the next day most supported it.[21]

Criticism was sparse until the later half of the 1970s, when censorship allegations hit a high point. In a personal letter from a friend of Diane Blair, a well-known and respected political science professor and writer who was appointed by Governor Clinton in 1980 to the Arkansas Educational Television Commission, the friend stated, "I refuse to have anything to do with AETN because of their censorship." This woman was concerned with the "bleeps" that were being used during programming. She ended the letter with the thought-provoking statement that if the commission was to truly look at AETN collections and figures and compare those to other states, even the commission would have to admit that there is a lack of representation.[22]

The programming that caused the greatest concern for controlling content was a film on former United States representative Brooks Hays and the Little Rock 1957 desegregation crisis. AETN stated on September 20, 1979, that they would not broadcast the film if they considered it to be biased in any way. Schmutz asserted that if it "plays up violence or sensationalism without showing the other side" that the film would be barred. Lee Reaves, the former director of the commission, made the concerns for the film public during a commission meeting. Reaves told the Associated Press that "anything embarrassing to Arkansas" would constitute grounds for not showing the film, although admitting that any account on the Little Rock High Crisis could be constructed in an embarrassing manner. What is of major concern here is that Schmutz said his apprehension for the film was raised when he found out the director of the film, David Solomon, planned to interview NBC television network about the problems they encountered when trying to cover the integration crisis. According to Schmutz, NBC took every chance during the event to "sensationalize and blow it up."[23]

As a result of this discontent, the executive board of the Arkansas Library Association approved a motion that expressed concerns about AETN's programming policies. The board requested the services of the association's Intellectual Freedom Committee to investigate how AETN decides what goes on air. Richard H. Reid, the assistant director of libraries at the University of Arkansas, headed the questioning into AETN action. In a letter to Lee Reaves, Reid wrote, "I find it unsettling that you and Mr. Schmutz seem to be acting as a two-man censorship board by reviewing material to determine its 'suitability' for Arkansas's audiences." Since Reid lived in northwest Arkansas he had access to both Arkansas and Oklahoma public television, and he stated in a letter to Governor Clinton that it was obvious that there were deletion of words and segments in Arkansas programming.[24]

Shortly after, the Arkansas Education Association's Representative Assembly joined with the Arkansas Library Association in expressing its concerns over AETN's programming policy in light of the Brooks Hays film. Mrs. Price, the former president of the AEA, also said that the focus of the investigation should be put on the "arbitrary decision" to not air portions of the Secondary Health Series that dealt with venereal disease. According to Price, one in three cases of all venereal disease in Arkansas are patients under twenty.[25]

Another group in the state also had concerns over the program of the 1957 Little Rock desegregation crisis. The Arkansas Association of College History Teachers adopted the resolution to protest AETN for basing their decision to show the program or not on whether it is considered "embarrassing" to the state. The resolution stated it "is gravely concerned about AETN procedures and policies for deciding what programs or portions thereof ought to be aired." They emphasize that educational programming is meant to "broaden intellectual horizons, not restrict them."[26]

The Editorial-Opinion piece on November 25, 1979, titled "The Censors," discusses briefly the results of the library association's research into AETN programming policies. It was deemed that the policy was found to be "fuzzy and vague," which is hardly surprising. As the piece states, vagueness is the only way in which censorship could be justified. Mrs. Neil Barnhard, then president of the library association, stated, "We do not question the no doubt excellent motives of the AETN censors ... but does looping off a program now and again serve the public interest or does it harm it?" It was the board's inclination to believe that more harm than good will always be the result of censorship in whatever form it takes.[27]

In response to the backlash on the Brooks Hays film, Schmutz said that the staff followed the commission policy that the network would not broadcast anything objectionable, obscene, or unacceptable in general circles. Governor Clinton believed that AETN has justification to cut "racy" material, but the commission must adopt a clear set of guidelines for this criteria and the public should be informed when a decision is made.[28] Clinton suggested that events in national and state history, though they may not always be positive, cannot be ignored.[29]

In a letter to the editor, D. L. Wilson of Fayetteville, Arkansas, discusses censorship on the Monty Python satire on the Messiah story in which the "letters" column of the paper was full of writers who thought that it should be suppressed. The main section of the paper reported on issues concerning the Brooks Hays film; therefore,

seemingly overshadowing letters of concern regarding the Monty
Python satire. Mr. Wilson called Senator Reaves a "self-appointed
protector of public sensibilities" after portions of "I, Claudius" were
blacked out on the grounds that they were salacious. After comparing
Arkansas's version of "I, Claudius" to Oklahoma, Wilson states, "I have
seen more salacious pantyhose commercials." He proceeded to discuss
moments in Arkansas history where free expression had clearly been
suppressed, including Muhammad Ali's troubles with speaking on the
University of Arkansas campus, the final legalization of teaching evolution in schools, and Bible readings still being conducted in schools
with blatant disregard for the concerns of others. He concludes, "The
central theme in all of this is, if most of us don't like what you say,
we're going to defend to the death our right to make you stop saying it."
According to our Founding Fathers, as Wilson stresses, America was
to be built on tolerance, not oppression, persuasion, and coercion.[30]

In June 1981, the Arkansas Education Television Network
Commission voted down the motion to give AETN staff and advisory broad discretion in censorship matters. The commission left
the decision up to Lee Reaves and Fred Schmutz. The Community
Advisory Board wanted to change the program policy, making the
acceptability of programming to be decided by Reaves, Schmutz,
and any appropriate members of AETN staff. It was also suggested
that anyone involved in the decision-making process could consult
the commission or advisory board.[31] With the policy staying intact,
Commissioner Diane Blair of Fayetteville did request that Reaves and
Schmutz keep the commission notified of any deletion of significant
portions of broadcasting.[32]

Another concerned Fayetteville citizen expressed his discontent
with educational television in Arkansas in comparison to neighboring
Oklahoma. He said he once considered himself a "friend" of AETN,
even a financial contributor, until March 2, 1982, when the ETV broadcasting of a Carl Sandburg poem bleeped out three stanzas, including
ending the poem in a bleep, which he considered to render the poem
meaningless. Angered by the censorship, he switched to Oklahoma
programming, which ran the programming without censoring. The
bleeped line of the poem was the phrase "son of a bitch," which he said
made the Arkansas institution childish and ridiculous.[33]

Political pressure on AETN came to light heavily in the latter half of the 1980s. The director of AETN at the time was Raymond Ho, who received much hostility from several state officials and one constitutional officer about how he was programming the statewide television network. AETN is supported through state-funded appropriations by the Arkansas General Assembly as well as private donations. State funding "thus gives legislators the opportunity to have a say about the type of programming the stations beam to the citizens of Arkansas, and they obviously exercise that privilege."[34]

A legislative subcommittee criticized two panelists on the political analysis program *Arkansas Week* that AETN aired in 1986 stating that, "officials should review the erosion of our ETV system and possibly a shakeup of the role and purpose and management of this program if it's to continue to receive public support." Senator Knox Nelson of Pine Bluff warned of more serious legislative action if the panelists on the program were to continue to be critical of public officials. Panelists John Starr and Meredith Oakley, both of the *Arkansas Democrat,* were the main targets of disapproval by the Review and Advice Subcommittee of the Legislative Council. Many viewers expressed concern about the programming and how panelists seemed critical of the state and some of its officials. Nelson notes that AETN was established to involve itself in education and not politics, and that there was "considerable legislative concern over ETV becoming a government-owned and operated propaganda system that would be used to promote political philosophies."[35]

In a response to the criticism of *Arkansas Week,* Raymond Ho sent a memorandum to the AETN Commission discussing rumors of the "politicizing" of educational television with the program. Ho noted two important considerations for the commission to remember: (1) *Arkansas Week* is *all* the week's news, not just the legislature and (2) *Arkansas Week* is not, and never will be, a forum for personal attacks on anyone. According the FCC rule 73.1920, anyone who has felt victimized must and will be given an opportunity to respond in their own defense. Ho states that, "free speech and freedom of the press are guaranteed."[36]

Another program that caused major concerns for AETN was a profile on the life of John Lennon. This PBS documentary had a "program flag" message sent along with the copy (a program flag is an indicator that the broadcast may not be suitable for all audiences). Mike Mottler, associate director and executive producer of programming, sent a memo to the commission apologizing for scheduling the programming despite the program flag. The program contained "sexually explicit language and frontal nudity."[37] On the same day, Mr. Mottler sent a follow-up letter to Ralph Caley concerning the Lennon program, "John Lennon: A Journey in the Life." Mottler states that he does not offer this letter as excuse-making, but more of an admittance that the program review process "didn't work right." According to Mottler, the PBS program description gave no suggestion that the program contained the language and obscenity that it did. This was an interim period for AETN as the program director had resigned earlier in November, and during this period a coworker was apparently suppose to "mind the store" as the job search for a replacement was underway. Mottler expressed regret that this program "slipped through the cracks" of what he deemed a usually rigorous process.[38]

A condensed list of AETN censorship over the years is as follows:

1. 1966: Tennessee Williams's *Ten Blocks on the Camino Real* was deemed "profane and lewd."

2. 1966: Hugh Hefner interview pulled and replaced.

3. 1967: Ten Mena ministers complain about Henrik Ibsen's *An Enemy of the People*, which contained "obscene, indecent, and profane" language. The play contained four "damns" and two "hells."

4. 1970: Viewers complain about AETN canceling a PBS program on rock because of brief nudity; a program on classical music replaced the program.

5. 1979: Schumtz states he will not air the documentary on former representative Brooks Hays and the 1957 desegregation crisis if it is biased in any way. Governor Bill Clinton expressed major concerns of the "advanced censorship."

6. 1981: State ACLU director, Sandra Kurjiaka, deemed AETN's editing policy "censorship. Pure and simple."

7. 1981: The Arkansas Educational Television Commission firmly asserts its position to air programs that "conform with accepted standards of the state and its communities."

8. 1986: Viewer complaints on *John Lennon: A Journey in the Life*.

9. 1991: AETN denies broadcasting *Tongues Untied*, a PBS documentary on homosexuality and African Americans. The language was said to be "way, way over the line."

10. 1993: Viewers complain when a program *The Sting* aired with uncensored expletives.

11. 1996: A "Version B" of Daniel Defoe's program "Moll Flanders" was criticized for several minutes of full frontal nudity and sexual situations.

In 1996, concerning what programming to air, Director Susan Howarth stated, "Today's AETN is more liberal than the AETN of 1966 or even 1984. Our real challenge is to put ourselves in the minds of our viewers. Obviously, there's a wide range of opinion about what's appropriate and what's not."[39]

The "AETN Programming Philosophy" in the Employee Handbook of 1986 states to judge programming based on technical quality as well as, "overall value of concept and content, aesthetic excellence, and appropriateness to the viewer." It provides written recognition that matters of taste or subjective and in the same breath reserve their right to reject material that lacks "literary, artistic, or intellectual merit."[40] The Proposed Program Policy was soon after adopted in April 1987, stating the four fundamental principles that shape the program service AETN provides as: editorial integrity, program quality, program diversity, and local station autonomy.

The policy further defines each of these concepts. PBS and its member stations are responsible to keep the programming process free of political pressure, program funders, or other sources shield editorial integrity. Program quality is full of ambiguous terms of judgment such as, "excellence, creativity, artistry, accuracy, balance, fairness, timeliness, innovation, boldness, thoroughness, credibility, and technical virtuosity." Diversity is defined to further goals of democracy. In providing diverse programming, AETN is to show a full range of ideas, information, and viewpoints. Finally, PBS sets forth local station autonomy as recognizing the unique needs of local communities by giving them timely information so that each station can exercise independent program decisions based on suitability for local broadcast.[41]

While censorship allegations have slowed in recent years, the AETN Program Policy, approved September 19, 2012, by the commission, still delegates power to the commission and executive director of AETN. Under the section headed "Programming Decision-Making," the executive director who acts as "editor" may make decisions under their discretion of the AETN mission statement; Arkansas's needs, problems, and interests; seasoned judgment; media research; comments of viewers/public; and consultation of programming experts. Under the First Amendment, state-owned public television stations, such as AETN, are allowed to place restrictions on what will and will not be aired, but are still to work in the "public interest" of Arkansans. AETN's Code of Editorial Integrity prides itself on trust, and that public confidence can be "strengthened by the regulations and legal requirements that accompany our FCC licenses to broadcast, our federal recognition as nonprofit educational and charitable organizations, and the federal funds that contribute to our work."[42]

Arkansas Educational Television's creation was a direct reflection of political and social unrest of perceived threats of communism in the state during the 1950s and 1960s. Paired with Orval Faubus's open opposition to the desegregation of Little Rock Central High School, his selection of the commission raises questions about the political pressure applied to AETN during its inception. Through constant assertion of power and control of content, Schmutz and Reaves highlight the negotiation of power between key decision makers of program selection. With the proclamation of governing content (Schmutz), and the little regard for public opinion, it is clear that few people were included in the discussion of content, and the population (Arkansans) whom AETN supposedly was to represent was being excluded from the programming conversation.

While program selection was and is to take into consideration a multitude of vague concepts of quality and this concept of public interest, it is hard to believe that Schmutz and Reaves were not asserting their own ideologies of what is considered appropriate. The public was never informed, still is not, of decisions to censor or what to broadcast prior to scheduling decisions—once again, an exclusion of the represented public. As critical discourse analysis stresses, power creates knowledge and they both in turn imply each other. Therefore, the few in control of information broadcasted on a publicly funded television station generates the information (knowledge) the represented public is to gain. This knowledge then reflects the ideologies of the editors in control of the selection process creating a somewhat spiral of silence of public interest as power relations on the end of those in control become stronger and the represented public's voice becomes stifled.

The First Amendment, in this case, raises unique questions of power and control. Since public access television is given authority to control content, protected by law, state action is allowed the control of content masked by vague terminology of what is deemed "public interest." This tension is certain to continue unless the AETN commissioners insist on adopting and enforcing a clear policy on program content that avoids viewpoint discrimination, and provides bright line guidelines to inform programming staff in executing public policy.

NOTES

1. Robert W. McChesney, "The Mythology of Commercial Broadcasting and the Contemporary Crisis of Public Broadcasting," Spry Memorial Lecture, Montreal, December 2, 1997.

2. James R. Bennett, "The Public Broadcasting Service: Censorship, Self-censorship, and the Struggle for Independence," *Journal of Popular Film and Television* 24, no. 4 (1997): 181–82.

3. Erwin G. Krasnow and Lawrence D. Longley, *The Politics of Broadcast Regulation* (New York: St. Martin's Press, 1973), 16; William Hoynes, *Public Television for Sale: Media, the Market, and the Public Sphere* (San Francisco: Westview Press, 1994), 38; James L. Baughman, *Television's Guardians: The FCC and the Politics of Programming, 1958–1967* (Knoxville: University of Tennessee Press, 1985); Michael P. McCauley, "The Contested Meaning of Public Service in American Television," *Communication Review* 5 (2002): 207–37; and Bruce A. Austin, "Public Interest Programming by Commercial Network Affiliates," *Journalism & Mass Communication Quarterly* 5 (1979): 87–91, 147.

4. Baughman, *Television's Guardians*, 4.

5. Christina Lefevre-Gonzalez, "Restoring Historical Understanding of the 'Public Interest' Standard of American Broadcasting: An Exploration of the Fairness Doctrine," *International Journal of Communication* 7 (2013): 89–109.

6. Patricia Aufderheide, "Public Television and the Public Sphere," *Critical Studies in Mass Communication* 8 (1991): 168–83.

7. Peter U. Hohendahl, "Critical Theory, Public Sphere and Culture: Jürgen Habermas and His Critics," *New German Critique* 16 (1979): 89–118; Aufderheide, "Public Television and Public Sphere," and Hoynes, *Public Television for Sale*, 172.

8. Bennett, "The Public Broadcasting Service," 182.

9. Public Broadcasting Station, "Funding Standards and Practicies," online resource at http://www.pbs.org/producers/guidelines/principles_iia.html.

10. "The Public Interest Standard in Television Broadcasting," http://govinfo.library.unt.edu/piac/novmtg/pubint.htm, and Hoynes, *Public Television for Sale*, 172.

11. "Broadcasting and Government Regulation in a Free Society: An Occasional Paper on the Role of the Mass Media in the Free Society" (Santa Barbara: Center for the Study of Democratic Institutions, 1959).

12. Hoynes, *Public Television for Sale*, 172.

13. Laura Linder, *Public Access Television: America's Electronic Soapbox* (Westport, CT: Greenwood Publishing Group, 1999), 52.

14. Alexandre Macmillan, "Michel Foucault's Contribution to a Critical Theory of Communication: The Case of Disciplinary Power," Paper presented at the International Communication Association conference, Phoenix, Arizona, May 26, 2012: 3.

15. Gulnaz Begum, "Critical Discourse Analysis of the Protesters' Language," *Language in India* 15, no. 3 (2015): 85–95.

16. Bernd Carsten Stahl, "Whose Discourse? A Comparison of the Foucauldian and Habermasian Concepts of Discourse in Critical IS Research." Paper presented at the Proceedings of the Tenth Americas Conference on Information Systems, New York, August 2004.

17. General Assembly of the State of Arkansas, *Acts of Arkansas, Act 359*. 1958–1959, vol. II 1604.

18. General Assembly of the State of Arkansas, *Act of Arkansas, Act 198*. 1960–1961, vol. I 732.

19. "A Brief History of AETN," Arkansas Educational Television Network, March 28, 2014. http://www.aetn.org/about/history (accessed April 12, 2015).

20. "'Profane' Play by Williams Canceled by KETS Official," *Arkansas Gazette*, December 10, 1966.

21. "Program Director of ETV Goes on the Radio to Defend Decisions, Finds Support," *Arkansas Gazette,* December 18, 1966.

22. Harriet [Jansma] to Diane Blair. Diane Blair Papers, series 2, subseries 6, box 1, folder 1. Special Collections, University of Arkansas Libraries, Fayetteville.

23. "AETN May Bar Film on LR Crisis," *Arkansas Gazette*, September 20, 1979, 1A sec.

24. "Association Board Is 'Concerned' about AETN's Censorship Policies," *Arkansas Gazette*, October 10, 1979, and "ETV Censorship Questioned," *Arkansas Times*, October 10, 1979.

25. "AEA Assembly Votes to Investigate Policies of Education Network," *Arkansas Gazette*, 1979, and "AEA Plans Review of AETN Policies," *Arkansas Times*, November 5, 1979.

26. "Teacher Group Criticizes AETN," *Arkansas Gazette*, November 1, 1979.

27. Editorial, "The Censors," *Arkansas Gazette*, November 25, 1979.

28. "'No Quarrel,' Chairman at AETN Says," *Arkansas Gazette*, December 19, 1979, 19A.

29. "A Word from Clinton," *Arkansas Gazette*, December 19, 1979, 28A.

30. D. L. Wilson, letter to the Editor, "Monty Python and a State," *Arkansas Gazette*, November 1, 1979.

31. "No Censorship by AETN Board," *Springdale News*, June 17, 1981.

32. "AETN Panel Reaffirms Censorship," *Arkansas Gazette*, June 17, 1981.

33. "Bowdlerizing on 'Educational' TV," *Arkansas Gazette*, January 1, 1982.

34. Editorial, "AETN Gets Flak," *Springdale News*, March 26, 1986.

35. Bill Simmons, "Legislators Critical of AETN Panelists: Comments on Political Analysis Program Draw Fire," *Log Cabin Democrat*, July 10, 1986.

36. Memorandum from Raymond Ho to the AETN Commission, July 11, 1986. Diane Blair Papers, series 2, subseries 6, box 1, folder 1. Special Collections, University of Arkansas Libraries, Fayetteville.

37. Memorandum from Mike Mottler to AETN Commission Members, December 18, 1986. Diane Blair Papers, series 2, subseries 6, box 1, folder 3. Special Collections, University of Arkansas Libraries, Fayetteville.

38. Mike Mottler to Ralph Caley, December 18, 1986. Diane Blair Papers, series 2, subseries 6, box 1, folder 3. Special Collections, University of Arkansas Libraries, Fayetteville.

39. Michael Storey, "Some Examples of AETN's 'Censorship' over the Years," *Arkansas Democrat-Gazette*, December 15, 1996.

40. "AETN Programming Philosophy," Employee Handbook, June 16, 1986. Diane Blair Papers (MC 1632), series 2, subseries 6, box 3, folder 4. Special Collections, University of Arkansas Libraries, Fayetteville.

41. "Proposed Program Policies," April 15, 1987. Diane Blair Papers (MC 1632), series 2, subseries 6, box 4, folder 1. Special Collections, University of Arkansas Libraries, Fayetteville.

42. "AETN Programming Policy," September 19, 2012.

CHAPTER 7

Off-Campus Speech and On-Campus Punishment for Student Websites

ANDREW LONG

Censorship, like charity, should begin at home; unlike charity, it should end there.

—CLARE BOOTH LUCE

"School slut." "Bitch." "Fuck Greenwood!! The Town from Hell." "Mrs. White can suck a big cock, choke on it, and drown in a pool of cum." These phrases, though vulgar and potentially offensive, would generally be protected by the First Amendment of the U.S. Constitution. Justice John Marshall Harlan, writing for the majority in *Cohen v. California*, notes, "one man's vulgarity is another's lyric," thereby enjoining state action against any individual merely because the words they speak might be of an offensive nature.[1] This theory is grounded in the idea that every word has a particular meaning, both in its literal and connotative sense, and that these words, though vulgar, carry in their meanings ideas that society benefits from by having expressed.

The situation becomes slightly more muddled when such speech is purported to have occurred on school grounds. When dealing with minors, the courts have traditionally recognized that schools do need a certain amount of disciplinary leeway since they are dealing with minors and need to maintain order among them. The right of schools to punish potentially disruptive student speech is limited, however. Even if the speech is potentially disruptive, schools must still tread lightly. As Justice Abe Fortas noted in *Tinker v. Des Moines*,

> Any word spoken, in class, in the lunchroom, or on the campus, that deviates from the views of another person may start an argument or cause a disturbance. But our Constitution says we must take this risk, and our history says that it is this sort of hazardous freedom—this kind of openness—that is the basis of our national strength and of the independence and vigor of Americans who grow up and live in this relatively permissive, often disputatious, society.[2]

Thus, schools generally are not permitted to mete out punishment for student speech, even if it is the kind of speech that will cause disruption. Student speech has been recognized to be valuable, and the courts have held that such speech deserves a large degree of protection.

The decision in *Tinker* has firmly established the limitations on schools' ability to censor student speech. It seems odd then that, more than three decades later, schools are once again beginning to crack down on speech they find to be offensive and disruptive. This new offensive is not aimed at black armbands or underground newspapers, but at student websites on the Internet. What is even more interesting is that these efforts cracking down on student cyber-speech are often directed at students who create their websites off school grounds, using their own equipment on non-school-affiliated web servers. In the wake of the *Tinker* decision, such actions would not seem to comport with the accepted boundaries a school may act within to punish speech, but the courts have not yet fully reached a consensus on how to handle cases involving off-campus student speech on the Internet. The purpose of this paper will be to examine two such cases—one past and one currently pending—that occurred in Arkansas. The first case, occurring in 2000, involved a fifteen-year-old student named Justin Redman who attended Valley View Junior High School in Jonesboro, Arkansas. The other case involves two students, Justin

Neal and Ryan Khul, who both attend Greenwood High School in Greenwood, Arkansas. This paper will first examine the background in each of these cases, showing the arguments the schools each used as justification for disciplining the students. Next, some substantial differences between these two cases will be examined in order to understand why these cases may have different outcomes. Analysis of how these cases—especially the Neal/Kuhl case—relate to applicable case law will also be offered. Ultimately, it will be shown that, despite the potential worries of school administrators, none of these students should have been punished for the websites they created.

On the evening of May 7, 2000, a fifteen-year-old Valley View Junior High student named Justin Redman signed onto the Internet from his home in Jonesboro and created a website parodying the one of his school.[3] Redman and two of his friends, John Alcorn and Greg Martin, had worked to create the official site for the Valley View School District earlier that semester.[4] After posting the parody site, he gave the address of the website to a few of his friends.[5] Redman figured that knowledge of the site's existence would stay within that small group, but word about it quickly spread to many of his class-mates.[6] Within several days, many students at Valley View had either seen or heard of the site. One student who was offended by the site's content printed it out and brought it to school with him to show the principal on May 15, 2000. After school officials reviewed the content of the site, several students, including Redman, were called in to meet with the dean of students, Gene Taylor. Taylor conducted a series of one-on-one "police style" interrogations with the students in order to determine who created the website.[7] Redman admitted to Taylor that he was the creator of the site, and that he alone was responsible for its content. At some point prior to this, Redman accessed the website from a computer in his school's library in an attempt to remove it, but was unable to do so from that location.[8]

After receiving Redman's confession of being the creator of this website, the school proceeded to discipline him in a variety of ways. They ordered that he would have to attend sexual harassment counseling before being readmitted into his classes. Redman was prohibited from using any of the school's computer equipment for eighteen weeks. He also received a ten-day suspension. This last part of the punishment was especially damaging to Redman, because the suspension would cause him to miss his final exams, thus resulting in him flunking the ninth grade.[9] Redman himself asked his principal, Sue Castleberry, to reconsider the decision, but she refused to do so.[10] When Justin told his parents, Marty and Patricia Redman, what had happened they felt that the school had overstepped their bounds concerning the discipline of their son. As they would later say in a press release, "Although we as parents do not condone what Justin did, we also do not feel the school has the right to control or discipline him for what he does off school grounds. That job belongs to us."[11]

The Redmans appealed the disciplinary action to Valley View School District superintendent Radius Baker to no avail.[12] They then requested that the Valley View School Board meet to discuss the disciplinary action concerning Justin in an attempt to appeal the superintendent's decision. The board met in a special closed-door session at the request of the Redmans on June 13, 2000. After meeting for over an hour, the school board upheld all parts of the disciplinary action against Justin. School board president Randy Woodruff would later note that the decision was upheld because the website created a "disruption of the school," and that even though the site was created off school grounds, it still "reached into the school. It involved the school."[13]

Shortly after Justin's suspension from classes, Jay Frankenberger, a friend of Justin's, wrote a letter to the American Civil Liberties Unions (ACLU) of Arkansas expressing concern over Justin's suspension.[14] Upon hearing the verdict of the Valley View School Board, the ACLU agreed to represent Justin in a lawsuit against the Valley View School District and the school administrators who punished him. On June 22, 2000, the ACLU filed a motion for an expedited hearing to get a restraining order enjoining the school district from carrying through with any of the proposed remaining punishments against Justin, to have the suspension he served removed from his record, and to allow him to make up his final exams and advance to the ninth grade.[15] The brief the ACLU filed with the court presented two major reasons that all punishments against Redman should have been vacated: the nature of the website and the reasoning the school gave for the disciplinary action.[16]

Concerning the nature of the website, the ACLU's brief submitted on behalf of Redman argued that both the way the site was posted as well as its content rendered the school unable to punish Redman for its creation. Redman's website "borrowed the format of the school's official website," thereby parodying its content.[17] Much of the content was either vulgar or sexual, prompting descriptions of the site to say that it was filled "with graphic nudity and explicit language."[18] The targets of the content of the site included the school itself, the school's administration and staff, and four students who attended the school.[19] Redman even dedicated a portion of this site to labeling one of the students, a fourteen-year-old female classmate, "the school slut."[20] Though the site was vulgar and potentially offensive, it was noted, however, that "the website contained no depiction of violence nor threat of intimidation."[21] This was a fact that the Valley View School District later stipulated.[22] Since the site's content did not contain violent threats against any of his classmates, the ACLU brief argued that the content was protected because even its offensive content contained "serious literary and political merit."[23] The brief explains:

> [The website] is the product of an average adolescent male. Yes, it is vulgar, and disrespectful, occasionally to the point of being offensively rude. Taken in isolation, some parts might even be called scurrilous. The work must be judged as a whole, however, as a parody of the school, its culture, its social life and its authority figures. It possesses social, political, and literary value. It is not obscene.[24]

This explanation, which notes the test set forth by the Supreme Court in *Miller v. California*, notes that even though the sites content might be patently offensive in certain parts, taken as a whole, the site is a commentary on the operations of the school and its officials and thus deserving of First Amendment protection.[25]

The ACLU's brief also noted that the way Justin Redman went about creating and disseminating information about his website should render the school's discipline of him invalid. The website was created by Redman "off school grounds, on his home computer, during his free time."[26] Since this activity was done away from school using no school equipment, the ACLU argued the school had no grounds on which to punish Redman. Additionally, Redman never attempted

to access the site from any school computer until the day of his suspension, May 15, 2000.[27] Further, the ACLU argued that Redman had
made reasonable attempts to keep the site from being widely dissemi-
nated. Both sides stipulated to the fact that Redman told only six of his
friends about the site, and never registered it with a search engine.[28]
This meant that "the website was not accessible to anyone unless he or
she had the site's specific address. It was not possible to accidentally
access Justin's site."[29] Since it would be nearly impossible for anyone
to stumble across Redman's site, the ACLU said that Justin attempted
to limit any exposure other students at Valley View would have to
it, and this made any knowledge or discussions other students had
about Justin's site an unforeseen consequence. Because the nature of
the website, both in its creation and dissemination was entirely an
off-campus activity, and because Redman sought to limit any exposure of the other students to the website, the ACLU argued that punishment of Justin for the site was beyond the scope of the school's
authority, comparing it to punishing a student for "disparaging the
principal at the local mall."[30]

The Valley View School District offered a myriad of reasons for
disciplining Justin, though the reasoning offered by different administrative officials at different points in time after they became aware of
Redman's website began to change. An analysis of materials related to
this case, both in the form of court documents and news items appearing during the time this matter was going on, reveals five distinct lines
of reasoning the Valley View School District and its administrators
used to justify their punishment of Redman. The main line of reasoning the school used was that, even though Redman's site was created
off school grounds, it still constituted a disruption to the educational
process. In a letter sent to the Redmans on May 18, 2000, Principal
Castleberry noted that "Justin's actions caused a disturbance in the
school and disrupted the learning environment."[31] Interestingly, even
though Redman had been suspended three days prior to the sending
of the letter, no mention of a disruption to the educational process had
been mentioned to Justin or his parents until that point. School board
president Woodruff also noted that even though the site was created
from Redman's home, "it also reached into the school. It involved
the school . . . it's just one of these situations with the dangers of the
Internet and how it affects the school."[32]

A second major cause of action the school used to justify disciplining Redman was his website sexually harassed other students, specifically the female student he referred to as a "slut." This was in violation of Title IX and the school's handbook. The Redmans were also advised in the May 18 letter they received that this was part of the reason for the punishment of Justin, and this violation also was the impetus for the sexual harassment counseling the school demanded Redman undergo before he would be readmitted to school.[33]

A third reason used by the school to punish Justin was the potential violence the website might have incited against Justin. Valley View's brief notes that the school feared that the students targeted on Redman's site might react violently in retaliation:

> It was foreseeably likely that these individuals would be upset and would want to retaliate against Justin Redman, and the evidence will show that the immediate and serious threat of violence was a major concern of Valley View school officials when they had to deal with the circumstances and suspended Redman.[34]

The brief filed by the ACLU similarly notes that school officials took action against Redman "to mollify two students who allegedly had demanded that action be taken, one of whom purportedly had threatened to 'take matters into his own hands' if the school did not act."[35] The school district used these incidences to claim they suspended Justin for his own protection against these students.

The fourth line of reasoning that was used to discipline Redman was the fact that the administrators were offended by the content on the site. Though this reasoning was not listed on the school's disciplinary form, testimony from the court proceedings and the defendant's brief indicate that administrators' personal feelings about the site's content certainly played a factor. In his court testimony, dean of students Taylor noted that he was "personally offended by the Web site"[36] and that he was angered that Redman could "use the Internet to attack people. [Redman] did damage to those students and he showed no remorse."[37] The school also argued that "Redman's website goes far beyond vulgarity and crosses the line into obscenity."[38]

A final justification the school used to punish Redman was that he did in fact access his site once from inside the school, thus violating the school's usage agreement for school computers since Redman's site contained pornography. On the morning of May 15, 2000, Redman asked to be excused from class to go to the restroom, but once excused went to the school's library where he attempted to delete this site.[39] Though Taylor said, "if he had asked me if he could use a school computer to take the site down, I probably would have let him," the school district still used this as a reason to suspend Redman and revoke his computing privileges.[40]

When the trial for Redman's case began in the Western Division of the Eastern District of Arkansas Federal Court in Little Rock on August 16, 2000, the ACLU sought to have a restraining order issued against the school to have all of Redman's punishments revoked. Dan Bufford represented the Valley View School District, and Nathan M. Norton represented Justin Redman as an ACLU cooperating attorney. U.S. district judge George Howard Jr. heard the arguments. Through the course of several days of trial, school officials, including Taylor, and several of Redman's friend's, including Greg Martin and John Alcorn, offered testimony.[41] After hearing testimony on August 16–August 18, 2000, both sides had a closed meeting with Judge Howard and worked out a settlement at his suggestion.[42] The agreement remains confidential,[43] but both sides claimed victory in the outcome. Valley View reportedly agreed to the settlement because they "were looking at sending six to eight teachers, seven to eight students and three sets of parents from Jonesboro to Little Rock to testify . . . The distractions and the expense of that was just too much."[44] The ACLU claimed victory, noting that "every school board and every school board attorney in the state is going to know about this case."[45] Due to the settlement, Howard dismissed the case and Redman was allowed to start school in the fall of 2000 in the tenth grade.[46]

Though the ACLU expressed hope that the Redman case would serve as a warning to other public schools in Arkansas that student activity on the Internet was not within the allowable bounds for school action, that hope was lost when on August 24, 2004, two students from Greenwood High School were suspended for their online activities. Justin Neal, seventeen, and Ryan Kuhl, eighteen, had worked together to create a website and a weblog (commonly referred to as a "blog") that lampooned their school and its administrators.[47]

On August 9, 2004, Ryan Kuhl created an online weblog called

"F_CK Greenwood" from his home on his family's computer. In addition to postings Kuhl himself put into the blog, other people could post comments, which were available by anyone to view as well.[48] After showing this blog to his friend, Justin Neal, Neal "thought that starting a site of his own wouldn't be such a bad idea . . . Justin and Ryan decided that the two sites could work in tandem."[49] Several days later, Justin created a website called "Greenwood" where he posted comics related to events going on at Greenwood High School. After the creation of these sites, Kuhl and Neal sent notice about the sites to "every [e-mail] address that could be had."[50] Word about the sites spread quickly among students at Greenwood High School, and several students posted comments of their own on Kuhl's blog.

When school began at Greenwood High School on August 19, 2004, Neal posted a cartoon on this site that "was to be the match to the fuse."[51] This comic, according to Greenwood High School assistant principal Jim Garvey, depicted "an image of my caricature shooting two students."[52] Shortly after the posting of this comic on Neal's site, the school started to receive a large number of comments from students who wanted to know what could be done about the site.[53] On August 24, 2004, Greenwood High School principal Jerry Efurd called Neal and Kuhl, along with several other students, out of class and questioned them separately for approximately thirty to forty-five minutes each about the websites. When talking to both Neal and Kuhl, Assistant Principal Garvey informed them that the police had been called about their websites, and that "jail time was a likelihood."[54] Later that day, both Neal and Kuhl were sent home from school, being told that they were receiving indefinite suspensions, the length of which would be determined at a later date.[55]

Neal's parents called their attorney, Chip Sexton, on the afternoon of August 24, 2004. Sexton told the Neals that it was unlikely either Neal or Kuhl would be suspended for these websites. However, when the Neals and Kuhls met with Efurd on August 25, 2004, he proceeded to suspend both Neal and Kuhl from school for three days. Sexton sent a letter to Efurd that afternoon demanding that he rescind the suspension of the students. When Efurd did not respond, Sexton filed a suit on behalf of both Neal and Kuhl in the Western District of Arkansas Federal Court in Fort Smith.[56]

The content of Neal and Kuhl's websites served as the basis for the suspensions each received. Both websites were created entirely from each boy's home on their own personal computer. On Kuhl's website, entitled "Fuck Greenwood!! The Town from Hell," Kuhl himself had several postings that contained some form of vulgar language, including one that said, "we received our yearbooks which is just 300 pages of shit . . . plain and pure shit."[57] There was also a posting of Kuhl talking about his displeasure with his class schedule, in which he says "fuck them" to people who viewed him as "rude or stuck up."[58] Kuhl's site also featured a cartoon he drew called "Bulldog death of the week," which featured a caricature of a bulldog with a "medieval type of weapon" immediately above it.[59] Other people also made postings on Kuhl's website. One student remarked, "I have a comment; Mrs. White can suck a big cock, choke on it, and drown in a pool of cum."[60] Kuhl was not aware of who made the comment.

Justin Neal's website contained a purpose statement on its homepage, stating, "this site's purpose is to express the author's view on life in the small town using crudely drawn . . . comics and generally horrible dialogue."[61] His intent was to "[experiment] with cartooning and writing while using opinions, school, life, etc. as material."[62] Before Greenwood High School was back in session in August 2004, Neal posted two comics on his site, one dealing with orientation and another with parking tags. The third comic that he posted after the first day of school is the one that seemed to cause the most concern among Greenwood High School administrators. It featured a caricature of Principal Efurd as an intercom being pushed around by a sasquatch-like caricature of Assistant Principal Garvey. The caption above the comic states:

> I've always found the first day of school to be quite . . . unappealing, but the two unlucky souls in this comic must find it to be almost annoying. Also, introducing Principal E-Firdcom and his lovable sidekick, the Abominable Vice Principal Garbo. Give them a hand (or Garbo might take it from you).[63]

The comic appearing on the aforementioned website contained the following cells (note: I have modified the size of the images to better fit within this paper):

Justin's website also had a forum where people could post comments. One of the topics on this forum was entitled "the creation of mayhem within the school . . . ,"[64] though none of the materials posted actually speaks of creating mayhem.[65] Another posting talks about how students need to "harass the school board," though the post actually "advocates a freely elected group to make recommendations to the School Board."[66] Neal's site also contained a link to Kuhl's site, but noted that "none of the above sites are mine."[67]

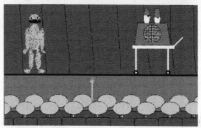

The school used several reasons for disciplining Neal and Kuhl, though the reasoning varied for each of them. According to the official suspension notices that were mailed to Neal and Kuhl after their suspension began, Neal was suspended for "Providing a web site and linking the site to an inappropriate web site [that] encouraged mayhem and dissension among GHS students," and also for "Providing images of school administration conducting violence toward students."[68] Kuhl was suspended for "Posting inappropriate web site. Inappropriate material on the web site."[69] Neither Kuhl nor Neal was ever given notice of which specific rule or regulation of Greenwood High School they had violated. Garvey testified that the suspensions were related to the "Violent Threats" policy in the Greenwood Student Handbook, also noting that they had to deal with these situations as they happened.[70] It seems that the school's worry about potential violence that they felt these sites incited were largely the official reason for the suspensions. The school also claimed that these websites disrupted the educational system. Garvey testified that the sites created a "disgruntlement" that "disrupted the harmony of the school."[71] Efurd testified that class time was lost because "students were wanting to talk or talking or arguing amongst themselves as to [the content of the websites.]"[72] Though these were the reasons expressed by the school as being the cause of the suspension for both boys, Neal and Kuhl's attorney, Chip Sexton, feels there might have been ulterior motives, saying the punishment was "related to who was complaining about the web sites and not about the content."[73]

When proceedings began on September 3, 2004, before U.S. magistrate Beverly Stites-Jones for a preliminary injunction against Greenwood High School to have the suspensions reversed, both Neal and Kuhl, as well as Principal Efurd and Assistant Principal Garvey, testified. Subject matter discussed in testimony included reasons the school suspended the boys, how the websites affected the school, and why Neal and Kuhl made their sites.[74] Ultimately, Neal and Kuhl lost their motion for a preliminary injunction against Greenwood High School. In her ruling, Magistrate Stites-Jones notes several reasons for her decision. She notes that the test for determining whether or not to issue the preliminary injunction is "whether the speech substantially interfered with school activities and/or discipline."[75] In applying this test, she notes that the "venomous hate-filled rantings . . . could be reasonably viewed by an administrator" as a potential cause of violence in the school.[76] Though the school's evidence of violence starting "was not particularly strong," she notes that "educators do not have to wait for substantial disruption to occur as long as it is reasonably foreseeable."[77] She concludes by noting that, although there is potential harm to Neal and Kuhl from stifling their speech,

> the harm to [Greenwood High School] will be greater if we grant
> to relief requested because we would be stripping the school
> administrators of the latitude to make disciplinary decisions
> where substantial interference is reasonably perceived.[78]

The proceedings seeking a permanent injunction against the school are scheduled to take place before Judge Jimm Hendron on January 5, 2005.

Though there are many similarities between the Redman case and the case involving Neal and Kuhl—including the fact that the websites were created off campus, they all dealt in some way with people or events at the school, and students at the schools found out about the sites and reported them to school officials—there are several important differences between these cases that may cause the outcome of the case involving Neal and Kuhl to be viewed differently than the case involving Redman. First, and most important, is the difference in the content of the websites, specifically as it relates to violence. Redman's site was devoid of all hints of violence, a fact not only asserted by his attorney, but also stipulated to by the Valley View School District.[79] The case involving Kuhl and Neal is not quite as straightforward. Neal and Kuhl assert that any mention of violence on their respective sites was done either as a form of satire or involved content that they themselves did not post. Greenwood High School asserts that they had to assume that this violence, even though potentially satirical, constituted a real threat against the school and its students. Though it was admitted that it was unlikely that anyone would perceive the threat to be a real one, it nonetheless was a "depiction of violence."[80] It was this perceived threat of violence that caused Neal and Kuhl to lose their bid for a preliminary injunction. Additionally, this perceived threat of violence could potentially be problematic to Neal and Kuhl's claim that their First Amendment rights were violated. A Pennsylvania court held in *J.S. v. Bethlehem Area School District* that violence depicted on a student website that was directed at a teacher constituted enough of a threat toward the school that school officials were justified in punishing the student.[81] This perceived violence by school officials is a major distinction between these cases, and it is one that may hurt the chances of Neal and Kuhl to prevail.

A second major difference between the cases involves who is responsible for the content on the websites. Redman's site was entirely his own creation, and he was responsible for all content on it. Though Neal and Kuhl were responsible for a large portion of the content that appeared on their respective sites, both of their websites allowed other users to post messages. Much of the content that the school claims to have found objective on the sites was posted to the sites by students other than Neal and Kuhl. Nonetheless, both Garvey and Efurd said they held Neal and Kuhl responsible for all content on their sites, regardless of who posted it.[82] The fact that the Greenwood High

School officials admit this may well serve to help Neal and Kuhl, as the Communications Decency Act requires that "no provider or user of an interactive computer service shall be treated as the publisher or speaker of any information provided by another information content provider."[83] Though this exception is not applicable to all of the content in question in this case, it may well account for enough of the content to show that there was not enough information posted by Neal or Kuhl for the school to have a reasonable threshold for believing violence was likely to occur in the school.

A final major difference between these two cases is the way the students went about informing others of the existence of the websites. In the Redman case, he only told a small select group of friends. This group of friends then went on to tell other students, creating a snowball effect. Nonetheless, Redman himself only intended for the site to be exposed to a very limited number of students. This is not the case with Neal and Kuhl. Neal and Kuhl admittedly attempted to send emails about their websites to anyone whose email address they had access to.[84] This action could potentially be seen as taking the website from an off-campus activity to one that is of a more on-campus nature. Though cases such as *Thomas v. Board of Education* have held that off-campus speech that would traditionally receive First Amendment protections is beyond the scope of a school's authority to punish, speech that is not traditionally protected or interferes with the school is a different matter.[85] The hints of violence, combined with the large student populace that Neal and Kuhl informed, could potentially be enough for a court to determine that their websites approached more traditional on-campus student speech.

Despite the potential differences that could serve as a hurdle for Neal and Kuhl's case, it is still likely that, given current case and statutory law, they will prevail in their bid for a permanent injunction for several reasons. First, their loss in the bid for a preliminary injunction should not serve as a basis to judge the merits of their case. Magistrate Stites-Jones notes that much of the speech on the sites is certainly worthy of constitutional protection. However, in seeking a preliminary injunction, the plaintiffs must show a "likelihood of success on the merits" in order to prevail, thus placing a very high burden on them.[86] Losing a motion for a preliminary injunction may not be a good indicator of how likely a plaintiff is to win a bid for a permanent injunction.

A second reason Neal and Kuhl are likely to prevail is because their activities were still largely done off campus. The officials at Greenwood High School say they do not believe that either website was accessed at the school, and both sides are in agreement that the site was completely created away from school grounds. Given this fact, precedent holds that the creation of these websites are beyond the school's authority to punish. In *Shanley v. Northeast Independent School District*, the Fifth Circuit held that an off-campus newspaper that was distributed near school grounds—some issues of which made it onto the school grounds—could not be used to punish the authors.[87] In drawing analogy to Neal and Kuhl, precedent holds that just because some byproduct resulting from off-campus speech finds its way into a school, that school may not use the off-campus speech to punish students.

A final reason that Neal and Kuhl are likely to prevail is that the case law most specifically related to this matter—that dealing with student websites that talk about a school but are not created in nor associated with that school—have been generally held to be protected speech that a school cannot punish.[88] In *Beussink v. Woodland R-IV School District*, the court held that an off-campus student website that parodied the school's official website and contained vulgar language was protected speech.[89] Similarly, in *Emmett v. Kent School District No. 415*, a student website created off campus that had a hit list of people he wanted killed was ruled to be protected speech.[90] In *J.S. v. Bethlehem*, the case Magistrate Stites-Jones used as a comparison for the one involving Neal and Kuhl, the facts do not seem to be parallel. In the Bethlehem case, the student in question had images of a teacher's severed head and the site solicited funds to hire a hitman to kill this same teacher, eventually causing the teacher to take a leave of absence. In the case involving Neal and Kuhl, no such graphic depiction of violence is offered, and any violence on their websites is either satirical or originates from a source other than Neal or Kuhl. Beyond that, at no point did any teacher or student take a leave of absence from Greenwood High School as a result of Neal or Kuhl's websites.[91] Thus, it would seem that with few exceptions, the courts have consistently held that student speech that is in the form of a website created off campus is speech that is beyond the scope of a school to punish.

With the advent of the Internet, schools have encountered a new area of student speech that they are finding hard to control. While schools can traditionally regulate some of what students says on campus, there is still a question as to whether or not schools have authority to regulate Internet speech that occurs off campus but spills onto school grounds. Though most case law now holds that students' speech on the Internet is beyond the bounds of a school's authority to regulate, many schools still insist upon being able to control what students say or write, even when what they say or write occurs outside of the schoolhouse gate. If students in public schools are ever to ensure that their First Amendment rights lie beyond the grasp of school officials, then there will need to be a challenge to the school's authority that works its way through the legal system. Former Arkansas state ACLU legal director John Burnett may have phrased the problem best when he said, "School administrators are bent out of shape that kids can enjoy free speech and know more about free speech than they ever had before. There is a lot of danger and responsibility there, but that doesn't mean it's something the schools get to control."[92]

NOTES

1. *Cohen v. California*, 403 U.S. 15 (1971).

2. Tinker v. Des Moines Independent Community School District et al., 393 U.S. 503 (1969).

3. J. Stengle, "Arkansas ACLU Sues School District on Behalf of Student," *Associated Press State & Local Wire*, June 22, 2000. Retrieved November 14, 2004, from Lexis-Nexis Academic Universe Database.

4. M. Nelson "Jonesboro Teen to Start School with Classmates," *Associated Press State & Local Wire*, August 16, 2000. Retrieved November 15, 2004, from Lexis-Nexis Academic Universe Database.

5. *Justin Redman v. Valley View School District, et al.* Case No. 4:00CV 00487-GH. Trial brief of plaintiff Justin Redman. (E.D. Ark. 2000 [Heard]). [Unreported].

6. S. Kondo, "School to Admit Web Spoofer: Student Suing District over Suspension Can Begin 10th Grade," *Arkansas Democrat Gazette*, August 17, 2000, B8. Retrieved November 14, 2004, from Lexis-Nexis Academic Universe Database.

7. *Redman v. Valley View*. Trial brief of plaintiff Justin Redman, 9.

8. L. Satter, "School Sued for Response to Mockery on Web Site," *Arkansas*

Democrat-Gazette, June 23, 2000, B1. Retrieved November 16, 2004, from Lexis-Nexis Academic Universe Database.

9. *ACLU of Arkansas Sues School District on Behalf of Student Expelled for Creating Off-campus Web Site,* June 22, 2000. Retrieved November 17, 2004, from http://www.aclu.org/StudentsRights/StudentsRights.cfm?ID=7991&c=160.

10. Stengle, "Arkansas ACLU Sues School District on Behalf of Student."

11. ACLU of Arkansas Sues School District on Behalf of Student Expelled for Creating Off-campus Web Site.

12. "Judge Rules in Favor of Newspaper," *Associated Press State & Local Wire,* July 1, 2000. Retrieved November 14, 2004, from Lexis-Nexis Academic Universe Database.

13. Satter, "School Sued for Response to Mockery on Web Site."

14. Nelson, "Jonesboro Teen to Start School with Classmates.".

15. ACLU of Arkansas sues school district on behalf of student expelled for creating off-campus web site.

16. *Redman v. Valley View.* Trial brief of plaintiff Justin Redman.

17. Ibid., 2.

18. "Hearing to Resume Wednesday in First Amendment Dispute," *Associated Press State & Local Wire,* August 14, 2000. Retrieved November 15, 2004, from Lexis-Nexis Academic Universe Database.

19. *Redman v. Valley View.* Trial brief of plaintiff Justin Redman.

20. Kondo, "School to Admit Web Spoofer."

21. *Redman v. Valley View.* Trial brief of plaintiff Justin Redman, 2.

22. *Justin Redman v. Valley View School District, et al.* Case No. 4:00CV 00487-GH. Findings of fact and conclusions of law. (E.D. Ark. 2000 [Heard]). [Unreported].

23. *Redman v. Valley View.* Trial brief of plaintiff Justin Redman, 11.

24. Ibid.

25. *Miller v. California,* 413 U.S. 15 (1973).

26. *Redman v. Valley View.* Trial brief of plaintiff Justin Redman, 2.

27. Kondo, "School to Admit Web Spoofer."

28. *Redman v. Valley View.* Findings of fact and conclusions of law.

29. *Redman v. Valley View.* Trial brief of plaintiff Justin Redman, 6.

30. Satter, "School Sued for Response to Mockery on Web Site."

31. *Redman v. Valley View.* Findings of fact and conclusions of law, 4.

32. Satter, "School Sued for Response to Mockery on Web Site."

33. *Justin Redman v. Valley View School District, et al.* Case No. 4:00CV 00487-GH. Defendants' trial brief. (E.D. Ark. 2000 [Heard]). [Unreported].

34. *Redman v. Valley View.* Defendant's trial brief, 5.

35. *Redman v. Valley View.* Trial brief of plaintiff Justin Redman, 9.

36. Kondo, "School to Admit Web Spoofer."

37. Nelson, "Jonesboro Teen to Start School with Classmates."

38. *Redman v. Valley View.* Defendant's trial brief, 7.

39. *Redman v. Valley View.* Defendant's trial brief.

40. Kondo, "School to Admit Web Spoofer."

41. Ibid.

42. M. Nelson, "School District Says It Settled Lawsuit to End Disruption,"

Associated Press State & Local Wire, August 18, 2000. Retrieved November 14, 2004, from Lexis-Nexis Academic Universe Database.

43. N. M. Norton, mnorton@wlj.com (December 10, 2004). RE: Any word [personal email].

44. Nelson, "School District Says It Settled Lawsuit to End Disruption."

45. Ibid.

46. Kondo, "District Settles Lawsuit by Teen Suspended for Web Site," *Arkansas Democrat-Gazette*, August 18, 2000, B4. Retrieved November 16, 2004, from Lexis-Nexis Academic Universe Database.

47. *Judge Supports Ark. Students' Suspension over Personal Web Sites*, October 6, 2004. Retrieved November 16, 2004, from http://www.splc.org/printpage.asp?id=878&tb=newsflash.

48. J. B. Reed, "Web Criticism, from Home, Prompts Suspension, Lawsuit," *Arkansas Times*, September 9, 2004. Retrieved November 2, 2004 from http://www.arktimes.com/Articles/ArticleViewer.aspx?ArticleID=50559043-c9f7-41e9-ab96-428a2ba6cb90.

49. J. Neal and R. Kuhl, email interview, December 5, 2004.

50. Ibid.

51. Ibid.

52. *Justin Neal & Ryan Kuhl v. Greenwood School District*. Case No. 2:04-2195. Transcript of proceedings. (W.D. Ark. 2004), 53. [Unreported].

53. *Neal & Kuhl v. Greenwood*. Transcript of proceedings, 29.

54. Neal and Kuhl, interview.

55. *Justin Neal & Ryan Kuhl v. Greenwood School District*. Case No. 2:04-2195. Plaintiffs' post-hearing brief. (W.D. Ark. 2004), 6. [Unreported].

56. Reed, "Web Criticism, from Home, Prompts Suspension, Lawsuit."

57. *Neal & Kuhl v. Greenwood*. Plaintiffs' post-hearing brief, 4–5.

58. Ibid., 5.

59. Ibid.

60. *Neal & Kuhl v. Greenwood*. Transcript of proceedings, 25.

61. *Neal & Kuhl v. Greenwood*. Plaintiffs' post-hearing brief, 2.

62. Neal and Kuhl, interview.

63. *Latest Comic*, 2004. Retrieved December 1, 2004 from http://www.angelfire.com/comics/greentree/comic.htm.

64. *Neal & Kuhl v. Greenwood*. Transcript of proceedings, 145.

65. *Neal & Kuhl v. Greenwood*. Plaintiffs' post-hearing brief, 3.

66. Ibid.

67. Ibid.

68. Ibid., 6.

69. Ibid., 6.

70. *Neal & Kuhl v. Greenwood*. Transcript of proceedings, 52.

71. Ibid., 30.

72. Ibid., 216.

73. C. Sexton, email interview, December 3, 2004.

74. *Neal & Kuhl v. Greenwood*. Transcript of proceedings.

75. *Justin Neal & Ryan Kuhl v. Greenwood School District*. Case No. 2:04-2195. Magistrate judge's report and recommendation. (W.D. Ark. 2004), 14. [Unreported].

76. Ibid., 15.

77. Ibid.

78. Ibid., 16.

79. *Redman v. Valley View*. Findings of fact and conclusions of law.

80. *Neal & Kuhl v. Greenwood*. Transcript of proceedings, 53.

81. *J.S. v. Bethlehem Area School District*, 757 A.2d 412 (Pa. Commonwealth 2000).

82. *Neal & Kuhl v. Greenwood*. Transcript of proceedings.

83. Communications Decency Act § 230(c)(1), 47 U.S.C.

84. Neal and Kuhl, interview.

85. *Thomas v. Board of Education*, 607 F.2d 1043 (2nd Cir. 1979).

86. Minnesota Association of Nurse Anesthetists v. Unity Hospital, 59 F.3d 80, 83 (8th Cir. 1995).

87. Shanley v. Northeast Independent School District, 462 F.2d 860 (5th Cir. 1972).

88. Subsequent to the writing of this essay, Judge Jimm Larry Hendren held that "the speech of Justin Neal and Ryan Kuhl under scrutiny in this case was protected by the First Amendment" and "that by subjecting Neal and Kuhl to punishment for the speech at issue, Jerry Efurd, in his capacity as Principal of Greenwood High School, and Greenwood School District violated rights of Justin Neal and Ryan Kuhl protected by the First Amendment." *Neal v. Efurd*, 2005 U.S. Dist. LEXIS 47296 (W.D. Ark. 2005).

89. Beussink v. Woodland R-IV School District, 30 F.Supp 2d 1175 (E.D. Mo. 1998).

90. *Emmett v. Kent School District No. 415*, 92 F.Supp 2d 1088 (W.D. Wash. 2000).

91. *Neal & Kuhl v. Greenwood*. Transcript of proceedings, 214.

92. Nelson, "School District Says It Settled Lawsuit to End Disruption."

CHAPTER 8

State v. Rodgers

The 1935 Anarchy Trial of
Ward Rodgers in Poinsett County

JAMIE KERN

*I believe in the organization of tenant farmers in
behalf of justice for themselves is one of the finest
examples of Americanism, one of the finest proofs that
the old American spirit of liberty and justice is not
dead, that I have seen.*

—NORMAN THOMAS

In American history, the 1930s are synonymous with the Depression.
Throughout the nation, the closing of factories and the failing of farms
marked this decade. Though the whole nation struggled, the situation in
the South was desperate. President Franklin Delano Roosevelt believed
the South's condition to be so dire that he commissioned *The Report on
Economic Conditions of the South* to discover not only why the South
was suffering so much more than the rest of the nation but also how
these problems might be resolved. In this report, the president's letter states, "It is my conviction that the South presents right now the
Nation's No. 1 economic problem—the Nation's problem, not merely

the South's. For we have an economic unbalance in the Nation as a whole, due to this very condition of the South."[1] This hopeless situation led to the creation of the Southern Tenant Farmers Union (STFU) in Arkansas. While this union was created to help the local sharecroppers and tenant farmers, its close association with socialism resulted in its members being persecuted based on their "radical" speech.

This chapter examines an incident that occurred in Poinsett County, Arkansas, during the mid-1930s, when Ward Rodgers was arrested based on a speech he gave on behalf of the STFU. This event serves as an effective case study because it illustrates the motives and actions of both the dissenters and the establishment. The examination of this case will aim to determine the pattern and extent of the damage brought forth by limiting free speech, asking: *What is the history and import of Ward Rodgers's arrest for anarchy? How do rhetorical agitation and control strategies manifest themselves in the messages presented in these case studies? What are the consequences of the establishment's silencing of protected speech for citizens of the United States? How do these laws shape our understanding of dissidents?*

To create an understanding of the way in which the state arrests dissenters, especially those dissenters who are affiliated with an anti-capitalist organization, the research will present an analysis of Ward Rodgers's arrest. In answering the previously posted research questions, the historical research will examine the events surrounding Rodgers's arrest as well as the creation of the STFU. Then, research will examine the background and rhetorical behaviors of the agitators and of the establishment. Next, this chapter will argue Rodgers's arrest under criminal anarchy is a violation of free speech and that limiting free speech serves to discourage dissenters. Then, using examples from the Rodgers case, the research argues that criminal anarchy charges serve as an effective economic punishment for dissidents. Finally, the research will argue that criminalizing dissent shapes the way society views the dissenters themselves.

Arrest of Ward Rodgers for Criminal Anarchy

Harry L. Mitchell and Henry Clay East founded the agitating group, the Southern Tenant Farmers Union, in mid-February of 1934. The two men had met in 1932 and discovered that they both shared a common interest in the Socialist Party. They began to organize local socialists. In 1933, Mitchell's and East's attention turned toward the plight of share-croppers.[2] The Agricultural Adjustment Act (AAA) of 1933—the New Deal's response to the South's depression—ended up only worsening the sharecropper's suffering. The act's most detrimental feature was the "disproportionate allocation of benefit payments to landlords, because of their greater equity in the crops produced."[3] Out of this heightened tension between landlords and tenants in Arkansas a need for organi-zation arose. In February 1934, Norman Thomas, the Socialist Party's nominee, visited Tyronza, Arkansas, and addressed both socialists and sharecroppers. Thomas met with East and Mitchell after his address where East and Mitchell recounted their futile attempts to run for office on the local Socialist Party ticket.[4] It was during this meeting that Thomas suggested to East and Mitchell that they should organize a sharecroppers' union.[5] This union was the first union to become both integrated and allow women.

Ward Rodgers, a young Methodist preacher from Texas, arrived in Arkansas in 1933 to take a preaching position near Paris. Rodgers was a well-known, well-connected, and active member of the Socialist Party. He was a native of Oklahoma and was a graduate of Vanderbilt University. When he heard about the union being organized he aban-doned his church in Paris and came to help.[6] Rodgers founded a local branch of the Socialist Party.[7] Rodgers, along with other members of the local Socialist Party, was also responsible for founding the eastern Arkansas branch of the Southern Tenant Farmers Union. The STFU was a federation of tenant farmers with the goal of reforming the sharecropping and tenant farming systems.[8]

East and Mitchell took the first delegation of sharecroppers to Washington in January 1935. They had wired Rodgers to notify the members of the STFU that members of the delegation would report at a meeting in Marked Tree, Arkansas.[9] East and Mitchell had antic-ipated only fifty or sixty people would attend the meeting, but when they arrived, there were so many people that they moved the meet-ing to the town square. The gathering ended up hosting about five hundred white and black members of the Southern Tenant Farmers Union.[10] Rodgers was acting as chairman of the meeting.[11] At the time, Rodgers had been working on the Federal Emergency Relief Administration (FERA) adult education program teaching adults to read, write, and do arithmetic. A number of the plantation owners objected to sharecroppers learning these skills. Lynch, the superintendent of schools in the area, advised Rodgers that he should stop teaching these classes and leave the county. Rodgers protested, and Lynch told him that he might "find himself strung up on a telephone pole, if he did not leave."[12] Rodgers recounts this encounter by stating

> I had been teaching in the FERA Workers Education program members of the STFU. I had two Negro classes and three white classes. I was teaching economics, current events, and English. On January 14 my Negro class near Tyronza was "investigated" by the school board, who had no authority to do so. They complained because I was a Socialist and because I was a white man teaching Negros. The latter was more unpardonable in their minds.[13]

It was this event that would lead to Rodgers's troublesome statements during the STFU meeting.

During the meeting, Rodgers referred to a black man as "Mister." The vice president of the union was a black man named McKinney, and during the meeting Rodgers had asked, "Is Mr. McKinney in the crowd? Will Mr. McKinney come to the platform?"[14] He repeated this a number of times. Fred Stafford, the prosecuting attorney, was standing at the edge of the crowd with a notebook having his stenographer write down everything Rodgers was saying. He even asked, "Did you hear that agitator call that nigger Mister?" To which an older sharecropper replied, "I'd rather call McKinney Mister than you."[15] The next "mistake" Rodgers made was failing to explain what Lynch had told him about his adult education class before saying, "You know if I wanted to do so, I could lead a lynch mob to lynch any plantation owner in Poinsett County."[16] The crowd cheered to this statement, and Mitchell knew that Rodgers had said the wrong thing. He recalls, "I got up on the platform and explained what had happened the night before. I got a little excited too by the crowd and said, 'Ward Rodgers is staying at my house, if anybody gets his head in a pillow case and comes around my place, he's gonna get the hell shot out of him.' Of course, I didn't have a shotgun."[17] After the meeting adjourned, everybody left, but Rodgers stayed around and was arrested by Sheriff J. D. Dubard based on the information Stafford had filed, and Rodgers was put in jail.[18]

The STFU's lawyer, C. T. Carpenter of Marked Tree, was a native of Virginia and a graduate of Washington and Lee College. He was not familiar with unions but he did believe in the teachings of Thomas Jefferson. Mitchell remembers Carpenter as "a lawyer of ability and a man of great personal courage."[19] In a letter to the Socialist Party Headquarters, members of the STFU expressed their deepest confidence in Carpenter, stating, "We are perfectly satisfied with methods and tactics employed by our attorney Mr. C. T. Carpenter and feel that he is wholly competent and worthy of our whole-hearted support. We authorize Mr. Carpenter and who ever he sees fit to use—to handle all cases involving the Southern Tenant Farmers Union."[20] The STFU was of the mentality that using only local defense for fighting these cases was ideal.

After his arrest, Rodgers was unable to make bail, which had been set at $3,000, so he was placed in Jonesboro to await trial.[21] On the day of the trial, Rodgers was brought back to Marked Tree by Sheriff Dubard, and before the court proceeding, the court ordered the sheriff and his deputies to search the crowd—which was about two-thirds sharecroppers—for firearms.[22] Rodgers was charged with anarchy, blasphemy, and barratry, among other things. The prosecuting attorney charged Rodgers with being "a foreign agitator from that Yankee school, Vanderbilt University."[23] The state contended that his speech to the sharecroppers was an attempt to incite a mob.[24] The state had six witnesses, W. P Frazier, Fred Bradsnor, Andy Smith, J. E. Hudgins, J. W. Hurley, and Sherrill Reeder. Reeder was the stenographer who made the report of Rodgers's speech. Each had testified that they were present at the meeting and that they had heard Rodgers make the alleged remarks.[25] Stafford, assisted by local attorney J. O. Waskom, asked the jury for the maximum penalty for anarchy, which consisted of $1,000 fine and six months imprisonment.[26] Rodgers was convicted on the charge of anarchy—a misdemeanor—in Justice J. C. McCroy's court.[27] The jury was packed with planters—seven of whom had been plantation owners in Mississippi—who were prejudiced against Rodgers. It is likely that the jury would have convicted him regardless of what the evidence against him was.[28] The jury deliberated for less than ten minutes before returning a guilty verdict. Rodgers was fined and given a prison sentence. After sentencing, Carpenter announced to the court that the case would be appealed to the circuit court.[29]

After Rodgers's arrest, the Farmers National Committee For Action (FNCA) and the STFU began a campaign to raise money for Rodgers's defense. The FNCA was a Communist Party front group. Lem Harris, the executive secretary of the FNCA and a Communist Party member, drafted a letter to "All Farm Groups and Organizations which Believe in Building the Unity of All Farmers."[30] In the letter, Harris described the situation as a "fierce attack" on the "courageous Southern Tenant Farmers Union."[31] He explained Rodgers's arrest and sentencing and asked the readers to "go out and take a collection from your friends and sympathizers and send it to H. L. Mitchell, secretary of Southern Tenant Farmers Union. Show your solidarity with our brothers in the South."[32] Harris also asked the farmers to write to the district judge in protest and demand the release of Rodgers because "that is one thing the bosses are afraid of,—the mass-power of the farmers and workers."[33] The STFU also sent a letter to the Socialist Party Headquarters explaining the situation and asking for support.[34] The National Headquarters of the Socialist Party responded to this plea by drafting a letter to all the branches of the Socialist Party. They asked for two things to be done: first, protests from all farm organizations telling Arkansas that human rights must be guaranteed, and second, that funds should be collected for the defense.[35]

Thomas also took up the cause of helping Rodgers. He wrote a letter to the editor of the *Commercial Appeal* on February 1, 1935. He wrote the letter in response to an article that portrayed Rodgers in a less than favorable light. In regard to the article, Thomas stated, "a story which definitely tries to cloud the issue of justice to share croppers and to Ward Rodgers by raising up a Red scare and by including the ancient bogey man of racial feeling."[36] It was not just Rodgers that Thomas is defending but the STFU. In a country founded on revolution, Thomas found it shocking that this organization would be considered un-American. He stated, "I believe in the organization of tenant farmers in behalf of justice for themselves is one of the finest examples of Americanism, one of the finest proofs that the old

American spirit of liberty and justice is not dead, that I have seen."[37]
He also addressed the fact that Rodgers's papers were confiscated and
used to demonize the STFU and Rodgers. Thomas believed that what
the newspapers were attempting to do would not work. He believed
that Americans were smarter than the papers had given them credit
for. To this end, Thomas stated:

> In this article which is before me the attempt is made to take
> the word "revolution" and possibly some other statements out of
> Mr. Rodgers' correspondence and use them to scare the public. I
> do not believe that an intelligent public will be so easily scared.
> It is to the credit of young men that their hearts revolt against
> injustice.[38]

Thomas's argument falls in line with the central charge of this
research, that the establishment and all those who work for the establishment have a vested interest in demonizing socialism.

Many sympathizers answered the call of the STFU to aid in
Rodgers's defense. The Highlander Folk School in Tennessee was one
of the organizations that sent Mitchell contributions for Rodgers's
defense.[39] Also, the Holiday Association of Nebraska sent a letter to
the district judge in Tyronza, Arkansas, demanding the immediate
release of Ward Rodgers and demanding that he be given a fair trial
since the STFU is merely defending the rights of American citizens.[40]

As mentioned by Thomas, the establishment also had authorities
raid the STFU's office in Tyronza. Lucien Koch, among others from
Commonwealth, rushed to Marked Tree to help Rodgers. When they
arrived they were abducted and pistol whipped by a group.[41] When
Rodgers was finally released on bail, he and Koch were arrested in
another community and thrown into jail on another charge of barratry.[42] They were held for two nights in a "filthy" jail cell with "inadequate heat, bedding, and food."[43] However, this time the charges were
dismissed. According to an article in the *Daily Democrat* titled "Tenant
Union Men Win Two Court Fights: Rodgers and Koch Freed of
Barratry Charges at Lepanto Today," the charges against Rodgers and
Koch were dismissed on February 6, 1935.[44] According to the article,
"Rodgers was on trial before a jury, and Koch was awaiting trial when
city attorney J. S. Mosby recommended the dismissals on 'technical

grounds,' and Mayor M. P. Smith who presided entered the dismiss-als."[45] Rodgers and Koch had been taken into custody during a rally of the Southern Tenant Farmers Union and were accused of spreading "false rumors and calumnies whereby discord and disquiet may grow among neighbors."[46] The mayor charged both Rodgers and Koch $50 on the city charge of obstructing streets and alleys. After the dismissal, Koch was free to go, but Rodgers was taken back into custody on the earlier anarchy charge. Koch announced after his dismissal that the "union would continue its rallies to organize sharecroppers to help them obtain their rights from the planters under the government's reduction contracts."[47] The American Civil Liberties Union issued a press release on February 8, 1935, which addressed the attack on the STFU in Arkansas and described both Rodgers's and Koch's arrests. They offered a list of a number of organizations that were already aid-ing in the defense of Rodgers. This list includes the League of Industrial Democracy, the Fellowship of Reconciliation, the Socialist Committee for the Promotion of Labor Defense, the Provisional Committee for Non-Partisan Labor Defense, the General Defense Committee of the I.W.W., and various labor unions.[48] The newly founded newspaper the *Sharecroppers Voice* also joined the fight by calling the case against Rodgers a "fight against the STFU because of his connection with this organization."[49]

Rodgers's appeal did not make it to the circuit courts until over a year later. On March 3, 1936, the charges against Rodgers were dis-missed in a circuit court in Harrisburg, Arkansas. He had appealed the case for a few rounds in court before it was dismissed. "He wasn't guilty of anything," Mitchell recalls. "It just sounded bad."[50] The STFU described this arrest as an "attempt to crush the growing tenants' union by which other methods have failed dismally."[51]

His appeal had been pending in civil court for several months. The *Fayetteville Daily Democrat* contends, "Rodgers denied attempting to lead a mob, but he said he told the crowd it would be possible to lead a mob because of alleged abuses he said sharecroppers had suffered. Denver Dudley, prosecuting attorney, said his recommendation for the dismissal of the action was all that was necessary to remove the case from the docket."[52] The article continued on to quote Dudley as saying, "I regard Rodgers as a meddler and agitator. There is no reason to distinguish that case between any other misdemeanor cases. I do not see any reason for spending the county's money to try that sort of case."[53] In regard to the Southern Tenant Farmers Union, Dudley said, "It is impolite to kick a corpse."[54]

In 1935, Rodgers wrote a piece about his arrest for the *Crisis*. It had been all too common for the public to get only the mainstream media's version of Rodgers's arrest. This article allowed Rodgers the rare opportunity to publish his counternarrative. One of the most import-ant things about the STFU was the fact that it was integrated. Rodgers recounts that there had been "practically no friction within the Union over the race question." He even went on to praise some of the best leaders as being black, mentioning E. B. McKinney.[55] Interestingly, Rodgers was arrested in part for referring to McKinney as "Mister," and yet, in this article Rodgers again refers to him as "Mister." Rodgers is making it clear that calling McKinney "Mister" was neither an acci-dent nor a mistake. He recounts the event by saying:

> I spoke of the violence being used against the Union and told of our policy of non-violence. But stated that violence is a weapon that two can use. And that if the planters continued their violent acts, eventually sharecroppers would stop turning their cheeks and start using lynch ropes. I, as chairman, had introduced two Negro organizers as "Mr.," an unpardonable sin in my homeland in the South. I was arrested on the absurd charges of "anarchy," "inciting a riot," "using profane and abusive language," and "con-spiracy to usurp the government."[56]

Rodgers contended that because the case had been given so much publicity all the additional charges were dropped and only the anarchy charge remained.

Ideologies of the Establishment and Agitators

Understanding the ideologies of the establishment and agitators at the time allows us to put these events into a larger context. The establish-ment is whoever is in control while agitators are whoever question or threaten that control.[57] In the case of Rodgers, the authorities in Poinsett County, Arkansas, represent the establishment. At this time,

the establishment represented the interests of the white, male, plantation owners. These plantation owners viewed dissenters as dangerous
to the "American" way of life. Whether they actually believed a threat
toward capitalism existed is irrelevant; the more important issue is
that they believed a threat existed to them personally and to the status
quo they had sworn to protect. This ideology can be seen both nationally and locally. On the national level, laws and Supreme Court rulings
punished dissenters.[58] Locally, this ideology was showcased through
the vague use of criminal anarchy and barratry laws.[59]

More specifically, the combination of the depression, the first Red
Scare of the 1930s, and the civil unrest in the South created the perfect
storm for dissenters to fight back and for the establishment to justify
oppression. The national and local government sought to uphold the
very system that the agitators opposed.

Agitation or dissent occurs when people outside the establishment advocate for any degree of social change.[60] The agitators, in this
instance Rodgers and members of the STFU, believed that governmental programs such as the AAA had given plantation owners an
unfair advantage over sharecroppers. They fought to right these gross
inequalities. There were a number of strategies employed by agitators
to fight the status quo and a number of strategies used by the establishment to respond.[61] Defining the strategies employed by both sides
during the events surrounding Rodgers's arrest is important so that
we can better understand the complexities of the relationship between
dissenters and the establishment.

Confrontation as the Central Strategy of the Agitators

The STFU, and Rodgers specifically, employed all the agitation strategies earlier defined. They petitioned, meaning the STFU approached
the establishment with evidence and arguments in support of their
position by taking meetings to Washington in regard to their plight.
The next stage, promulgation, was used as they attempted to recruit
sharecroppers to become members of the union. The STFU also
used their gatherings as a way to solidify and reinforce the viewpoint
and beliefs of its members and to unite them under a common goal.
However, the central strategy—especially in regard to the Rodgers

arrest—was that of escalation or confrontation. This strategy involves escalating the tension until the establishment responds.[62] During the STFU gathering, Rodgers was upset at being threatened. Though the STFU had always taken a nonviolent stance, Rodgers decided to make the strong point that violence could indeed be fought with violence. While his statements were not threats, they were enough to garner the attention of the establishment.

Suppression as the Central Strategy of the Establishment

The major rhetorical strategy used by the establishment in the Rodgers case was that of suppression which "demands not only an understanding of the opposing ideology but a firm resolve and commitment on the part of the decision makers to stop the spread of that ideology by hindering the goals and personnel of the agitative movement."[63] In Rodgers's case, it seems fairly obvious that the establishment tried to silence or suppress the agitator's ideology. Rodgers's case showcases all the tactics of suppression that an establishment can use. One of those strategies is harassment of the leaders. By arresting Rodgers, the chairman of the meeting, the establishment was able to weaken his cause by portraying him and his movement as one of unnecessary violence. The media attention given to the case also served as an attempt to scare the public from joining the cause for fear that they might also be arrested or even killed.

Rhetorical Assessment

The aim of this thesis is to historically reconstruct criminal anarchy arrests in order to create a forgotten picture of an important artifact. This artifact serves to highlight the consequences faced by dissenters. I will discuss these consequences in more detail by using Supreme Court opinions and First Amendment theories.

At the time of his arrest, Rodgers was using his First Amendment right to speak on behalf of an organization he believed was correct. He was arrested merely for speaking words that the establishment disagreed with and this showcases the harm the *Brandenburg v. Ohio* decision addressed. While *Brandenburg* did not come until thirty years after Rodgers's arrest, it is important to call upon its opinions to support the argument that Rodgers's First Amendment right was violated. The opinion of the court, delivered per curiam, stated "the constitutional guarantees of free speech and free press do not permit a State to forbid or proscribe advocacy of the use of force or of law violation except where such advocacy is directed to inciting or producing imminent lawless action and is likely to incite or produce such action."[64] Basically, the court is arguing that speech is not protected when it crosses the line from speaking hypothetically to becoming likely to produce actual results. This decision was groundbreaking and a great victory for free speech. It seems that had this mentality existed before the Rodgers case that Rodgers might not have been charged with such a vague criminal anarchy law.

However, the question is less *would* Rodgers have been arrested had the *Brandenburg* opinion been issued and more even if Rodgers's speech had been likely to produce such "imminent lawless action," *should* he have been arrested? The First Amendment does not say, "The government shall make no law abridging the freedom of speech except in instances of violence." It seems quite clear that the First Amendment should protect any and all speech. The problem is that any type of restriction on free speech becomes an excuse to constrain all free speech. In the 1930s, the United States witnessed some of the grossest attempts to silence dissenters with excuses of "communist scares" and "threats" to the United States. In the present-day United States, the threat being used to limit free speech has moved from communists to terrorists. The point being that the United States has always and will always have a seemingly endless amount of scapegoats to use in order to justify attacks on the First Amendment. The solution then should be to stop trying to interpret the First Amendment as one that has implied exceptions, but rather to interpret it at its word. Free speech should have no restrictions. The restrictions on free speech seem superfluous considering the other laws in place. Why should speech be prosecuted for being "violent?" Do we not have laws against violence? Should we not just punish the actual acts of violence rather than the abstract speech said to have caused such violence? As the Rodgers case illustrates, dissenters will only truly be able to speak freely when we eliminate any law that limits the First Amendment.

Any type of limitation does not fully protect the dissenter, and protecting the dissenter should be of the greatest importance to all United States citizens. While limitations continue to exist the dissenter will likely always be concerned—at least to a certain extent—about whether or not his or her speech is likely to break some arbitrary exception. These exceptions play one of the most powerful roles in shaping citizens' view of the First Amendment.

The First Amendment plays an important role as a cultural symbol. Knowing the First Amendment exists creates in all of us some level of desire to protect our interests.[65] However, this desire has been and will continue to be stifled by the existing limitations. Progress can only exist if free speech is absolute. Speech and dissent are social events and progressive in nature, and free speech has always had progressive implications.[66] Thus, the Rodgers case demonstrates the ways limiting free speech in any way is not only unconstitutional but serves the more powerful role of encouraging United States citizens to become passive about the society they live in.

Arguably, the most important thing this case illustrates is the fact that limiting free speech always punishes dissenters in a number of ways. Rodgers's later release is irrelevant; because he and his organization faced economic punishments he was sufficiently deterred. These economic punishments are of some of the greatest importance when studying free speech in contemporary times. Even if dissenters are acquitted or later released, they still face time off work, lawyer fees, and a number of other financial consequences. These financial consequences send a message that is consistent with the capitalist society: the wealthy are granted the privilege of using their First Amendment right because they can afford any financial determents. However, the poor and working class are beaten into submission with their inability to afford time off work or First Amendment lawyers. These financial punishments serve to contradict what we are taught about the meaning of the First Amendment. Conceptually, we are taught to value free speech but concretely we are taught to fear dissent.[67] The financial punishment is just another way to privilege the voice of one group over that of another. The only real way to eliminate this inequality is to eliminate limitations thereby freeing all Americans to voice their opinions without fear of retribution.

A final and extremely important consequence of punishing

dissenters is the rhetorical shaping of dissenters into a negative conno-
tation. Even in 2012, the words "socialist," "communist," and "anarchist"
are often viewed as both negative descriptors and insults. The question
becomes: why is an ideology that conflicts with capitalism spoken
about as if it is a threat to democracy? This idea is especially ludicrous
in regard to socialism. Socialism is an economic system competing
only with capitalism. It is in no way, shape, or form a threat to the
current political system. It is likely that this can be traced back to the
laws we used to arrest dissenters. The law is one of the most powerful
rhetorical texts through which groups are defined. Legal scholar James
Boyd White contends that the law "is a language in which our perceptions of the natural universe are constructed and related, in which our
values and motives are defined, and in which our methods of reasoning are elaborated and enacted."[68] The law is created to maintain and
privilege the status quo. Laws should change and evolve as members
of a society change and evolve. The problem is that most people are
unaware that the law is a way to rhetorically shape groups of people.

Even in present times, the United States' laws have constructed a
narrative using an "either/or" philosophy. We all remember the infamous words of President George W. Bush when he stated, "Either
you are with us, or you are with the terrorists."[69] This logical fallacy
translates into the law and people become either law-abiding citizens,
which means they are champions of the capitalist way of life and the
American dream, or they are disobedient, un-American, and criminal.
Thus, those who voice their point of view, which may be ideologi-
cally opposed to what the law has defined, become what rhetoric has
termed the "other." The "other" has become an important concept in
critical studies and from that has emerged the idea of the "rhetorical
construction of the other."[70] Humans find their individual identities
through their interactions with people in society and the groups of
which they have membership. Being different is viewed as a negative, but we are taught to define those that are different from us. "Like
its closely related strategic 'cousins,' the enemy and the scapegoat, the
other is increasingly recognized by critical scholars as a central vehicle
in forms of constitutive rhetoric or those discourses that create individual and group identity."[71]

In the case of dissenters, the law not only defines and "others" these people, it asks citizens to do the same. An example of this in contemporary times would be the Occupy Wall Street movement. The country was quickly split into two either/or groups. You became either supportive of the movement or adamantly opposed to the movement. We watched as the law and all acting agents of the law became champions of the status quo. We watched as protestors were pepper sprayed and arrested. However, the laws support the existing situation so this reaction to the protestors was almost unsurprising. What became surprising was the countermovement that developed: a movement by people who financially would be categorized as part of the 99 percent, but who claimed that being a part of the "99 percent" was a choice. This countermovement attempted to shame the members of the movement by calling them "lazy" or "complainers." This example showcases how effectively the law can demonize one group and how quickly it can garner support from the public to champion its cause.

By using the law to define dissenters as criminals, it serves to also define them as outsiders or "others." The law serves to define and maintain the ideal citizen. In Rodgers's time and today, this ideal citizen was and continues to be someone who keeps quiet. A person who supports the system at hand is ideal. The dialogue of the dominant group creates and demonizes the "other." The dominant group or establishment provides dissenters with certain characteristics and habits, usually negative.[72] Once the stereotype of the "other" has been constructed, it remains for long periods of time as is evidenced by the way dissenters are still discussed in a negative manner by contemporary society. It is the creation of a group as the other that grants power in society.[73]

Foucault argues that the law is used as a means to achieve power. [74] In the case of Rodgers's criminal anarchy charge, this was a way to silence and punish dissenters. Thus, the concept of "illegal" serves as a way to "sum up symbolically all the others" who fall outside the conventional boundaries of the law.[75] These others are automatically defined as "criminals," which stirs the idea of a "bad citizen" in the mind of all other citizens. This is a powerful punishment for dissenters because it affects not only how they are viewed personally, but also how the rest of the society views them. This hurts their message, cause, and any attempt at revolution.

NOTES

1. National Emergency Council, *Report on the Economic Conditions of the South,* The President's Letter (1938): 1.

2. Jarold S. Auerbach, "Southern Tenant Farmers: Socialist Critics of the New Deal," *Arkansas Historical Quarterly* 27 (1968): 112–15.

3. Ibid., 115.

4. Ibid., 116.

5. Ibid.

6. H. L. Mitchell, "The Founding of the Early History of the Southern Tenant Farmers Union," *Arkansas Historical Quarterly* 32 (1973): 354.

7. Erik S. Gellman and Jarod Roll, *The Gospel of the Working Class: Labor's Southern Prophets in New Deal America* (Urbana: University of Illinois Press, 2011), 53.

8. Gellman and Roll, The Gospel of the Working Class, 55.

9. Mitchell, "The Founding of the Early History of the Southern Tenant Farmers Union," 354.

10. "FERA Worker Held After Speech Here," *Marked Tree Tribune,* January 17, 1935, 4.

11. Mitchell, "The Founding of the Early History of the Southern Tenant Farmers Union," 354.

12. Ibid., 355.

13. Ward H. Rodgers, "Sharecroppers Drop Color Line," *Crisis* 42 (1935): 168, 179.

14. Mitchell, "The Founding of the Early History of the Southern Tenant Farmers Union," 355.

15. Ibid.

16. Ibid.

17. Ibid.

18. "FERA Worker Held after Speech Here," *Marked Tree Tribune,* January 17, 1935, 4; Harold Preece, "Anarchy in Arkansas," *New Masses* (1935): 14.

19. Mitchell, "The Founding of the Early History of the Southern Tenant Farmers Union," 356.

20. Letter to Socialist Party Headquarters, Southern Tenant Farmers Union Papers, Reel January 1934–March 1936, Microfilm Collection, University of Arkansas.

21. "Rodgers Given $500 Fine, 6 MO. Jail Sentence," *Marked Tree Tribune,* January 24, 1935, 1.

22. Ibid.

23. Mitchell, "The Founding of the Early History of the Southern Tenant Farmers Union," 356.

24. "Rodgers Given $500 Fine, 6 MO. Jail Sentence," *Marked Tree Tribune,* January 24, 1935, 1.

25. Ibid.

26. Ibid.

27. Ibid.

28. J. Davis Story Publishers, *New York Post,* February 8, 1935, Southern Tenant

Farmers Union Papers, Reel January 1934–March 1936, Microfilm Collection, University of Arkansas.

29. "Rodgers Given $500 Fine, 6 MO. Jail Sentence," *Marked Tree Tribune,* January 24, 1935, 1.

30. FNCA Letter to Members, Southern Tenant Farmers Union Papers, Reel January 1934–March 1936, Microfilm Collection, University of Arkansas.

31. Ibid.

32. Ibid.

33. Ibid.

34. STFU Letter to Socialist Party Headquarters, Southern Tenant Farmers Union Papers, Reel January 1934–March 1936, Microfilm Collection, University of Arkansas.

35. Letter to *Commercial Appeal* from Norman Thomas, Southern Tenant Farmers Union Papers, Reel January 1934–March 1936, Microfilm Collection, University of Arkansas.

36. Ibid.

37. Ibid.

38. Ibid.

39. Ibid.

40. Ibid.

41. Gellman and Roll, The Gospel of the Working Class, 58.

42. M. S. Venkataramani, "Norman Thomas, Arkansas Sharecroppers, and the Roosevelt Agricultural Policies, 1933–1937," *Mississippi Valley Historical Review* 47 (1960): 225–46.

43. Southern Tenant Farmers Union Papers, Reel January 1934–March 1936, Microfilm Collection, University of Arkansas.

44. "Tenant Union Men Win Two Court Fights: Rodgers and Koch Freed of Barratry Charges at Lepanto Today," *Fayetteville (ARK) Daily Democrat,* February 6, 1935, 4.

45. Ibid.

46. Ibid.

47. Ibid.

48. Southern Tenant Farmers Union Papers, Reel January 1934–March 1936, Microfilm Collection, University of Arkansas.

49. ACLU Press Release, September 1935, *Sharecroppers Voice,* Reel 1935–1937, Microfilm Collection, University of Arkansas.

50. Mitchell, "The Founding of the Early History of the Southern Tenant Farmers Union," 356.

51. Southern Tenant Farmers Union Papers, Reel January 1934–March 1936, Microfilm Collection, University of Arkansas.

52. "State Drops Counts against Ward Rodgers," *Fayetteville Daily Democrat,* March 3, 1936, 1.

53. Ibid.

54. Ibid.

55. Rodgers, "Sharecroppers Drop Color Line," 168.

56. Ibid., 179.

57. This framework is derived from John W. Bowers, Donovan J. Ochs, and Richard J. Jensen, *The Rhetoric of Agitation and Control* (Prospect Heights, IL: Waveland Press, 1993), 4.

58. See *Schenck v. United States*, 249 U.S. 47 (1919); *Gitlow v. New York*, 268 U.S. 652 (1925); *Abrams Et al. v. United States*, 250 U.S. 1616 (1919).

59. Ark. Acts, 1919, 388–89.

60. Bowers et al., The Rhetoric of Agitation and Control.

61. Ibid., 89.

62. Ibid.

63. Ibid., 54.

64. *Brandenburg v. Ohio*, 395, U.S. 444 (1969).

65. Steven H. Shiffrin, *The First Amendment, Democracy, and Romance* (Cambridge, MA: Harvard University Press, 1990), 89.

66. Ibid.

67. Ibid., 89.

68. James Boyd White, "Law as Rhetoric, Rhetoric as Law: The Art of Cultural and Communal Life," *University of Chicago Law Review* 52 (1985): 692.

69. George W. Bush, "Address to a Joint Session of Congress and the American People," September 2001, The White House Archives, http://georgewbush-whitehouse.archives.gov/news/releases/2001/09/20010920-8.html.

70. This line of argument is supported by James Jasinski, *Sourcebook on Rhetoric: Key Concepts in Contemporary Rhetorical Studies* (London: Sage Publications, 2001), 411–12.

71. Ibid.

72. Ibid.

73. Ibid., 412.

74. Michel Foucault, *Society Must Be Defended*, ed. Mauro Bertani and Alessandro Fontana, trans. David Macey (New York: Picador, 1997).

75. Foucault, *Society Must Be Defended*, 277.

CHAPTER 9

Johnson v. State

God, Country, and Joe Johnson

REBEKAH HUSS FOX

A moth-eaten rag on a worm-eaten pole,
It does not look likely to stir a man's soul.
'Tis the deeds that were done 'neath the moth-eaten rag,
When the pole was a staff, and the rag was a flag.

—GENERAL SIR E. HAMLEY,
cited in Justice Smith's dissenting opinion in
Johnson v. State, 163 S. W. 2d 153 (1942)

It is the nature of a constitutional democracy to face the tension of balancing the majority's will and the individual's rights. Although the Constitution seems clear in its provisions for protecting the individual's innate rights, historically and contemporarily, the clash between the two has required legal intervention. Historically, especially during times of war, individual liberties have been thwarted in the name of national security. The case that is the focus of this chapter, *Johnson v. State* 163 S.W. 2d 153, took place in July 1941, just five months before the U.S. entry into World War II. The climate of the United States at this time was marked by uncertainty about involvement in the war abroad and a heightened sense of the need for national unity. This emphasis on unification led to voluntary public displays of patriotism, and occasionally pressure on individuals to participate involuntarily in these public displays.

During this time, the Jehovah's Witnesses often found themselves having to defend their religious faith against the majority's call for national unity. Because the Witnesses, of which Johnson was a member, believe that the Bible prohibits saluting the flag or any other like emblem, they often found themselves in the middle of controversy. The American Civil Liberties Union reported that between May and October of 1940, one year prior to Joe Johnson's case, "almost 1,500 Jehovah's Witnesses had been the victims of mob violence in at least 355 communities in 44 states" (Goldstein 1993, 510).

The Johnson case fell between the two notorious "flag salute cases" *Minersville School District v. Gobitis,* 310 U.S. 586, which ruled that students attending public schools could be compelled to salute the flag (regardless of religious objection), and *West Virginia State Board of Education et al. v. Barnette et al.* 319 U.S. 624, which overturned the ruling in Gobitis. Both of these cases were important in shaping our nation's history, and the rejection of *stare decisis* in the Barnette ruling reveals how citizens and the courts were wrangling with how to balance liberty and authority.

The purpose of this chapter, however, is to position the Johnson case between the two other flag salute cases, and to preserve details of the case that were obtained through personal interviews with people involved directly or indirectly with the case. The timing in the Johnson case is interesting because if the events of the case would have happened even a few months later, Johnson would have been acquitted under the Barnette ruling. The remainder of this chapter will be devoted to exploring the case narratives and arguments in each of the cases.

Minersville School District v. Gobitis, 310 U.S. 586

GOBITIS CASE NARRATIVE

On November 6, 1935, Lillian Gobitis, age twelve, and her brother William, age ten, were expelled for insubordination from the public schools of Minersville, Pennsylvania, for refusing to salute the flag as part of a daily school exercise. The ceremony consisted of placing the right hand over the heart and reciting the following pledge in unison: "I pledge allegiance to my flag, and to the Republic for which it stands; one nation indivisible, with liberty and justice for all." At this time, recitation of the pledge was accompanied by the "stiff-arm" salute, which requires individuals to extend their right hands in salute to the flag. The Gobitis children were Jehovah's Witnesses, and they and their families believed that participation in the flag-salute ceremony, or saluting any flag of any state or nation, would be a violation of God's command found in Exodus 20:2–6.[1]

Walter Gobitis, the father of the Gobitis children, was forced to move his children to private schools, which presented a financial burden to the family. The Watchtower Society of the Jehovah's Witnesses sued on behalf of the Gobitis children. The U.S. district court and the court of appeals ruled in favor of the children, but in an 8–1 decision the Supreme Court ruled in *Minersville School District v. Gobitis,* 310 U.S. 586, that the requirement of such a school exercise was not beyond the powers of the states to enforce. This ruling echoed the unanimous decisions of four previous Supreme Court cases.[2]

ARGUMENTS IN GOBITIS

Because of the popularity of the Gobitis case, the arguments are fairly well known, but it is important to revisit them here briefly to discuss the two subsequent cases.

Acknowledging the gravity of the court's decision, and pinpointing the hinge issue, Justice Felix Frankfurter opens the court's opinion with, "A grave responsibility confronts this Court whenever in course of litigation it must reconcile the conflicting claims of liberty and authority" (*Minersville School District v. Gobitis,* 1940, 591). Frankfurter cites the dilemma presented by Lincoln in his first message delivered to Congress in 1861, "Must a government of necessity be too strong for the liberties of its people, or too weak to maintain its own existence?" to show that the issue facing the court was not new, and to position the Gobitis case as representative of that dilemma.

In the court's opinion, Frankfurter supports strength in government as the victor in the "balancing test" by arguing along three intertwined lines. First, he argues that individual religious exercise should not trump such an important and effective way to engender patriotism. Second, he argues that it is inappropriate for the court to overrule the states' rights to decide educational policy. And finally, he argues that it is inappropriate for the courts to trump legislative power in general.

Frankfurter argues, "Our present task then, as so often the case with courts, is to reconcile two rights in order to prevent either from destroying the other" (594). However, the majority of the opinion argues for the subjugation of individual liberty. He writes, "The mere possession of religious convictions which contradict the relevant concerns of a political society does not relieve the citizen from the discharge of political responsibilities . . . the question remains whether school children, like the Gobitis children, must be excused from conduct required of all the other children in the promotion of national cohesion" (594–95).

Frankfurter bridges the (in)actions by the Gobitis children with a threat to national security by first arguing,

> The ultimate foundation of a free society is the binding tie of cohesive sentiment. Such a sentiment is fostered by all those agencies of the mind and spirit which may serve to gather up the traditions of a people, transmit them from generation to generation and thereby create that continuity of a treasured common life which constitutes a civilization. "We live by symbols." The flag is the symbol of our national unity, transcending all internal differences, however large, within the framework of the Constitution. (596)

To further support the importance and legitimacy of the flag-salute ceremony, he answered criticism that had been leveled against the "commonly accepted" flag-salute procedure (the stiff-arm salute) for appearing as if it were drawn from the symbolic repertoire of fascists and might accomplish the same ends by writing, "It mocks reason and denies our whole history to find in the allowance of a requirement to salute our flag on fitting occasions the seeds of sanction for obeisance to a leader" (598). He then offers a now infamous line revealing the connection between the flag-salute case, unity, and national security, "National unity is the basis of national security" (595).

Second, he blends the arguments that the states have the right to determine their own educational standards with the idea that national unity can be secured through public declarations and ceremonies when he wrote about the Pennsylvania Legislature,

> They indicated a belief in the desirable ends to be secured by having its public school children share a common experience at those periods of development when their minds are supposedly receptive to its assimilation, by an exercise appropriate in time and place and setting, and one designed to evoke in them appreciation of the nation's hopes and dreams, its sufferings and sacrifices . . . The precise issue, then, for us to decide is whether the legislatures of the various states and the authorities in a thousand countries and school districts of this country are barred from determining the appropriateness of various means to evoke that unifying sentiment without which there can be no liberties, civil or religious. (597)

Finally, he argues that the court of public opinion, made manifest through the legislative process is the proper venue for shaping, changing, or overturning law, not the court system. He writes, "education in the abandonment of foolish legislation is itself a training in liberty. To fight out the wise use of legislative authority in the forum of public opinion and before legislative assemblies rather than to transfer such a contest to the judicial arena, serves to vindicate the self-confidence of a free people" (600).

At once, in his closing statements, Frankfurter appears to briefly consider the usefulness of entertaining "the most crochety beliefs" only to dismiss that notion on grounds of jurisdiction:

> For ourselves, we might be tempted to say that the deepest patriotism is best engendered by giving unfettered scope to the most crochety beliefs. Perhaps it is best, even from the standpoint of those interests which ordinances like the one under review seek to promote, to give the least popular sect leave from conformities like those here in issue. But the court-room is not the arena for debating issues of educational policy. . . . So to hold would in effect make us the school board for the country. That authority has not been given to this Court, nor should we assume it. (598)

The dissenting opinion in the Gobitis case was written by Justice Harlan Fiske Stone. His dissenting arguments answer issues brought

up in the Frankfurter opinion. He first argues that compelling participation in the flag-salute ceremony represents a violation of both the
First and Fourteenth Amendments. Second, he argues that the Gobitis
case is qualitatively different from other cases that rendered a verdict
supporting the authority of government to compel speech because
the Gobitis case did not meet the "clear and present danger" standard.
Third, he argues national unity can be achieved in ways other than
compelling belief. And finally, he argues that the court's duty to protect
constitutional freedoms trumps state power if it runs counter.

First, Justice Stone argues:

> The law which is thus sustained is unique in the history of
> Anglo-American legislation. It does more than suppress freedom
> of speech and more than prohibit the free exercise of religion,
> which concededly are forbidden by the First Amendment and
> are violations of the liberty guaranteed by the Fourteenth. For
> by this law the state seeks to coerce these children to express a
> sentiment which, as they interpret it, they do not entertain, and
> which violates their deepest religious convictions. (601)

Related to the first argument, Stone also argues that each previous time the court had voted to limit expression it had been for
public safety, health reasons, or good order, but that this danger was
not present in the Gobitis case, "But it is a long step, and one which I
am unable to take, to the position that government may, as a supposed
educational measure and as a means of disciplining the young, compel
public affirmations which violate their religious conscience" (602).

Criticizing the idea that national unity leads to national security,
Stone argues that we can achieve national unity in other ways and that
compulsory professions may work against the notion of patriotism.
He writes:

> So here, even if we believe that such compulsions will contrib-
> ute to national unity there are other ways to teach loyalty and
> patriotism which are the sources of national unity, than by com-
> pelling the pupil to affirm that which he does not believe and by
> commanding a form of affirmance which violates his religious
> convictions. (603–4)

Answering the issue of judicial authority, Stone insists upon the

importance of freedom of expression above the interests of conformity, when he wrote,

> I cannot conceive that in prescribing, as limitations upon the
> powers of government, the freedom of the mind and spirit
> secured by the explicit guaranties of freedom of speech and
> religion, they intended or rightly could have left any latitude or
> a legislative judgment that the compulsory expression of belief
> which violates religious convictions would better serve the pub-
> lic interest than their protection. (605)

Finally, he specifically critiques the means-ends trade-off of limiting expression in public schools in order to maintain discipline when
he wrote:

> I am not prepared to say that the right of this small and helpless
> minority, including children having a strong religious convic-
> tion, whether they understand its nature or not, to refrain from
> an expression obnoxious to their religion, is to be overborne by
> the interest of the state in maintaining discipline in the schools.
> (606)

Johnson v. State 163 S.W. 2d 153

On July 1, 1941, Joe Johnson walked into the welfare commissary
in Marshall, Arkansas, to obtain commodities for his family. He
approached Mrs. Nell Cooper, a clerk at the dispensing office, and
asked her if his commodity slip had run out. Mrs. Cooper, whose complaint filed on July 3 led to Johnson's conviction, later testified that she
had heard rumors that he was drawing commodities for more people
than were actually in his family, and asked Johnson if the rumor was
true. Johnson replied he was only drawing for the members of his
family. Mrs. Cooper testified that she had found it difficult to believe
that particular rumor but turned her attention to a rumor she apparently did. She testified that she then said, "It is also rumored that you
don't believe in saluting the flag. Is there anything in that?" (*Johnson
v. State* 163 S.W. 2d 153, 3). During the testimony she clarified that she
"didn't demand" but "merely requested" of Johnson "just to quiet the
rumor" by saluting the flag (4).

Both Cooper and Johnson testified that he then walked toward a United States flag that was hanging over the steps of the commissary, pointed to it, and delivered a short oration concerning his beliefs. However, their testimonies differ as to what Johnson said and did at that time. Cooper claimed that Johnson said, "He would die before he would [salute the flag]" and turned to the others in the commissary and said, "You can't get anything here unless you salute the flag. It don't have eyes and can't see, and has no ears and can't hear, and no mouth and can't talk, it doesn't mean anything to me. It is only a rag" (4). To this, Cooper replied, "You can't talk that way here" (4). When questioned about whether or not Johnson touched the flag, Cooper's testimony went from confident to less so. She said, "He did. I don't know whether he touched it or not, but his hand was in touching distance of the flag, and he reached toward the flag" (5). Cooper also testified that the entire event, when Johnson entered the commissary to the time he left, took perhaps five minutes.

Because of the events at the commissary, Mrs. Cooper filed an affidavit in the justice of peace court of W. M. Heard. Lawrence E. Exum, commander of Treadwell-Allen American Legion Post 117, signed the prosecution bond and an arrest warrant was issued for Johnson. Johnson was charged with unlawfully, willfully, and publicly exhibiting contempt for the flag of the United States based on a 1919 Arkansas Flag Statute.[3] Johnson understood how he was viewed in his township and asked for a change of venue for his circuit court hearing. His attorneys argued that "the inhabitants of Bear Creek Township are so prejudiced against him that he could not obtain a fair and impartial [trial] in said township, not in Wileys cove Township, and he asks the court for an order removing this cause to some other township in said county" (43). After a change of venue, the case came to trial in the justice of the peace court. Howard Hensley, who was a deputy sheriff during the time of Johnson's arrest, reported details of the JP trial in a personal interview in August 2000. He said that the JP trial was held in Eli Jordan's living room in Tomahawk Township. He also noted that although there was no "ruckus" twenty-five people stood outside, including "bull-headed people" and a few "hot-headed people from the Legion." He mentioned that Jordan only allowed other Witnesses to enter the house/court to keep Johnson from "getting hurt" but that Johnson did not seem scared. He said Johnson did not testify, but stood in the doorway the entire time. The "court" found Johnson guilty and ordered him to pay a fine of $60 and spend thirty days in jail.

The case was appealed and came for hearing to the Searcy County Circuit Court on August 25, 1941, and was abandoned because of insufficient bond costs. The same day, the prosecuting attorney, Len Jones, filed the necessary information to continue with the trial, which ended in a hung jury. On February 9, 1942, the prosecution refiled the charge, and a second trial began in Searcy County Circuit Court. Nell Cooper and Ogle Horton testified for the state, and Johnson and W. E. Tharp testified for the defendant. This time Johnson was found guilty, ordered to pay a fine of $50, and imprisoned in the county jail for a twenty-four-hour period.

Meanwhile, the local newspapers began to cover the Johnson case, and included opinion pieces from local residents that directly or indirectly addressed the issue. On January 30, 1942, the *Marshall Mountain Wave* included an article by the Christian Church pastor, the Reverend Joe A. Detherage, titled "What the Churches Can Do for the Defense" in which he argues that the United States is in war "to defend the right: (1) To worship God in our own way and as our reason and conscience dictate, being responsible to God alone in this matter; (2) To write or speak our opinions without fear of arrest" (1). On February 20 the same newspaper reported, "Jehovah Witness Fined $50" and that "Johnson was arrested at the instigation of the American Legion Post" (2). The adjacent article's headline read "605 Men Register in Searcy County Selective Service." The same day, the *Marshall Republican* reported "Minute Men to Organize" and provided details for an upcoming meeting to be held at the school gym (1).

During cross-examination in the trial, Nell Cooper was asked if she had received "any instructions from any superior officer not to let Jehovah Witnesses have any commodities unless they would salute the flag?" to which she replied, "No cult was named. They were sworn by affidavits that you wouldn't receive any unless they were a loyal American citizen" (*State of Arkansas v. Johnson* 163 S.W. 2d 153, p. 7). Mrs. Cooper then revealed that Johnson's actions angered her and that "It might be that I over stepped in asking him to salute. We were sworn not to give to anyone who wasn't a loyal American citizen. I think saluting the flag comes under being a loyal American citizen" (7).

However, Johnson's testimony about what occurred that July

morning differs in considerable ways. Johnson testified that Mrs. Cooper asked if he was taking groceries to other Jehovah's Witnesses and he said he was not, but only "drawing for the actual members of my family" (483). He went on to say,

> Before I had time to finish she said "Prove yourself and salute the flag." It stunned me so that I just stood there . . . I told her I wouldn't salute the flag. I walked to the door and pulled off my hat and made a little speech. I didn't want to talk to the lady; some of them make things bigger than they are. I said, "This flag means as much to me as to you. My forefathers died for it the same as yours" . . . I do not recall saying that the flag didn't mean anything to me, because it does. It means all to me, [but] it hasn't any life or being, [such] as a God. . . . I was not angry at Mrs. Cooper. Her statement surprised me and shocked me—like going out a door and having somebody throw a bucket of water on you. (26)

Johnson denied saying most of what Mrs. Cooper said, but when directly asked if he called the flag a rag, or a piece of cloth, he said, "I said it, but I meant to finish the statement. I meant that it wasn't a God. That is what I meant" (27).

Two other witnesses were called in the case, Ogle Horton, who was also a WPA commissary clerk at the time of the events, and W. E. Tharp, a citizen who was at the commissary to obtain goods. Mr. Horton's testimony was similar to Mrs. Cooper's but differed in a few important ways. Mr. Horton testified that Johnson "had hold" of the flag and said "in very harsh words," "Gentlemen, you can't get your commodities unless you salute this flag. It is nothing but a piece of rag. I don't believe in anything. I don't believe in no kind of church" (11). Although his unguided testimony did not include biblical references, the state's attorney, Mr. Henley, asked, "Did he make another statement about the flag? I will ask if he said anything about it having eyes or ears?" To which Mr. Horton replied, "He said it had no eyes, ears, or nose, and couldn't see, hear or smell, and don't have no sign of life about it" (11). However, the information that came out during cross-examination by Johnson's lawyer, Mr. Shouse, reveals that there was much more going on behind the scenes in Marshall concerning Johnson's case. During questioning, Mr. Shouse asked Mr. Horton, "Have you taken a right smart interest in the case?" To which Mr.

Horton replied, "No, sir, just a witness is all." Mr. Shouse then asked, "Didn't you go—you with some others—go to a lawyer's place here in Marshall and tell him that you wanted to go take this boy out by force and take him to Little Rock and Court Martial him?" Objections were raised and overruled. Mr. Horton replied, "No, sir, I didn't. It was my brother. He came to me and asked if I would. My brother was in the United States Army, and he was pretty hot about it" (12). During the course of his testimony, Mr. Horton explained that he did go with his brother and one other person to Frank Reeves's place, but that Mr. Reeves advised them that they would be guilty of kidnapping if they took Johnson to Little Rock by force. Then Mr. Shouse asked Mr. Horton, "Were you aiming to go with them if Mr. Reeves endorsed it and take him out by force and take him to Little Rock?" To which Mr. Horton replied, "If there was a law to that effect, Yes, I might have been American enough to do it" (13).

The other witness who testified, W. E. Tharp, said that he did not hear the exchange between Mrs. Cooper and Johnson, but explained that when Johnson stepped outside he pointed to the flag and said, "That flag means as much to me as anybody else. My forefathers fought for the flag . . . It doesn't see, smell, taste, talk, nor walk" (30). During cross-examination, Mr. Henley asked Mr. Tharp specifically if he heard Johnson call the flag a rag. Mr. Tharp said he was outside and did not hear that, to which Mr. Henley asked, "You wouldn't deny that he said it?" Mr. Tharp replied, "I wouldn't say he did, or didn't, because I didn't hear that part of it" (31).

Climate in Marshall

When Joe Johnson's case was reported in the *Marshall Mountain Wave* in late July, the headlines didn't feature the Johnson story, but instead said, "For defense, buy United States savings bonds and stamps—America on Guard," and "10 more men from Searcy county to be inducted into Army" (July 25, 1941). The June 9, 1942, copy of the *Arkansas Democrat Gazette* also reported on the case. The article was placed directly beside a map of the Japanese attack on Midway and began with an ode to Francis Scott Key and included all of the words to the national anthem.

Wartime propaganda was everywhere, and American citizens

were being urged to help out the war effort in any way possible. During these times, people were scared, skeptical, and worried about national security. This public sentiment was made apparent by the trial proceedings themselves and other political influences including the fact that the circuit court elections were to be held in February, a timely six months after the trial. The events in Marshall and the subsequent trials regarding Johnson's case reveal an undercurrent of religious intolerance and the relationship between local religious preference and local legal proceedings. Writing about this type of issue just five years later, professor and theologian Willard L. Sperry said, "the religious affiliation of the majority of the voters in any given state does much to influence legislation and the administration of the law" (1946, p. 63).

ARGUMENTS IN THE JOHNSON CASE

The court opinion was delivered by Jack Holt on June 8, 1942. He argued that the trial court "very clearly and properly" instructed the jury that the appellant could not be convicted for refusing to salute the flag of the United States; that he was within his constitutional rights if he did not desire to do so" and that "To constitute the crime with which he is charged required some voluntary action or statement on his part in contempt of the flag" (*Johnson v. State* 163 S. W. 2d 153, Court Opinion, p. 479).

Holt explained that Johnson's behavior clearly exhibited such contempt. He wrote, "The strange and unnatural conduct of this man at the very time he was receiving, from the hands of a most generous government, supplies to aid him in sustaining a large family, may not be explained away on the grounds of ignorance or religious beliefs" (479). Holt leaned on the decision from the *Minersville v. Gobitis* case to argue that the flag was a symbol of our national unity, and that any assertion of religious liberty would not provide an exemption from the law.

The dissenting opinion was delivered by Griffin Smith, in which he began by reminding the court that the events of Johnson's case occurred six months before the attack on Pearl Harbor, and the Flag Statute under which Joe was convicted was approved February 10, 1919, right after World War I was concluded. He argued: "It was natural that realism of war would amalgamate with the fervor of peace when members of the Forty-second general assembly convened in Little Rock to plan the economy of a world they thought had been made safe for democracy" (481).

After setting this tone, Smith addressed the specific events of the case. He said,

> It is clear that the controversy into which the appellant was drawn had its inception in Mrs. Cooper's assumption that she had a right to require those whom she conceived to be on the shady side of patriotism to make proffer of some loyal act, the nature of which should satisfy the tension of her emotion ... She must have thought that somewhere in the Decalogue of things prohibited and things commanded it was requisite that those receiving bread in consequence of government bounty should stand at attention when so directed. (484)

Although Smith went on to argue for Johnson's innocence under the 1919 Flag Statute, he not only distanced himself from Johnson's actions throughout the proceedings, but also did not attempt to argue against the constitutionality of the statute.

Smith presented arguments along three lines. First, he argued that the court misjudged Johnson's motive. Second, he argued that during times of war, we are more likely to commit these types of errors. And third, that the rights of the individual, especially that of expression, must be guarded at all costs.

To support his first argument, that the court did not properly ascertain Johnson's purpose, he argued, "I do not agree with appellant's point of view. To me it is mawkish ... *The statute is intended to prevent a person, by word, or act, from publicly exhibiting contempt for the flag.* [italics original] Johnson's aversion was not to the flag. His conduct was based upon his religious belief; and while to me it appears vapid, to him it was real" (484). Smith then attempts to tap into notions of patriotism by citing Sergeant York as an example of another conscientious objector who in 1918 "held doggedly to the conception that the Bible banned war; yet when he became convinced that national safety was threatened he used rifle and pistol with deadly effect" (485).

Smith worked to create more distance from Johnson as a person, while arguing that his actions still did not violate the 1919 Flag Statute.

He said, "It is a strange philosophy—if appellant's belief may be digni-
fied by that term—which blunts a citizen's patriotic sensitivities when
in the presence of his country's emblem, or dulls his comprehension
of its status" (485). He concludes his point about the court misjudging
Johnson's motive by saying,

> In spite of my own lack of sympathy with appellant's attitude,
> irrespective of an entrenched belief that a country would not
> endure if peopled by men entertaining the ideas appellant
> expounded as interpreted by the state, the fact remains that we
> are engaged not only in a war of men, machines, and materials,
> but in a contest wherein liberty may be lost if we succumb to the
> ideologies of those who enforce obedience through fear, and who
> would write loyalty with a bayonet. (486)

To support his second line of reasoning, that during times of war,
we often loose cite of individual liberties that need protecting, he cites
Attorney General Francis Biddle, who on December 10, 1941, said,
"The United States is at war. Every American will share in the task of
defending our country. It is essential at such a time that we keep our
heads, keep our tempers—above all, that we keep clearly in mind what
we are defending . . . It therefore behooves us to guard most zealously
these principles at home" (486).

Smith also cites President Roosevelt's December 15, 1941, address,
"We will not under any threat or in the face of danger surrender the
guarantees of liberty our forefathers framed for us in the Bill of Rights.
We hold with all the passion of our hearts and minds to those com-
mitments of the human spirit" (487).

To support his third argument, that no rights of the individual are
more important than those relating to free expression, he connects
free expression with the pursuit of happiness, positions it as necessary
for the dissemination of intelligence, and argues that it is essential if
we are to correct errors. He cites an excerpt from senior United States
circuit judge John Parker's *Democracy in Government,*

> While all of these rights are of the first order of importance,
> I would speak particularly of freedom of speech, because it
> is always in danger . . . The history of human thought is one
> continuous process of the triumph of ideas which upon their
> first expression were condemned as error by the learned and

the powerful. Progress is dependent upon the advance of truth; and this in turn is dependent upon the right of men to give free expression to any view they may entertain. (488)

In his concluding remarks, Smith again distanced himself from Johnson's actions, but argued, "If ignorance were a legal crime the judgment would be just. But witch-hunting is no longer sanctioned. The suspicions and hatreds of Salem have ceased. Neighbor no longer inveighs against neighbor through fear of the evil eye" (489).

West Virginia State Board of Education v. Barnette, 319 U.S. 624

BARNETTE CASE NARRATIVE

One year after the Japanese attack on Pearl Harbor, and two years after the Gobitis decision, the West Virginia legislature responded to the renewed wave of public displays of patriotism by amending its statutes on January 8, 1942, to require the State School Board of Education to select and prescribe curriculum for all public schools in the state in history, civics, the Constitution "for the purpose of teaching, fostering and perpetuating the ideals, principles and spirit of Americanism, and increasing the knowledge of the organization and machinery of the government" (*West Virginia State Board of Education v. Barnette*, 319 U.S. 624, p. 626).[4]

The statute required all children, from kindergarten through twelfth grade, to salute the flag and recite the Pledge of Allegiance daily. Students who refused to salute the flag or to recite the Pledge of Allegiance were considered "insubordinate" and subject to expulsion from school. The children would then be considered "delinquent," which meant that their parents were also subject to prosecution.[5]

The resolution originally required the "commonly accepted salute to the Flag," which at that time was criticized for "being too much like Hitler's" by the PTA, Boy and Girl Scouts, the Red Cross, and the Federation of Women's Clubs. These groups complained about the form of the salute, but not over the inclusion of the ceremony in general. At the time of the Barnette case the commonly accepted salute was the "stiff-arm salute" (the saluter to keep the right hand raised with palm turned up while the following is repeated "I pledge alle-giance to the Flag of the United States of America and to the Republic for which it stands; one Nation, indivisible, with liberty and justice for all" (628–29).[6]

The Jehovah's Witnesses offered the following alternate pledge that they agreed to "periodically and publicly" deliver; however, no accommodations were made for them.

> I have pledged by unqualified allegiance and devotion to Jehovah, the Almighty God, and to his Kingdom, for which Jesus commands all Christians to pray. I respect the flag of the United States and acknowledge it as a symbol of freedom and justice to all. I pledge allegiance and obedience to all the laws of the United States that are consistent with God's law, as set forth in the Bible. (628)

In addition to a number of parents who had been prosecuted for their children's (in)action, Walter Barnette, Lucy McClure, and Paul Stull sued in U.S. district court and won an injunction against the state when their children were expelled from the Kanawha County schools for their refusal to salute the flag. The West Virginia State School Board appealed to the U.S. Supreme Court, who heard the case on March 11, 1943.

ARGUMENTS IN THE CASE

Three of the Supreme Court justices who had ruled in the Gobitis case had been replaced, changing the make-up of the bench, and in a 6–3 decision, the court struck down the West Virginia statute because "while it is the Fourteenth Amendment which bears directly upon the State it is the more specific limiting principles of the First Amendment that finally govern this case" (639). The decision represented a major shift in the court's trajectory and subsequently, our nation's trajectory.

Justice Robert Jackson delivered the opinion of the court. He opened by arguing that the Barnette case was similar to the Gobitis case and other flag-salute cases, but that it differed in five major ways. First, the refusal of the Barnette children to salute did not interfere with the rights of others. He argues,

The freedom asserted by these appellees does not bring them into collision with rights asserted by any other individual. It is such conflicts which most frequently require intervention of the State to determine where the rights of one end and those of another begin. But the refusal of these persons to participate in the ceremony does not interfere with or deny rights of others to do so. Nor is there any question in this case that their behavior is peaceable and orderly. The sole conflict is between authority and rights of the individual. The State asserts power to condition access to public education on making a prescribed sign and profession and at that same time to coerce attendance by punishing both parent and child. The latter stand on a right of self-determination in matters that touch individual opinion and personal attitude. (630–31)

Second, the Gobitis case ruled that the state may require teaching by instruction, but the Barnette case dealt with a compulsion of students to declare a belief. He also wove in criticism about the educational value of the salute when he argued, "Here, however, we are dealing with a compulsion of students to declare a belief . . . The issue here is whether this slow and easily neglected route to aroused loyalties constitutionally may be short-cut by substituting a compulsory salute and slogan" (631).

Third, he argued that the flag salute, a form of "primitive but effective" symbolic communication, still counts as utterance and should not be coerced. He wrote,

Symbolism is a primitive but effective way of communicating ideas. The use of an emblem or flag to symbolize some system, idea, institution, or personality, is a short cut from mind to mind. Causes and nations, political parties, lodges, and ecclesiastical groups seek to knit the loyalty of their followings to a flag or banner, a color or design . . . Associated with many of these symbols are appropriate gestures of acceptance or respect: a salute, a bowed or bared head, a bended knee. A person gets from a symbol the meaning he puts into it, and what is one man's comfort and inspiration is another's jest and scorn. Objection to this form of communication when coerced is an old one, well known to the framers of the Bill of Rights. (632–33)

Fourth, refusing to salute the flag does not represent a clear and present danger. He wrote,

> It is now a commonplace that censorship or suppression of expression of opinion is tolerated by our Constitution only when the expression presents a clear and present danger of action of a kind the State is empowered to prevent and punish. It would seem that involuntary affirmation could be commanded only on even more immediate and urgent grounds than silence. But here the power of compulsion is invoked without any allegation that remaining passive during a flag salute ritual creates a clear and present danger that would justify an effort even to muffle expression. To sustain the compulsory flag salute we are required to say that a Bill of Rights which guards the individual's right to speak his own mind, left it open to public authorities to compel him to utter what is not in his mind. (633–34)

And finally, it was assumed in Gobitis that the state held the power to impose the flag salute but assumption needs to be questioned. He argued,

> The question which underlies the flag salute controversy is whether such a ceremony so touching matters of opinion and political attitude may be imposed upon the individual by official authority under powers committed to any political organization under our Constitution. We examine rather than assume existence of this power and, against this broader definition of issues in this case, re-examine specific grounds assigned for the Gobitis decision. (635–36)

After addressing what he considered to be substantive differences between the Gobitis case and the Barnette case, Justice Jackson reviewed the grounds for the Gobitis decision. He argued that Lincoln's dilemma, "Must a government of necessity be too strong for the liberties of its people or too weak to maintain its own existence," the answer to which was "strength," was inappropriately applied to the flag-salute cases. He argued that it was an oversimplification of what Lincoln was discussing. He wrote,

> It may be doubted whether Mr. Lincoln would have thought that the strength of government to maintain itself would be impres-

sively vindicated by our confirming power of the state to expel a handful of children from school. Such oversimplification, so handy in political debate, often lacks the precision necessary to postulates of judicial reasoning. If validly applied to this problem, the utterance cited would resolve every issue of power in favor of those in authority and would require us to override every liberty thought to weaken or delay execution of their policies. (636)

In addition to arguing that Lincoln's dilemma was inappropriately applied, he also argued that a limited government need not be weak. He argued,

Assurance that rights are secure tends to diminish fear and jealousy of strong government, and by making us feel safe to live under it makes of its better support. Without promise of a limiting Bill of Rights it is doubtful if our Constitution could have mustered enough strength to enable its ratification. To enforce those rights today is not to choose weak government over strong government. It is only to adhere as a means of strength to individual freedom of mind in preference to officially disciplined uniformity for which history indicates a disappointing and disastrous end. (636–47)

Justice Jackson also responds to the charge that to interfere with the school board's decision would make the court the "school board of the country." He argues,

The Fourteenth Amendment, as now applied to the States, protects the citizen against the State itself and all of its creatures— Boards of Education not excepted . . . That they are educating the young for citizenship is reason for scrupulous protection of Constitutional freedoms of the individual, if we are not to strangle the free mind at its source and teach youth to discount important principles of our government as mere platitudes. (637)

In the Gobitis case, the justices reasoned that the courts were the wrong place for a debate over the constitutionally of a law and that the appropriate place to discuss legislative authority is "in the forum of public opinion and before legislative assemblies rather than to transfer such a contest to the judicial arena" (638). However, Justice Jackson argued that

The very purpose of a Bill of Rights was to withdraw certain subjects from the vicissitudes of political controversy, to place them beyond the reach of majorities and officials and to establish them as legal principles to be applied by the courts. One's right to life, liberty, and property, to free speech, a free press, freedom of worship and assembly, and other fundamental rights may not be submitted to vote; they depend on the outcome of no elections. (638)

Justice Jackson directly addressed the argument that was the hinge of the Gobitis opinion—that national unity is the basis of national security and that the authorities have the right to select appropriate means for its attainment—by arguing that "Authority here is to be controlled by public opinion, not public opinion by authority" and that these types of efforts to secure nationalism are dangerous. He argued,

As first and moderate methods to attain unity have failed, those bent on its accomplishment must resort to an ever-increasing severity. As governmental pressure toward unity becomes greater, so strife becomes more bitter as to whose unity it shall be. Probably no deeper division of our people could proceed from any provocation than from finding it necessary to choose what doctrine and whose program public educational officials shall compel youth to unite in embracing. . . . Those who begin coercive elimination of dissent soon find themselves exterminating dissenters. Compulsory unification of opinion achieves only the unanimity of the graveyard. (640)

He concludes by arguing that "The case is made difficult not because the principles of its decision are obscure but because the flag involved is our own" (641) and "If there is any fixed star in our constitutional constellation, it is that no official, high or petty, can prescribe what shall be orthodox in politics, nationalism, religion, or other matters of opinion or force citizens to confess by word or act their faith therein" (642).

CONCURRING OPINIONS

The concurring opinions in this case are especially interesting because two of the justices, Black and Douglas, originally sided with the Minersville school district in the Gobitis case, but supported the Barnette children in the West Virginia case based on the First and Fourteenth Amendments, a lack of a clear and present danger, and because a compulsory flag salute is equal to a test oath. They wrote,

> Long reflection convinced us that although the principle is sound, its application in the particular case was wrong. . . . We believe that the statute before us fails to accord full scope to the freedom of religion secured to the appellees by the First and Fourteenth Amendments . . . The duty is a solemn one, and in meeting it we cannot say that a failure, because of religious scruples, to assume a particular physical position and to repeat the words of a patriotic formula creates a grave danger to the nation. Such a statutory exaction is a form of test oath, and the test oath has always been abhorrent in the United States. (643–44)

Also concurring, Justice Frank Murphy expanded the arguments of the aforementioned justices by explaining that the First Amendment does not only protect the expression of an individual but also the right to refrain from expressing and that compulsory expression may have the opposite effect. He argued that freedom of thought and of religion

> includes both the right to speak freely and the right to refrain from speaking at all . . . Any spark of love for country which may be generated in a child or his associates by forcing him to make what is to him an empty gesture and recite words wrung from him contrary to his religious beliefs is overshadowed by the desirability of preserving freedom of conscience to the full. It is in that freedom and the example of persuasion, not in force and compulsion, that the real unity of American lies. (645–46)

DISSENTING OPINION

The dissenting opinion, offered by Justice Frankfurter, was built on the arguments that the actions of the State of West Virginia were proper ones used to promote good citizenship. He also argued that the framers of the Constitution did not "grant to this Court supervision over legislation" (650) and that the United States has compelled obedience to general laws that have created religious scruples in other instances (citing compulsory vaccination, food inspection regulations,

obligation to bear arms, testimonial duties, compulsory medical treatment). He goes further to say that compulsion is the nature of laws—
"Law is concerned with external behavior and not with the inner life
of man. It rests in large measure upon compulsion" (655).

Although it seems to be built on slippery slope fallacy, he also
argued that the government would be forced to provide alternative
arrangements and accommodations for anyone who disagreed with
the teachings of the public schools. He wrote, "All citizens are taxed
for the support of public schools although this Court has denied the
right of a state to compel all children to go to such schools and has
recognized the right of parents to send children to privately maintained schools . . . What of the claims for equity of treatment of those
parents who, because of religious scruples, cannot send their children
to public schools?" (660).

Justice Frankfurter also attempted to silence the criticism that
the flag salute seemed fascist or equal to oath tests when he argued,
"And surely only flippancy could be responsible for the suggestion
that constitutional validity of a requirement to salute our flag implies
equal validity of a requirement to salute a dictator" (662). And, "The
flag salute exercise has no kinship whatever to the oath tests so odious
in history" (664).

In what seemed to be the most controversial part of his dissent, he
argued that the court had previously been in agreement but that the
new configuration of the bench led to this decision. He argued that
the court had already heard three similar cases and ruled that they had
no "federal question" and ruled on a fourth based on the decisions in
the other three. "Only the two Justices sitting for the first time on this
matter have not heretofore found this legislation inoffensive to the
'liberty' guaranteed by the Constitution" (665).

Finally, he closes by arguing that the court is overstepping its jurisdiction and being disrespectful to the legislature and to the citizens by
overruling this statute. He cites James Bradley Thayer, "A just respect
for the legislature requires that the obligation of its laws should not
be unnecessarily and wantonly assailed" (666). He explained that the
people also lose out because they do not get to participate in the creation of laws that govern them and must learn to correct their errors
though the established methods. He concludes by saying, "Of course

patriotism cannot be enforced by the flag salute. But neither can the liberal spirit be enforced by judicial invalidation of illiberal legislation" (670).

Conclusion

A little over one year prior to the Johnson case the Supreme Court of the United States had found other Jehovah's Witnesses guilty of similar offenses. In the case of *Minersville School District v. Gobitis*, 310 U.S. 586, two children were expelled from school because they would not participate in a mandatory flag-saluting exercise. The court reasoned that because the children were in a formative time of their lives they needed to be taught about patriotism and loyalty. Just as in the *Johnson* case, these children were trying to obtain a government-supported, state-ran service. The fact that these individuals were of the Jehovah's Witnesses group forced them into a bind by making them either dismiss their own religious conviction or not get the service they needed. One step further, the children in the *Gobitis* case were lawfully required to attend school or obtain an equivalent education elsewhere, therefore they were expelled into an unlawful position. The prosecution in the Johnson case used the *Gobitis* case as a precedent to convict Johnson, mentioning that "the flag is the symbol of the nation's power . . . it signifies a government resting on the consent of the governed; Liberty regulated by law; the protection of the weak against the strong" (154). The *Gobitis* case, although it is not identical to the *Johnson* case was used to convict Johnson. Less than one year after Johnson's conviction, and only three years after the *Gobitis* decision, the U.S. Supreme Court ruled in favor of the Jehovah's Witnesses (*West Virginia State Board of Education et al. v. Barnette et al.* 319 U.S. 624) and recognized that saluting the flag does entail a religious belief and that by making it mandatory in order to get a public service it is in conflict with the very freedom the flag stands for.

Because they happened so close chronologically, it is hard to determine why the court reversed its decision between *Gobitis* and *Barnette*, but at least three factors may have contributed. First, the reconfiguration of the bench after the *Gobitis* trial opened the door for new arguments to emerge. Second, after the *Gobitis* decision, there was quite a bit of negative public opinion in response. According to K. L. Hall and J. J. Patrick, authors of *The Pursuit of Justice: Supreme Court Decisions that Shaped America*, "More than 170 newspapers throughout the country opposed the Court's decision" (2006, 98). Finally, the *Gobitis* decision seemed to have given misguided patriots a license to ill. The newspapers and the courts were busy with a flood of cases involving the persecution of Jehovah's Witnesses, which no doubt caught the attention of the justices.

As for Johnson, it seems that since *Barnette* was decided less than one year after *Johnson*, it is hard to imagine why he was convicted other than the fact that the court simply did not exercise any legal imagination and were acting upon pressures and prejudices of the time.

BIBLIOGRAPHY

Arkansas Gazette. 1942. "Johnson Case." June 9, p. 4.

Goldstein, R. J. 1993. "The Great 1989–1990 Flag Flap: An Historical, Political, and Legal Analysis." In *The Constitution and the Flag: The Flag Salute Cases,* ed. Michael Kent Curtis, 483–571. New York: Taylor & Francis.

Hall, K. L., and J. J. Patrick. 2006. *The Pursuit of Justice: Supreme Court Decisions That Shaped America.* New York: Oxford University Press.

Johnson v. State 163 S.W. 2d 153 (1942).

Marshall Mountain Wave. 1942. "What the Churches Can Do for the Defense." January 30, pp. 1–2.

Marshall Mountain Wave. 1942. "Minute Men to Organize." February 20, p. 1.

Marshall Mountain Wave. 1942. "Jehovah Witness Fined $50." February 20, p. 2.

Minersville School District v. Gobitis, 310 U.S. 586 (1940).

Sperry, W. L. 1946. *Religion in America.* New York: Macmillan Company.

West Virginia State Board of Education et al. v. Barnette et al. 319 U.S. 624 (1943).

NOTES

1. I am JEHOVAH thy God, . . . Thou shalt have no other gods before me. Thou shalt not make unto thee any graven image, or any likeness of anything that is in heaven above, or that is in the earth beneath, or that is in the water under the earth; thou shalt not bow down thyself to them, nor serve them; for I JEHOVAH thy God am a jealous God, visiting the iniquity of the fathers upon the children unto the third and fourth generation of them that hate me; and showing mercy unto thousands of them that love me, and keep my commandments.

2. Leoles v. Landers, 302 U.S. 656; Hering v. State Board of Education, 303 U.S. 624; Gabrielli v. Knickerbocker, 306 U.S. 621; Johnson v. Deerfield, 306 U.S. 621.

3. Act. February 10, 1919, p. 34, section 1.

Whoever shall in any manner for display, place or cause to be placed upon the flag, colors, coat of arms, or other insignia of the United States, or of the State of Arkansas, any word, picture of device of trade advertising, or who shall sell, have in possession, or display any flag, colors, coat of arms, or insignia of the United States or of the State of Arkansas, so marked or mutilated for advertising or trade purposes; or who shall in any manner place on, attach to, or associate with any article of commerce any flag, colors, coat of arms or insignia of the United States or of the State of Arkansas, or offer for sale or have in possession any such article so associated; or who shall in any manner mutilate, deface of by word or act publicly exhibit contempt for the flag, colors, coat of arms, or other insignia of the United States, or the State of Arkansas, or any representation thereof; or shall in any manner display, place or cause to be placed, in or in connection with any advertisement of any kind, any representation of the flag, colors, coat of arms, or other insignia of the United States, or the State of Arkansas, shall be deemed guilty of a misdemeanor and on conviction shall be punished by a fine not exceeding $100, or imprisonment for not more than thirty days, or both.

4. § 134, West Virginia Code (1941 Supp.):

In all public, private, parochial and denominational schools located within this state there shall be given regular courses of instruction in history of the United States, in civics, and in the constitutions of the United States and of the State of West Virginia, for the purpose of teaching, fostering and perpetuating the ideals, principles and spirit of Americanism, and increasing the knowledge of the organization and machinery of the government of the United States and of the state of West Virginia. The state board of education shall, with the advice of the state superintendent of schools, prescribe the courses of study covering these subjects for the public elementary and grammar schools, public high schools and state normal schools. It shall be the duty of the officials or boards having authority over the respective private, parochial and denominational schools to prescribe courses of study for the schools under their control and supervision similar to those required for the public schools.

The text is as follows:

WHEREAS, The West Virginia State Board of Education holds in highest regard those rights and privileges guaranteed by the Bill of Rights in the Constitution of the United States of America and in the Constitution of West Virginia, specifically, the first amendment to the Constitution of the United States as restated in the fourteenth amendment to the same document and in the guarantee of religious freedom in Article III of the Constitution of this State, and

WHEREAS, The West Virginia State Board of Education honors the broad principle that one's convictions about the ultimate mystery of the universe and man's relation to it is placed beyond the reach of law; that the propagation of belief is protected, whether in church or chapel, mosque or synagogue, tabernacle or meeting house; that the Constitutions of the United States and of the State of West Virginia assure generous immunity to the individual from imposition of penalty for offending, in the course of his own religious activities, the religious views of others, be they a minority or those who are dominant in the government, but

WHEREAS, The West Virginia State Board of Education recognizes that the manifold character of man's relations may bring his conception of religious duty into conflict with the secular interests of his fellow man; that conscientious scruples have not, in the course of the long struggle for religious toleration, relieved the individual from obedience to the general law not aimed at the promotion or restriction of the religious beliefs; that the mere possession of convictions which contradict the relevant concerns of political society does not relieve the citizen from the discharge of political responsibility, and

WHEREAS, The West Virginia State Board of Education holds that national unity is the basis of national security; that the flag of our Nation is the symbol of our National Unity transcending all internal differences, however large, within the framework of the Constitution; that the Flag is the symbol of the Nation's power; that emblem of freedom in its truest, best sense; that it signifies government resting on the consent of the governed, liberty regulated by law, protection of the weak against the strong, security against the exercise of arbitrary power, and absolute safety for free institutions against foreign aggression, and

WHEREAS, The West Virginia State Board of Education maintains that the public schools, established by the legislature of the State of West Virginia under the authority of the Constitution of the State of West Virginia and supported by taxes imposed by legally constituted measures, are dealing with the formative period in the development in citizenship that the Flag is an allowable portion of the program of schools thus publicly supported.

Therefore, be it RESOLVED, That the West Virginia Board of Education does hereby recognize and order that the commonly accepted salute to the Flag of the United States—the right hand is placed upon the breast, and the following pledge repeated in unison: "I pledge allegiance to the Flag of the United States of America and to the Republic for which it stands; one Nation, indivisible, with liberty and justice for all"—now becomes a regular part of the program of activities in the public schools, supported in whole or in part by public funds, and that all teachers as defined by law in West Virginia and pupils in such schools shall be required to participate in the salute, honoring the Nation represented by the Flag; provided, however, that refusal to salute the Flag be regarded as an act of insubordination, and shall be dealt with accordingly.

5. § 1851(1), West Virginia Code (1941 Supp.):

> If a child be dismissed, suspended, or expelled from school because of refusal of such child to meet the legal and lawful requirements of the school and the established regulations of the county and/or state board of education, further admission of the child to school shall be refused until such requirements and regulations be complied with. Any such child shall be treated as being unlawfully absent from school during the time he refuses to comply with such requirements and regulations, and any person having legal or actual control of such child shall be liable to prosecution under the provisions of this article for the absence of such child from school.

6. During the course of the trial, on December 22, 1942, Congress amended the Flag Code to make the official salute the hand-over-heart salute to distance it from the symbolic repertoire of fascists.

CHAPTER 10

United States v. Burch

Freedom of Speech
in the Ouachita National Forest

DAVID R. DEWBERRY

The distinction between the public and private sphere for freedom of expression is incontrovertible. In the law, however, there are subtle nuances on the continuum. This article examines one such nuance based on Justice William O. Douglas's opinion in *Evans v. Newton* (1966): What is private and what is state action is not always easy to determine. The question addressed here is, does a private individual, who has leased land from the federal government, have the right to invoke a restraining order to prohibit someone from being on that land and exercising their free expression.

Property, Privatization, and Public Oversight

There has always been tension between property ownership and free speech. Specifically, interests in news gathering and the free dissemination of information are increasingly coming to a contention with property claims.[1] Access to public sites for the purpose of interaction is often ignored within the scholarly research in lieu of First Amendment literature dominated by the growing electronic era.[2]

One of the staples of the United States is the First Amendment's protection of free speech, but property rights are also imperative. As Justin Hughes notes, "For every pilgrim who came to the New World in search of religious freedom, there was at least one colonist who came on the promise of a royal land grant."[3] Recently, however, that balance may have shifted. That is, those with property and means might be seen as having more power. As the *New York Times* reported, "Business Does It Better. That is the rallying cry on Capitol Hill and in statehouses across the country, where legislators are turning over to private company's traditional government functions ranging from running jails to exploring outer space."[4] This privatization leads to decisions to be made based on factors that do not necessarily prioritize civil liberties.

Privatization is a term that has recently become common around the world as a phenomenon and as a figure of speech. Outside the United States, the term refers specifically to the selling of government land to the private sector; in the United States, however, the term takes on the additional meaning of disinvolvement, which is the amount and nature of any continuing governmental involvement that does not remain constant.[5] One method of privatization is the "use of contractual rearrangement of control over some, but not all, aspects of an activity."[6] The government accomplishes this type of privatization through the means of a lease.

The federal, state, and local governments are under increased pressure to privatize operations (e.g., prisons, hospitals, schools, film commissions, development agencies, daycare, trash collection, policing, transportation services, and drug treatment facilities) to simplify operations and to cut budgets.[7] Subsequently, "businesses operating privatized governmental functions have attempted to deny the public access to a wide variety of records."[8] The State of Arkansas defines public records in Arkansas code 25-19-103 5(a) as:

> Writings, recorded sounds, films, tapes, electronic or computer-based information, or data compilations in any medium, required by law to be kept or otherwise kept, and which constitute a record of the performance or lack of performance of official functions which are or should be carried out by a public official or employee, a governmental agency, or any other agency wholly or partially supported by public funds or expending public funds.

When the government turns over its operations to private companies, "public oversight of the new provider may be important, this is particularly true when public awareness and public pressure may be an important way to prevent corruption and abuse by private providers."[9] Due to the nature of private enterprise, public access suffers, for private enterprise is the tool of managers, owners, and shareholders, not taxpayers.[10] As Robin Rose posits, "It has been a strange epiphany to realize that real forest stewardship is a private matter where individuals, not governments, serve the public good [for] no government can bond with the land."[11]

The False Dilemma: Public and Private Land

The First Amendment is for the ban of federal, state, and local government on restrictions on speech; the First Amendment does not exclude private abridgement.[12] There is public land and there is private land where speech can and cannot occur. However, there is always a gray area. Banerjee posits the term "publicized private spaces" and defines such places as not truly public and the use is not a right rather a privilege.[13]

Increased privatization of public space shifts the site of social interaction, and important interactional situations are being lost; thus, the individual and the community's well-being is harmed.[14] The extensively cited *Marsh v. Alabama* (1946) is one of the hallmark cases of freedom of speech on private property.[15] It was declared that if a corporation owns a town or a municipality, the public has an identical interest in the operation in such manner that the channel of communication remain free.

In 1966, the Supreme Court declared that private conduct may become so entwined with governmental policies and permeated with governmental character that the subject becomes an agency or instrument of the state and are under the same constitutional limitations placed thereon.[16]

THE CHRIS BURCH STORY: BACKGROUND

Chris Burch moved to Montgomery County, Arkansas, in the winter of 1977 after graduating high school and has lived around the Joplin

Campground in the Ouachita National Forest to this day. Burch states that he had walked "on that land for over twenty years . . . and had seen eagles there"[17] and "has biked, hiked and bird watched in the park."[18] Currently, Burch works in a grocery store adjacent to the Colonial Motel, which is owned and operated by his parents, Charlie and Shirley.

On June 23, 24, and 27, 1997, meetings were held in Mount Ida and Hot Springs, Arkansas, regarding the April 2, 1996, 200-acre lease expansion requested by Bill Barnes, who is the president of Mountain Lake, Inc. (MLI). Barnes is, also, the proprietor of the Mountain Harbor Resort. Unfortunately, Chris Burch was unable to attend the meetings, but obtained transcripts of the meetings from the court and "became familiar with the opposition to the lease."[19]

On 27 acres of the 200-acre lease expansion, Mountain Harbor Resort was permitted over a period of ten years to build thirty cabins, one motel suite, five boat docks (with 123 slips), two boat docks for overnight lodging and guest use (with 22 slips), and a parking area (325 spaces).[20] Burch states, "a lot of politicians come up here and play . . . they just raised $20,000 for the governor up there . . . Sen. Blanch Lincoln, who I contacted when she was first elected and talked to her about this, what was going on up here, she never heard of Mountain Harbor, now someone told me she had a house up there."[21] According to Burch, 98 percent of the public opposed the lease, yet the Army Corps of Engineers carried out the lease.

In April 1999, Burch began working on a pamphlet that included information regarding the lease expansion by the Army Corps of Engineers. The pamphlet explained that "the acres were proposed for lease to Mountain Harbor Resort for private development . . . [and] feared that this private development would destroy the animal habitat around the lake."[22] The pamphlet also noted the amount of money that would be paid for the lease, which was 9.3 cents per acre. With the aid of the Arkansas Sierra Club, Burch began distributing pamphlets to anyone who was willing to receive them (i.e., campers, hikers, and walkers). The pamphlet announced a public meeting to be held on July 21, 1999, to discuss the lease.[23]

On July 2, 1999, Burch was hit by a pickup truck while distributing the pamphlets. Rex Ennis was driving the truck; Ennis was a security guard for MLI. The incident resulted in Burch being transported to St. Joseph's Hospital. Burch claims he has "incurred over \$2,000 in medical expenses and continues to have chronic neck problems."[24] Subsequent to the attack, Sheriff Williams and Deputy Whittle visited Burch on July 3, 1999. They took his statement and informed Burch that he should not go somewhere he thought his life could possibly be in danger. Ennis was not charged.

On July 4, 1999—Independence Day—Burch and approximately twelve individuals continued passing out pamphlets regarding the lease and the public meeting. Burch was stopped by an Army Corps of Engineer park ranger and was asked to cease. Ranger Greg Clemons cited 36 C.F.R. § 372.17, which reads as follows: "Advertising by the use of bill boards, signs, markers, audio devices, hand bills, circulars, posters or any other means whatsoever, is prohibited without written permission of the District Engineer."

Despite the warning, Burch continued to distribute pamphlets and was reported in his citation as saying if Ranger Clemons wanted to stop him, he would have to arrest him. Burch continued to the next campsite and handed out more pamphlets; Ranger Clemons asked Burch again to cease and desist, and Burch, again, replied that Clemons would have to arrest him. Ranger Clemons then contacted the sheriff's office for assistance. State trooper Wendell Adams was dispatched to the scene. Ranger Clemons, accompanied by Trooper Adams, then proceeded to issue a citation to Burch under title 36 C.F.R. § 372.24(B) (failure to comply with a lawful order issued by a federal employee). The fine was \$100.00.[25] Later that day, Bill Barnes, president of MLI, sent letters to Sheriff Williams. Barnes states, "At some point I am afraid we are going to have to request some kind of action by the prosecuting attorney to keep Chris [Burch] off our property since his actions are purely for negative and damaging purposes."[26]

On July 5, 1999, Burch reported to Sheriff Williams that Rex Ennis, while driving a Mountain Harbor truck, threatened him. Burch requested information about the attack on him from Sheriff Williams; Williams refused to give any information except that Ennis was not charged.

On July 20, 1999, Burch went to the area under development to take pictures of the process. Later that day, Bill Barnes sent letters

to Sheriff Williams claiming that photographing in the area constituted "harassment . . . serious discomfort . . . apprehension and
nervousness."[27]

On July 28, 1999, Burch returned to the area under development with a video camera. Mark Whisenhunt, a Mountain Harbor
employee, confronted Burch while holding a pistol behind his back.
Whisenhunt informed Burch that he was on private property. Deputy
Whittle arrived on the scene and also informed Burch that he was on
private property and gave Burch a citation for criminal trespassing.
Burch videotaped the entire incident himself.

On September 8, 1999, Sheriff Williams arrived at Burch's house
and arrested him for the criminal trespassing. Shirley Burch, Chris's
mother, asked Sheriff Williams why he was being arrested. Sheriff
Williams replied that it was to ensure Burch would show up for his
court date. Burch paid $575.00 for bond.[28]

Rex Ennis was eventually charged with assault in the second
degree. Ennis states, "I revved my engine to get his attention . . . he
either ran into my left front fender area or my foot slipped off the
brake."[29] However, the prosecutor opted for *nolle prosequi* to the charge
against Ennis. Judge McKimm instructed Ennis that violence was not
the appropriate reaction to any provocation and that if someone upset
him, he should hit a tree or board but not to hurt his knuckles.[30] Judge
McKimm convicted Burch of two counts of criminal trespassing and
fined Burch $250.00.

On October 26, 1999, Burch appealed. Clayton Blackstock, who
was contacted by the Arkansas ACLU, took the case on *pro bono*. On
March 3, 2000, the Honorable Bobby E. Shepherd overturned Burch's
convictions. Then, 208 days later Burch received a check from Judge
McKimm for $250.00. On October 23, 2000, Sheriff Williams was
relieved as sheriff of Montgomery County after being convicted of felony tampering with public documents. Nevertheless, after the reversal
Burch has been physically assaulted, he has traveled one thousand
miles to court only to find out that a hearing was dismissed and no
one contacted him, and had an employee of MLI expose himself in
front of Burch. Burch continues to go about the area documenting the
destruction of bald eagle perching sites. Recently, Burch was videotaping a bald eagle, and the new sheriff informed Burch that he needed

to leave or he would go to jail. Burch replied, "What for?" The sheriff replied, "I'll find something."[31]

THE MOUNTAIN HARBOR STORY: BACKGROUND

Tenure is widely recognized as a basic component of sustainable forest management, and policymakers generally prefer privatization.[32] Bill Barnes is continuing the work his father started in 1955, when the Army Corps of Engineers offered twenty total leases of which only fourteen were sought. The lease was good for twenty-five years and was automatically renewed if the leaseholder met the public needs and there were no outstanding complaints.[33]

Barnes's father started Mountain Harbor with eight floating docks, a bait shop, one hundred fishing boats, and a motor room. Two and a half years later, Mountain Harbor filed for Chapter 12 reorganization. In 1968, Bill Barnes, who was studying commercial and hotel management, dropped out of college and came to the aid of his father. Bill Barnes worked alone building cottages, marinas, and boat storage facilities to generate revenue year round. Barnes continued to improve the land over the next ten years, which paid off as the lease came for renewal in 1980, and Mountain Harbor met the Army Corps of Engineers provisions of adding to the land and having no outstanding complaints.

Barnes continued his work, and eventually built a small general store. Across the street, the Burch family ran their store and motel. Barnes related, "If they didn't have it, we had, and if we didn't have it, they had it."[34] Both Barnes and Burch state that prior to 1977, they both referred consumers to each other; the Colonial Motel displayed brochures for Mountain Harbor, and Mountain Harbor displayed brochures for the Colonial Motel.

In 1977, Barnes received a telephone call from a former visitor of Mountain Harbor. The visitor wished to move to the area and was looking for a business to buy. Barnes offered the general store, and the visitor bought it. After the general store opened with new owners, Barnes continued to make his regular visits to the Colonial Motel and Grocery. Things, however, changed. One time Barnes walked in and Chris Burch cursed Barnes and told him to get out of the store.

Barnes refused and asked to speak with his mother. Shirley Burch, whom Barnes describes as a very kind level-headed lady, came to the store and asked Barnes to leave. He did and such interactions became more frequent.

The Restraining Order

According to Barnes, since the incident, Burch swears at, spits on, and gives the middle finger to him every time they meet, even in the bookstore in nearby Hot Springs. Bill Barnes said that he can handle the abuse and frequently walks up to Burch and asks, "Do you have anything to say to me, Chris?"[35]

Bill Barnes and his wife, Debi, walk through Lake Ouachita during the morning. One day, Debi Barnes went walking with Sam, the family dog. Debi wears contacts but did not put them in for her morning walk. She came upon Burch videotaping (Burch's method of documenting eagles), and she recognized him as she approached. Sam ran up to Burch and sniffed him. Debi told Bill that Chris proceeded to growl at her and the dog, Burch later claimed that he was saying "greed, greed, greed."[36]

During the construction on the leasehold, Barnes states that Burch would enter into areas that had been marked "Construction Area—Authorized Persons Only" and document the construction workers all the while yelling "and trying his best to start an incident."[37]

Barnes admits that Burch's activities bothered him, but he could handle it, but when Burch created anxiety among his family, something had to be done. Barnes filed a restraining order. That day the Honorable Judge Gayle Ford ordered that Burch could not come about Bill or Debi Barnes, nor any person of Mountain Lake, Inc., and Burch was temporarily restrained from coming upon property of Mountain Lake, Inc., including its leasehold interests.[38]

Burch strongly contests the restraining order for several reasons. First, on the claim that Burch trespasses into areas where a marina was then under construction marked "authorized personnel only," Burch points to the June 13, 1983, lease from the Army Corps of Engineers to Mountain Harbor that states, "No attempt shall be made by the leasee to forbid the full and free use by the public of the water and areas of the reservoir." Therefore, Burch should be allowed on the property.

Secondly, Barnes posits that Burch walks in the middle of the road; Burch, nevertheless, claims that he walks on the side of the road. Barnes, in his interview, mentioned that when Burch does walk in the middle of the street, he follows him slowly and waits for an area where he can safely drive around. Barnes continues by explaining that he asks Burch, if he has anything to say, Barnes claims that Burch screams, "Yeah, leave me the fuck alone," which Burch affirms in his interview.

As for the charge of harassment, Burch claims the definition from the United States Code Title 18 §1514 (c) (1) as "a course of conduct directed at a specific person that causes substantial emotional distress in such a person and serves no legitimate purpose." Burch contends his journeys into the leasehold and subsequent video documenting are legitimate and are done so to ensure his own safety.

Also, Burch points out that none of the affidavits include "statements are true to the best of my knowledge, information and belief." Burch also maintains that no law enforcement officer ever cited him for any conduct described in the restraining order. Nevertheless, Barnes claims that Burch was in violation.

Discussion

On July 4, 1999, a park ranger issued Burch a ticket for violating 36 CFR § 327.24(B) in the Army Corps of Engineer's Joplin Recreation Area. On March 3, 2000, the Honorable Bobby Shepherd found 36 C.F.R. § 327.17 unconstitutional and ordered that Burch be acquitted of the charge, and the Army Corps of Engineers, subsequently, revised 36 CFR § 327.17. The Army Corps of Engineers sent Burch a copy of the policy promulgated under the regulation.[39]

The Joplin Campground is located on a small peninsula on Lake Ouachita. For an individual to get to the campground without a boat or aircraft, they must travel through the Mountain Harbor's leasehold. That is, to get to the public campground, one must travel through government land, which is leased to a private individual, who has a restraining order against a man who wants to go to the campground. The existing roads provide an easy method of access to the campground and "the public is permitted to enter and walk through the campground on the roadway which serves the area."[40] Unless, of course, you are prohibited from the leased land as is the case with Burch.

A United States magistrate judge declared that Burch has the right to distribute flyers without prior restraint. The Honorable Bobby E. Shepherd found that the 36 CFR § 327.17 (1999) gave the district engineer "'unbridled and absolute power to prohibit' the distribution of leaflets in Corps controlled areas."[41]

"Looking, gazing, and watching are all part of our normal stimulus-seeking behavior," and this is exactly what Burch was doing.[42] Ostensibly, "forests are not possible without capitalism, private ownership, forest regulations, and enforcements of forest management laws. Public forests of all sorts are being carried off every day to fuel fires, feed families, provide cash, make figurines for tourists, satisfy the greed of poachers, and build homes"; however, one could feel differently and state that forests should be entirely public.[43] Yet, if a forest were to be public entirely, could one man not cut down all the trees, for it is his as much as another's? Rose posits this argument and sums it up by saying, "It [is] public land, not *his* land."[44]

The Freedom of Information Act was passed in 1966 with the central purpose "to insure that the Federal Government's activities be opened to public scrutiny."[45] And "in the past few years, businesses operating privatized governmental functions have attempted to deny the public access to a wide variety of records."[46] In this case, Congress did not make a law abridging the freedom of speech, but private entities did.

Chris Burch simply wants to go about the leasehold of Mountain Harbor and document the activities of Mountain Lake, Inc. In *Marsh v. Alabama* (1946), Justice Hugo Black stated in the opinion of the court, "The more an owner, for his own advantage, opens up his property for use by the public in general, the more do his rights become circumscribed by the statutory and constitutional rights of those who use it."

Arkansas code 25-19-103 5(a) defines public records as recorded sounds, films, and tapes, which constitute a record of the performance or lack of performance of official functions which are or should be carried out any that are wholly or partially supported by public funds. Burch receives no compensation for his efforts to document the destruction of eagle perching sites at Lake Ouachita, which he believes is a matter of public concern. Burch simply wishes to videotape what he sees as the destruction of the natural beauty around the lake. He has numerous videotapes, but he has no immediate available means of disseminating the information.

The restraining order against Burch is abrogating his rights to demonstrate and comment on what he sees as a public harm. The United States Supreme Court has stated in *Evans v. Newton* (1966) and *Marsh v. Alabama* (1946) that the more a person is endowed with government functions and opens his property for the public, the more that person is subject to the constitutional limitations of the government. Barnes is operating under the pretense of the government, for he is operating a campground at Lake Ouachita National Park and lives on that land. Barnes is acting indirectly on behalf of the government, and based on the cases above, Barnes is stopping Burch by the means of a restraining order that prohibits Burch from entering the leased land.

Perhaps a hypothetical situation can be used for an analogy. If a government agency is suffering from poor media depiction from news gatherers who are investigating misconduct, the government could lease out the operation of the government agency to the private sector and have the private sector issue a restraining order against the press from being on their premises. Could this stop the reporters from undermining the authority of government operations? Is this realistic? If so, the protection of the First Amendment has met its match—the catch-all restraining order. And we can see this in the case with Chris Burch.

The First Amendment clearly allows Burch to petition the government for a redress of grievances. The Arkansas state constitution in Article 2, Section 2 gives Burch the inherent and inalienable right to protect property, and it must be duly noted the same section gives Barnes the right to possess and acquire property. As for the restraining order that prohibits Burch from entering the leasehold due to his harassment of Barnes is problematic for it is based on no real evidence. Yes, Burch admits to scowling at Debi Barnes and saying greed three times on a public road; yes, Burch admits to taking pictures of construction at a national park. Yet, are these acts of speaking and taking pictures sufficient to issue a restraining order? Apparently, yes.

In 1998, Senator Dianne Feinstein and Senator Orrin Hatch proposed the Personal Privacy Protection Act. Bill S.2103 states, in part, that capturing any image of a personal or familial activity through the use of a visual enhancement device, even if no physical trespass has occurred, is prohibited. The intent of the legislation was not aimed at the mainstream, but at abusive behavior from individuals who do not respect where the line is between what is public and what is private.[47] This raises the question of who is the First Amendment directed at: the majority or the minority? Is it the majority that needs protection of their freedom of expression? According to Supreme Court justices Black, Murphy, and Douglas, and Chief Justice Stone, freedom of expression does belong to the majority and to the "dissident minorities who energetically spread their beliefs."[48] Quite simply, the line between public and private is not always a clear one.

Based on past court decisions, the Constitution, the Arkansas Constitution, and past legislative activities, it is evident that the restraining order preventing Burch to enter a national park should be revoked, but Burch says that he would be happy just to get his hearing in court.

Conclusion

Restraining orders can prevent a person from harassing and being on another's property. But this case has a peculiar twist. The person being protected by the restraining order *lives* on public land. Under Justice Black's opinion of the court in *Marsh v. Alabama*, Burch, ostensibly, has a right to be on the land and to document what he sees as destruction of perching sites for bald eagles.

I had the privilege of visiting the small town and interviewing both parties involved. Before I left, I asked each one the same question, "What do you want?" Burch replied that he wanted to document what was going on and to be left alone; Barnes claims that he too wants to be left alone and improve the property as this lease dictates under the Arkansas Constitution. Both Burch and Barnes have legitimate claims in this battle.

In February 27, 2001, the Army Corps of Engineers stated that visitation had grown dramatically over time.[49] In 1972, 2,992,200 people visited Lake Ouachita; in 1999, 4,378,443 people visited the lake. In contrast, Yosemite National Park had 300,919 in 2002. Lake Ouachita has approximately 670 miles of shoreline. Including islands, there is a total shoreline of over 1,000 miles, of which only 3.5 percent of that is developed. Burch just wants something done.

Burch is financially exhausted from fighting his battle and cannot afford an attorney and must defend himself, yet he is currently waiting for a hearing regarding his temporary restraining order: a temporary order issued over eight months ago; the order was issued the same day it was requested. Burch has never been cited for any criminal activity and claims that Barnes's request was processed quickly and his long wait for a hearing violates his Fifth Amendment rights.

In his most recent declaration, Chris Burch states:

> For over 20 years I had regularly and freely accessed these lands and observed American bald eagles. In 1999, I witnessed, in horror, numerous bald eagle perching sites destroyed at what is now called Harbor North. There is substantial evidence that this lease and development is illegal and in violation of The National Environmental Policy Act, Endangered Species Act and The Code of Federal Regulations.[50]

As Burch waits for his hearing, Mountain Harbor continues to build. If it is true that those with the most resources have the most power, Chris Burch is in for a long, long battle.

This article has shown that with the increased privatization that is occurring within the government, there are some obstacles to overcome. The ambiguity of the private and public contexts of freedom of expression needs to be addressed in order to overcome these obstacles. If the court upholds the restraining order, the order will do what very few laws have been able to do—silence an individual.

NOTES

1. M. Bunker, "Trespassing Speakers and Commodified Speech: First Amendment Freedoms Meet Private Property Claims," *Journal and Mass Communication Quarterly* 77 (Winter 2000): 713–26.

2. S. Drucker and G. Gumpert, "Public Spaces and the Right of Association," *Free Speech Yearbook* 36 (1998): 25–38.

3. Justin Hughes, "The Philosophy of Intellectual Property," *Georgetown Law Review* 77 (1988): 287–366.

4. L. Eaton, "A Billion at Risk: A Special Report. Public Money Foots the Bills for 'Privatized' Foreign Aid," *New York Times*, February 7, 1996.

5. Robert Cass, "Privatization: Politics, Law, and Theory," *Marquette Law Review* 71 (1988): 449–523.

6. Ibid., 458.

7. Matthew Bunker and Charles Davis, "Privatized Government Functions and Freedom of Information: Public Accountability in an Age of Private Governance," *Journalism and Mass Communication Quarterly* 75 (1998): 464–77.

8. Ibid., 464.

9. Ibid., 471.

10. Ibid., 473.

11. R. Rose, "Back from the Future, and I Didn't Like What I Saw," *Journal of Forestry* 100 (2002): 60.

12. W. Freedman, *Freedom of Speech on Private Property* (New York: Quorum Books, 1988).

13. T. Banerjee, "The Future of Public Space: Beyond Invented Streets and Reinvented Places," *Journal of the American Planning Association* 67 (Winter 2001): 9–24.

14. Drucker and Gumpert, "Public Spaces and the Right of Association," 25.

15. Cf. *Brentwood Academy v. Tennessee Secondary School Athletic Association*, 531 U.S. 288; *PruneYard Shopping Center v. Robins*, 447 U.S. 74; *Columbia Broadcasting System, Inc. v. Democratic National Committee*, 412 U.S. 94; *Dennis v. United States*, 341 U.S. 494; *Everson v. Board of Education*, 330 U.S. 1.

16. Cf. *Evans v. Newton*, 382 U.S. 296.

17. Chris Burch, telephone interview by author, September 21, 2002.

18. *United States v. Chris Burch* (Criminal No. 99-A226584 WA-33) Memorandum of Law in Support to Dismiss.

19. Chris Burch, telephone interview by author, September 21, 2002.

20. Chris Burch, email to author, September 27, 2002.

21. Chris Burch, telephone interview by author, September 21, 2002.

22. *United States v. Chris Burch*, Criminal No. 99-A226584 WA-33, Memorandum of Law in Support to Dismiss.

23. Ibid.

24. Chris Burch, Chronology of Events by Chris Burch (modification #8): September 27, 2001.

25. United States District Court, Violation Notice A22658. DD Form 1805. September 1998.

26. B. Barnes, Letter to Prosecuting Attorney, Tim Williamson. July 4, 1999.

27. Ibid., July 20, 1999.

28. Burch, 5.

29. Ibid., 6.

30. Ibid.

31. Chris Burch, Videotape of Confrontation with Sheriff Spivey, October 8, 1999.

32. K. Tucker, "Private versus Common Property Forests: Forest Conditions and Tenure in a Honduran Community," *Human Ecology* 27, no. 2 (June 1999): 201–30.

33. Bill Barnes, interview by author, October 19, 2002.

34. Ibid.

35. Ibid.

36. Affidavit of Debi Barnes. Petition Requesting Temporary Restraining Order and Permanent Injunction Against Chris Burch. (# CV 2002-22) Exhibit B. Montgomery County Circuit Court. March 29, 2002.

37. Affidavit of Bill Barnes. Petition Requesting Temporary Restraining Order and Permanent Injunction Against Chris Burch. (# CV 2002-22) Exhibit A. Montgomery County Circuit Court. March 29, 2002.

38. Order of Temporary Restraint. (# CV 2002-22). Montgomery County Circuit Court. March 29, 2002.

39. Judgment of Acquittal. *United States v. Chris Burch* (99-A226584 WA-33), March 3, 2000.

40. Ibid.

41. Judgement of Acquittal. Citing: *Shuttlesworth v. City of Birmingham, AL*, 394 U.S. 147, 150 (1969).

42. Bannerjee, "The Future of Public Space," 22.

43. Rose, "Back from the Future," 60.

44. Ibid.

45. United States Dept. of Justice *et al. v. Reporters Committee For Freedom of the Press et al.* 489 U.S. 749 (1989).

46. Bunker and Davis, "Privatized Government Functions and Freedom of Information," 464.

47. R. Feingold, Introduction of the Personal Privacy Protection Act. Speech presented at Judiciary Committee of the U.S. Senate, Washington D.C., May 1988.

48. *Jones v. Opelika*, 316 U.S. 584 (1942).

49. Army Corps of Engineers Proposed Management of Aquatic Plants at Lake Ouachita and Degray. Page 9, par. 32 EA. February 27, 2001.

50. Public Statement by Chris Burch, November 25, 2002. Subsequently, many of Burch's claims were dismissed by federal judge Robert Dawson, *Burch v. Naron*, 333 F. Supp. 2d 816 (W.D. Ark., 2004).

CHAPTER 11

Nichols v. Chacon

Rhetoric, Law, and the Gesturing Man

RYAN GLISZINSKI

In contemporary usage the displaying of one's middle finger to another is an act that carries many connotative meanings including, but not limited to, anger, defiance, disdain, frustration, and protest, but also camaraderie,[1] comfort, and even excitement.[2] Anthropologists have suggested that the gesture is one with a history that predates written language and exists even as an observable behavior in primate species.[3] The history of the gesture is one that has been relatively well documented; the first documented usage of the gesture stretches back over 2,000 years when it was first mentioned in ancient Greece by Aristophanes in his play, *The Clouds*.[4] In a fictional account of a meeting between Socrates and a character by the name of Strepsiades, wherein Socrates asks his counterpart to define "finger-rhythm," Strepsiades displays to him his middle finger, saying, "Why it's tapping time with this finger. Of course, when I was a boy I used to make rhythm with this one (displaying his erect phallus)."[5]

However, Aristophanes was not the only ancient Greek philosopher documented to have employed the gesture, the self-proclaimed Cynic and father of modern Stoicism, Diogenes, is also documented as having used the gesture,[6] as part of a larger process of morally critiquing the social structures, institutions, and culture of his time through disruption and acts of public "obscenity."[7] Appropriated by the Romans, like so much of Greek culture, the gesture came to take on a very specific meaning, one that indicated anal intercourse in a threatening and violent manner.[8] Indeed, the gesture was so popular among the Romans that they gave it its own name,[9] *digitus impudicus*, meaning, "impudent finger,"[10] and even Emperor Caligula was known to regularly extend it, in a humiliating manner, for his subjects to kiss.[11] Although the gesture appears to have relatively disappeared during the Dark Ages, a fact which historians attribute to the influence and rising moral order of the established Christian church, it nonetheless reemerged sometime before the end of the Enlightenment, though its first documentation on American soil did not appear until 1886 when a baseball pitcher was recorded in a photograph utilizing the expression to "communicate" a sense of rivalry with the opposing team.[12] Since then the gesture has enjoyed widespread usage in the United States and around the world, being deployed in a variety of manners and intended to convey a variety of meanings.[13]

Given the frequent use of the gesture in our culture, and as evidenced across time, it should not surprise us that the gesture appears in a variety of cultural institutions, not least of which is the law. In the United States a number of state and federal cases have concerned themselves with the gesture,[14] and most of these cases have focused on the use of the gesture as a form of symbolic speech protected by the First Amendment. Although this paper will not deal explicitly with the various courts' framing of the gesture in relation to the First Amendment, it will attempt nonetheless to delve into one specific case relevant to this issue.

On August 6, 1998, Wayne Nichols, driving down a major Arkansas highway, flipped the bird to a state trooper, whom he believed to be officer Joe Hutchens,[15] driving in the opposite direction.[16] Apparently Hutchens had recently removed Nichols, who owned and operated a towing service in Benton County, from the list of service providers that the county calls upon to assist in clearing traffic wrecks.[17] Nichols had been a regular contact of the county for over thirty years and had regularly been depended upon to clear traffic wrecks by a former deputy friendly to Nichols and his family.[18] After displaying the gesture numerous times, Nichols was pulled over by the passing officer, Jose Chacon, a sixteen-year employee of the Arkansas State Police, and issued a citation for disorderly conduct,[19] despite Nichols's profuse apologies.[20] Nichols appeared in the Bentonville Municipal Court on December 1, 1998, and after a fifteen-minute trial he was declared not guilty because his exercise of expressive conduct did not constitute "fighting words" as determined by a landmark 1942 Supreme Court case *Chaplinsky v. New Hampshire*.[21] After the verdict was issued, Nichols filed a civil rights suit against Chacon, suing him in both his individual and official capacities, seeking a declaratory judgment and compensation for punitive damages and attorney's fees, and arguing that his First, Fourth, and Fourteenth Amendment rights had been violated.[22] Nichols was awarded two thousand dollars in compensatory damages and an additional two-thousand in punitive damages[23]—a shock to both Nichols and his attorney,[24] and to the court.[25] More shocking than the punitive damages, however, was the fact that the jury had written that they would also like a written apology from the arresting officer—a request Judge Franklin Waters[26] deemed "unenforceable."[27] During the Supreme Court trial Chacon's representing attorney filed a motion for judgment as a matter of law,[28] claiming that her client had not demonstrated the "evil motive or callous indifference" required to impose punitive damages, a motion that was upheld by the court and later appealed by Nichols's lawyer to no avail.[29]

Conducting a close reading of the trial transcript and subsequent appeal by Nichols's representing attorney, Doug Norwood, this essay seeks to answer a number of questions. In what ways did the rhetoric espoused by the defending and prosecuting attorneys determine the outcome of this case? What rhetorical features, or forms, were called upon to persuade the jury? How was Nichols's representing attorney capable of encouraging the jury to reach the decision that they did? How were Wayne Nichols and Jose Chacon constructed rhetorically throughout this case and what bearing did this have, if any, on the outcome? Why did the court ultimately decide to grant judgment as a matter of law and vacate the punitive damages verdict? What sort of arguments pertaining to this issue were made by Nichols and refuted by the defense in the court of appeals? In what ways, if at all, did the court potentially undermine judicial process by granting judgment as

a matter of law? Finally, what sort of precedent does this case set for
future First Amendment cases related to the gesture?

To answer these questions it will be necessary to examine this
case from a rhetorical standpoint and to examine the very discourse
operating throughout the trial, and to do so I will draw upon Kenneth
Burke's *A Rhetoric of Motives*[30]—specifically this issue of consub-
stantiation, or identification—an issue that appears to be incredibly
pertinent in determining the outcome of this case. Also pertinent to
the analysis will be a brief discussion of Louis Althusser's concept
of "hailing" or interpellation[31]—a concept that also appears to factor
heavily into the case, especially considering the frequent mention of
"The Gesturing Man" during the appeal.[32] Finally, an in-depth look
at the precedent set forth by the Eighth Circuit Court of Appeals was
conducted to determine whether or not the court erred in its granting of judgment as a matter of law, effectively vacating the punitive
damage award determined by the jury. Relying upon this methodolog-
ical framework I will assert three claims: first, that Chacon's attorney
interpellated Nichols as "The Gesturing Man" so as to undermine his
ethos and present him as morally deficient, narrowly limiting the issue
to one of unwarranted damages; second, that Nichols's representing
attorney Doug Norwood engaged in a complex process of identification and dis-identification, framed the issue as one of responsibility,
and raised the "specter of the state" so as to warn the jurors of the
potential threat posed to the U.S. Constitution in their decision; and
finally, that the entire judicial process was undermined when the court
granted judgment as matter of law and vacated the punitive damages
against Trooper Chacon.

After engaging in a close-textual analysis of the trial transcript, and
investigating the rhetoric employed by Chacon's representing attorney,
Sherri Robinson, it becomes clear that Robinson interpellated Nichols
as "The Gesturing Man" so as to undermine his ethos and present him
as morally deficient, narrowly limiting the issue to one of unwarranted
damages. Interestingly, the first time Wayne Nichols is acknowledged
during the trial as "The Gesturing Man" it is in reference to himself.[33]
In response to the questioning of his attorney who inquired if Nichols
had been damaged, "other than just by direct out of pocket expenses,"
Nichols responded, "Yeah everywhere I go people flips me the bird.

They call me the gesturing man."[34] Norwood affirmed this statement by asking, "So you started some kind of trend or something or another?" to which Nichols agreed. [35] Inquiring as to whether this provided any source of anxiety for him when he presented himself at the criminal court proceedings, Wayne answered, "Yeah, I didn't know whether I was going to get fined a big fine or get put in jail or get put in the Benton County Jail. I didn't know."[36] Quickly changing the direction of questioning after this statement, Norwood began to inquire after Nichols's otherwise unblemished criminal record,[37] but what is interesting to note is that Nichols is the first to acknowledge himself as "The Gesturing Man" during the trial. However, this was not the first time that Wayne Nichols had been called into being as "The Gesturing Man," and it appears that credit for this title should be attributed to the local media, which reported the proceedings as early as November 1999 when Wayne was identified as one of two "gesturing men" in an article written by Rebecca Pilcher for the *Arkansas Democrat-Gazette*.[38.] At that time Wayne was not the only member of his family involved in a legal battle with the Benton County police force; his nephew John Christopher Nichols[39] had also displayed the gesture to an officer,[40] though the charges against him were later dropped. This notion of "The Gesturing Man" appears to be one that Wayne initially relished, as evidenced by a subsequent article in the *Arkansas Democrat-Gazette*[41] that claimed that following the municipal court proceedings, at which time the charges against Nichols were dropped, Wayne is cited as claiming that he planned to have t-shirts printed with the name, "Gesturing Man" across the front, and "Protected by the First and Fourteenth Amendments" across the back.[42]

Unfortunately for Wayne, the media coverage of the incident appears to have had a negative impact in the court proceedings, and the next time he was acknowledged as "The Gesturing Man" during the trial was by the defense. During cross-examination Robinson acknowledged Wayne's claim that he had suffered damages as a result of the title, when she asked him, "You've said that you've had other damages, people flipping you off, calling you the gesturing man?" to which Nichols agreed. "You were the gesturing man, though, weren't you?" to which Nichols answered yes. "You did flip Mr. Chacon off, didn't you? [Nichols confirms] . . . *So you are the gesturing man. And in fact you said you received one hundred phone calls saying good job?*"[43] to which Nichols claimed that a number of people had called him, "and congratulated [him] for not being put in jail and . . . being found not guilty," and that neighbors frequently drove by his business and flipped him the bird, to which Robinson responded by stating, ". . . there's no bad publicity or bad worry with that, is there . . . that's protected speech so it's okay if they do that, isn't it?"—a statement with which Wayne was forced to agree.[44]

This moment during the trial is pivotal and reflects a larger process identified by social theorist Louis Althusser concerning the ways in which ideologies interpellate subjectivities; writing in 1971 about the role of ideology in perpetuating and maintaining oppressive relationships between labor and producers, Althusser claimed that ideologies act as *interpellating* forces; that is, they call persons into being by recognizing them as subjects.[45]

Elaborating upon this process, Althusser writes:

> I shall then suggest that ideology "acts" or "functions" in such a way that it "recruits" subjects among the individuals (it recruits them all), or "transforms" the individuals into subjects (it transforms them all) by that very precise operation which I have called interpellation or hailing, and which can be imagined along the lines of the most commonplace everyday police (or other) hailing: "Hey, you there!" Assuming that the theoretical scene I have imagined takes place in the street, the hailed individual will turn round. By this mere one-hundred-and-eighty-degree physical conversion, he becomes a subject. Why? Because he has recognized that the hail was "really" addressed to him, and that "it was really him who was hailed" (and not someone else).[46]

This process of hailing, or interpellation, Althusser argues, is one that is extremely effective, because in recognizing oneself as being "hailed" the now-subject affirms this reality as legitimate for both him and his "hailer"; he recognizes himself as he was addressed and in doing so participates in a larger system of identification and being—a system that Althusser dubs "ideology."[47]

In calling "The Gesturing Man" into being Robinson interpellated Wayne Nichols in a particular way, as a subject with a title that carried with it a series of connotative values, values then present in the larger culture thanks to the media coverage of the case. In calling "The Gesturing Man" into being Robinson was also able to construct Wayne in a particular way, as someone who was lacking in credibility and, moreover, as someone who was morally deficient. During her closing argument Robinson again calls into being "The Gesturing Man," this time to undermine his ethos and present him as morally wanton. Discussing the fact that Wayne had failed to produce any sort of documentation during discovery or during trial examination, she appeals to the jury saying, "There is no credible evidence to support his allegations,"[48] and the jury should "think about that when [they're] assessing the credibility that Mr. Nichols has displayed on the witness stand."[49] She goes on to acknowledge that Nichols apologized to Trooper Chacon for being disrespectful, and that he even went out of his way to write him a letter of apology,[50] but then deftly dismisses this act by saying:

> But then he tried to say, well, it was a little embarrassing. I was labeled the gesturing man. But then he admitted, well, yeah, I was the gesturing man so, you know, that was truthful in the media. He said that he got phone calls but, you know, those were not bad phone calls. They congratulated him on getting out of it. He wasn't really offended when people flipped him off. That was okay, but he was a little embarrassed. Do you know what *he should be embarrassed about making that gesture? He should be embarrassed to make that gesture to anyone and Mr. Norwood said he would do that to anyone.*[51] I don't think any of us would do that to anyone . . . This could have been over in 1998. If he suffered any embarrassment, it's his own fault. It's his own fault for giving the gesture. It's his own fault that he kept this thing going in the media.[52]

After shaming Wayne and presenting him as morally wanting, Robinson juxtaposed "The Gesturing Man" against the obligations of the state and claimed that police officers "put their lives on the line for us every single day," and that "If the law says it's okay for us to cuss a police officer. It's okay to display a rude or offensive gesture to a police officer. It's okay to *show a total lack of respect to a police officer.*[53] But you know something, that doesn't make it right. That doesn't make it something we should all run out and do."[54] Cementing her argument against the plaintiff and reifying her attack upon his ethos Robinson concluded by framing the issue as one that could potentially reward dubious and morally decrepit behavior when she said, "Don't reward Wayne Nichols for showing that he has a total lack of respect for law enforcement officers. He doesn't deserve any damages at all. He hasn't shown you by a preponderance of the evidence. Don't give him any."[55]

Robinson's arguments here demonstrate the power of interpellation, of hailing, and in doing so, constructing a subject in a particular way. After having called into being the subject as "The Gesturing Man," she undermined his ethos and attacked his credibility. She shamed "The Gesturing Man" and argued that, regardless of the law, the gesture he displayed is not one that *should* be displayed. Her appeal here is to the moral nature of the jury, an appeal to their common decency. Her appeal to the moral delicacies of the jury was a strategic one in that it allowed her to narrowly restrict the issue of the trial to one of damages. Now, to be sure, the issue in this trial was explicitly one of damages, but, of course, and as we'll soon see, the trial in question acted in a larger way, and in a way in which both attorneys were highly conscious of[56] in that the outcome of the case would determine the way courts, generally, interpret and handle issues pertaining to the gesture and the First Amendment.

In undermining the credibility of "The Gesturing Man," Robinson was able to downplay the significance of the case, and indeed in her closing argument she did just that when she claimed, "this case is not the issue. It's the municipal court case. It's the traffic stop. That's the issue. That's what you have to focus on when you're talking about damages. *This whole process is irrelevant.*[57] It's that issue that you want to look at."[58] Robinson struggled to narrowly restrict the issue to one of damages, of essentially *rewarding* "The Gesturing Man" for acting immorally and obscenely. In constructing Wayne Nichols as "The Gesturing Man" she called him into being as an incredible entity, a morally bankrupt subject, and in doing so was able to frame the issue as one of unwarranted and nonexistent damages.

The rhetorical approach taken by Nichols's representing attorney was distinctly different, and based on the outcome of the case, decidedly more effective. Throughout the case Nichols's representing attorney, Doug Norwood, engaged in a complex process of identification and dis-identification, framing the issue as one of responsibility while raising the "specter of the state" and warning the jurors of the potential threat posed to the Constitution in their decision. The notion of identification is one rhetoricians have acknowledged as fundamental to the persuasive art of rhetoric—a driving force in all matters related to effective argumentation. In his 1950 text, Kenneth Burke outlined the concept of identification and argued that this process is fundamental to the art of persuasion. Outlining the method by which this process occurs, he writes:

> A is not identical with his colleague, B. But insofar as their interests are joined, A is *identified* with B. Or he may *identify himself* with B even when their interests are not joined, if he assumes that they are, or is persuaded to believe so. Here are ambiguities of substance. In being identified with B, A is "substantially one" with a person other than himself. Yet at the same time he remains unique, an individual locus of motives. Thus he is both joined and separate, at once a distinct substance and consubstantial with another.[59]

Burke would further elaborate upon this process when he wrote:

> As for the relation between "identification" and "persuasion": we might well keep it in mind that a speaker persuades an audience by the use of stylistic identifications; his act of persuasion may be for the purpose of causing the audience to identify itself with the speaker's interests; and the speaker draws on identification of interests to establish rapport between himself and his audience.[60]

Identification, then, lay at the heart of persuasive rhetoric, and indeed, is *the* driving force in all matters of persuasion, a force that operates by intimating a sense of shared interest, of creatively persuading others that interests, and consequently, identities, are similar.

Throughout the case the process of identification is deployed strategically by Norwood. Norwood strategically identifies and dis-identifies with his client, Trooper Chacon, the jury, and as we'll soon see at least one fictitious and constructed rhetorical entity. The first instance of this process of identification occurred soon into Norwood's closing argument; gesturing to his client, he said, "Now you see Mr. Nichols over here and he's pretty rough looking. I mean he's got long hair and he looks just like an old country boy and he works in a junk yard."[61] Here Norwood identifies his client as a "country boy," a salt-of-the-earth-type fellow, with a few rough edges. In his rebuttal to Robinson's closing argument he would again identify his client in a similar way when he stated, "Wayne Nichols . . . looks rough and maybe he's a little different than everybody else . . . he pushes the envelope a little too far."[62] Strategically identifying his client as he does Norwood quickly distances himself from his client's actions and claims that Wayne "was being disrespectful, Mr. Nichols was. There's no doubt about that . . . Would I have personally done what he did? Not in a million years."[63] Further emphasizing his respectable nature and pure intentions, Norwood asserted that he "[didn't] expect to get a lot of money off of this," and that, "This is not the biggest case I've ever had."[64] In identifying his client as he does and then distancing himself from his clients' actions and stating clearly to the jury that he wasn't in this for the money, Norwood was able to identify himself as someone the jury could trust, that is, as someone vested in protecting the constitutional rights of others, regardless of how those persons choose to exercise those rights. In doing so he effectively claimed that, like the jury, he was vested, indeed had made a career out of, doing the right thing, and in this way was able convey a sense of identification with the jury, and a sense of dis-identification from his client and his actions.

At another point in the case Norwood makes yet another strategic identification, this time on behalf of his client. Stating that there are clearly damages to compensate for, he argued that his client "[was] not a guy who got up there and said as a result of this I've lost my business. I've become—you know, I was a psychic before and all my psychic powers have gone away from me now and I mean just come up with some ludicrous amount of damages that are just so outrageous. This guy has lost true out of pocket expenses."[65] What's interesting here is that Norwood juxtaposes the statements of his client during the trial against those of perhaps the most arguably incredible persons in our society—psychics. This is a strategic move, of course, especially given that the defense had striven hard to undermine the ethos of "The Gesturing Man." Here Norwood is effectively claiming that although his client may not be the most "well-adjusted" member of our society, he nonetheless should be dis-identified with persons who make

dubious claims to irk a living. In this way, having dis-identified himself from his client, he uses the process of identification to further
dis-identify his client from charlatans, and in doing is able to re-assert
the credibility undermined by Robinson.

Even more interesting than the way Norwood dis-identified his
client's statements from the actions of psychics is the way in which he
identified the defendant Jose Chacon. Instead of attacking Trooper
Chacon's character Norwood strategically and persistently did just
the opposite. For example, in his closing statement he claimed that
"Trooper Chacon, as far as I can tell, is a good man. He works a difficult job. There is nothing out of the ordinary about him whatsoever."[66] To further highlight the discrepancy between his client and
Trooper Chacon, strategically dis-identifying them from each other,
he even went so far as to say, "I don't have a really spit shined client
like the trooper sitting over there. [And] I'm not here to vilify Trooper
Chacon."[67] Near the end of his first closing argument Norwood would
further hyperbolize Chacon's character:

> There is not a black mark on Jose Chacon's record that I know of.
> Nice guy. No doubt in my mind that if you called Jose Chacon in
> the middle of the night and said "Jose somebody is breaking into
> my house," he'd strap that gun on, get in the patrol car, drive as
> fast as he could to your house, and if he had to, he'd whip three
> grizzly bears in your yard to get in there to help you. He's just that
> kind of guy. Jose Chacon is not a bad guy.[68]

Here Norwood identifies Chacon as an upstanding police officer, as someone that can be trusted, a characteristic which the jury,
Chacon, and Norwood purportedly share. Of course, this process of
identification between Chacon and the jury is strategic, and is in fact
a larger process of assigning responsibility to Trooper Chacon.

The notion of responsibility is pivotal to Norwood's argument,
and the word itself is liberally peppered throughout his closing arguments. In his closing statements he mentions the term at least four
times and even begins his closing statement by stating, "this case is
about accepting responsibility for what you do."[69] Arguing that the
average citizen is forced to accept the responsibility of their actions
when they are stopped by the police, Norwood argued that despite

Chacon's outstanding character he had not yet accepted responsibility for his actions and that he still "[did] not think that he . . . did something wrong," and that "in his mind he still thinks that he still should have written that guy a ticket and stopped him."[70] Norwood argued that if he were to theoretically run someone over on his way to lunch that day he would have to accept the full responsibility of the law, and that he wouldn't be shown any favors on account of his being a lawyer, and furthermore that Chacon "has to be treated like everybody else when he messes up."[71] In his rebuttal argument Norwood would again state that the average citizen had a responsibility to the law and that when one commits a crime, "[Law-enforcement] expect[s] you to take responsibility."[72] Deftly marrying the processes of identification to that of the issue of responsibility Norwood argued, "I'm not trying to give you the idea that Jose Chacon is a bad guy. But . . . on this particular issue he was wrong and it is time for him to face up to his responsibility. To do otherwise is basically to say the Constitution doesn't apply to Wayne Nichols . . . because we don't like these people; we like these people over here . . . Jose, you're a great guy but on this day you made the wrong call."[73]

Aside from identifying Chacon as an upstanding character, as one who wouldn't shirk from accepting responsibility for his actions, Norwood also raised the "specter of the state" and warned the jurors of the potential threat posed to the Constitution in this case. Norwood relied heavily upon the element of fear to make his argument persuasive and he frequently warned against not taking the case seriously, despite it being "a quirky case . . . almost like a man bites dog case."[74] In his closing argument he said:

> Ladies and gentlemen, I assure you that whatever you do here today is going to be reported in the press and every officer in northwest Arkansas is going to look at it . . . If the message is this that the juries do not take these cases seriously, the police are not going to take them seriously . . . I can assure you if you give this man nothing, that's going to be in the press. The police are going to read that and they're going to go what incentive do we not have to arrest somebody that's up there flapping their gums at me or they flipped me off or they say something I don't like or they cuss me. They're going to go, hey, I remember this case a few years ago. The jury just blew it off, didn't give the guy a

dime. I ain't got nothing to worry about. And that's the danger in these kind of cases because the great majority of police officers are just like Jose Chacon . . . if you all don't be fair to this man and fairly compensate him, the word is going to get out, and the word is that juries don't care and I think that's going to be a very bad thing.[75]

At the end of his rebuttal argument Norwood would further fuel the metaphorical fires of fear he had instilled in the jury, though in a bit more-subtle and indirect manner. Norwood says, at the very end of his rebuttal argument, "Now I give you credit, he didn't haul him off to jail and handcuff him. *He didn't stomp on him, try to break his fingers, poke his eye out, or nothing like that.*[76] Jose Chacon ain't that kind of guy."[77] What is interesting to note here is the placement of these final lines and the vivid imagery they suggest. Indeed, the entirety of Norwood's rebuttal to Robinson hinged on the notion of fear and violence, and this was the last argument that the jury heard before they began deliberation. Here Norwood raised the metaphorical "specter of the state," explicitly warning the jurors of what could be, assured the jury that violence done by that state is an inevitability, and then commenced by painting a very heinous picture for the jury to contemplate during deliberation. Of course, soon after he crafts this image he makes it very clear that "Jose Chacon ain't that kind of guy,"[78] but this only strengthens his argument, as it suggests that just because Chacon isn't "that kind of guy" it doesn't guarantee that another officer won't be. Norwood had already established that the decision of the jury is one that will not be taken lightly by law enforcement, and earlier in the case he alluded to the gravity of Supreme Court decisions and their importance in professional legal circles when he said, "When the Supreme Court says something, a lot of people in the street they don't think too much about it. All the lawyers listen. Supreme Court says something, my what's the new law."[79] Like lawyers, it was intimated that members of law enforcement are going to be paying attention to the jury's decision and that it was going to have a very tangible effect upon their behavior. The only thing standing between the potentially heinous violation of the Constitution and the average citizen was the jury's decision in this matter. And just as he had deployed the notion of responsibility to criticize Chacon, Norwood extended the notion to include the jury's *responsibility* to defend the Constitution just like "the

Constitution is defended in little courthouses across America every
day on little cases like this."[80] An adept, if not impassioned rhetor,
Norwood identified the players in this case in extremely pragmatic
terms—he didn't attempt to justify the nature of his client's actions
or even undermine the ethos of Chacon, he simply argued that they
were who they were, and that one of them had yet to own up to his
responsibility. Conveying an ethos of fear to the jury he raises the
ugly "specter of the state," crafting a heinous picture of possibility, nay,
inevitability, and saddles the jury with the responsibility of protecting
that most sacred of documents.

And his rhetorical strategy proved effective. Despite the insis-
tence of the presiding judge that the trial would be a quick one and
would commence that day,[81] the jury took all evening and even part
of the following morning to deliberate before issuing their verdict.[82]
As mentioned previously, the verdict stating that Chacon owed $2,000
in compensatory damages and $2,000 in punitive damages[83]—replete
with a request that Chacon write a letter of apology to Mr. Nichols—
was a shock to both Nichols, his attorney,[84] and the court. It seems that
Norwood's arguments carried some weight and that the jury took to
heart his appeal to take the case seriously.

Yet despite the jury's explicit stance on the issue of damages, as
evidenced by their request for a written apology from Chacon, the
court decided to vacate the punitive damages award and in doing
so, effectively undermined the judicial process, setting an ominous
precedent for future Supreme Court cases dealing with the gesture.
During the trial on damages there seem to have been some discrepancies between the amount and nature of damages as determined during
discovery and the damages claimed by Nichols during examination.[85]
After Norwood's initial examination of Nichols, Robinson requested
to approach the bench, and questioned the veracity of Nichols's claims,
stating:

> Your Honor, we conducted discovery in this case where I specif-
> ically asked for any notes or anything that had been taken, any
> itemized account of damages or anything sought in connection
> with this complaint. I was told there wasn't anything written
> down. I was told that damages would be determined by a jury.
> We have not seen any sort of financial sheet or information to
> support these losses. We asked questions in discovery in deposi-

tion and weren't given any of this information in the discovery phase . . . none of this diary that Mr. Nichols is referring to has not been disclosed to the defendant. This is the first time that we've heard of any of the information that he's told us about here, about detailing the damages.[86]

Arguably confused as to how to proceed, Waters responded to Robinson's argument, saying, "I'm not sure how detail [*sic*] he has. The jury can decide that," and, "You're going to have to cross-examine the witness, and the jury will decide," and even, "It's certainly a little speculative, I would agree with that, but that is something the jury will have to determine."[87] After a considerable grilling of Nichols and repeated cross-examination by both lawyers, Robinson concluded by asking the plaintiff if he was aware that discovery was an ongoing process, to which he answered no.[88] During a short recess the court conferenced again to discuss possible motions and Robinson also admitted that she was unsure how to proceed in this matter, not having tried a trial on damages before; she claimed:

> I'm not exactly sure if it's proper for me to ask for judgment as a matter of law on the entire issue of damages since there has not been any evidence provided. But at least on the way of punitive damages, I would certainly ask for judgment as a matter of law. There has been no demonstration of evil motive, reckless disregard, callous indifference, anything that's required in the punitive damage instruction. At most we've seen that Mr. Nichols may have some out-of-pocket expense, if that, but we haven't seen any documentation to support that either. So I would at the very least ask for a judgment as a matter of law on the punitive damages and if it's possible, then on the entire issue as well.[89]

In response the court agreed that the damages were "somewhat speculative," and said that if the court needed to investigate it further they would do so after the jury reached a verdict.[90] Denying the motion, Waters decided to reserve ruling on the punitive damages, and again asserted, "We are going to let the jury consider it . . . we are . . . going to let the jury decide the case."[91] Soon after addressing the issue to the jurors Waters would state:

> I am going to go ahead and let the jury consider, while we're here, the punitive damages issue. I, however, recognize the defendant's

record in respect to that. I think the jury could decide, it may be thin, but I think the jury could decide that the defendant was callously indifferent to the plaintiff's free speech rights there. I would agree that the other things such as motivated by evil and motivated by interest is obviously not present, but I think the callous indifference might be a jury question . . . if we need to, we will look at it at the close of the jury verdict.[92]

As evidenced, the court explicitly stated on numerous occasions that they were going to let the jury decide this case, and indeed, even the issue of punitive damages. Yet in conference the court also claimed that following the verdict they would determine whether or not motions for judgment as a matter of law were necessary. What does this imply? Well, it suggests that if the jury was to reach a verdict not approved of by the court, then, and only then, could motions be made to vacate the jury's decision and grant judgment as a matter of law. Here is the first instance of judicial process being undermined; as evidenced, the court meditated upon this issue and decided to reserve judgment until after the verdict had been reached.

After the jury reached its verdict the following day, Robinson again raised the issue of motions, to which Waters agreed he would allow in the form of a written, post-trial motion.[93] In a memorandum opinion on September 6, 2000, the court acknowledged the motion of the defendant to vacate both the compensatory and punitive damage awards and grant judgment as a matter of law, or in the alternative, a new trial, and outlined its decision to vacate the punitive damages award.[94] Concerning the motion, Judge Waters described his decision:

> While there was testimony that Chacon was angered by Nichols' action and did not realize the action was considered constitutionally protected speech, we do not believe these facts, standing alone, support an award of punitive damages. Aside from his having been angered by the gesture, a reaction no doubt common to those on the receiving end of the gesture, there is little else to suggest that Chacon's conduct was serious enough to warrant punitive damages. *After carefully watching defendant as he testified, and after listening to his testimony, this court is convinced that he sincerely believed that he was enforcing the law when he stopped plaintiff and issued a citation.*[95] The fact that he turned out, in this court's view, to be wrong, does not mean that his con-

duct was "motivated by evil motive or intent" or was in "reckless or callous indifference to the federally protected rights of others." In short we believe that, as a matter of law, Chacon's conduct is not the sort that calls for deterrence and punishment over and above that provided by compensatory damages. *We believe the imposition of punitive damages should be reserved for conduct more egregious than that involved in this case.*[96]

Rationalizing his decision to both allow the jury to deliberate on the issue of punitive damages and to inevitably vacate the punitive damages, in a footnote to his Memorandum, Waters writes:

Thus, although the court had serious doubt about the punitive damages claim, the jury was allowed to consider this issue at the same time to avoid the possibility of having to retry that issue in case of a reversal on appeal. The Court of Appeals for the 8th Circuit has advised trial courts that this is the better practice.[97]

Citing two former cases tried by the Eighth Circuit,[98] Waters rationalizes his decision by claiming that there is a precedent that has been set by the Eighth Circuit, and that his decision was a strategic one preventing the possibility of having to retry the issue in the court of appeals. While this may be the true, and for the sake of efficiency may indeed be pragmatic, it doesn't negate the fact that the issue of punitive damages was nonetheless vacated by the courts. It appears that the precedent and practices of the Eighth Circuit created an opportunity by which judicial process and the role of juries in determining cases was severely undermined. An Eighth Circuit technicality undermined the power of the jury to assess damages and in doing so undermined the very principles upon which the Sixth Amendment was founded.[99] This was the second moment following the trial in which judicial process was undermined.

Additionally, Waters acknowledges his own subjective interpretation in determining the character of Chacon when he states, "After carefully watching defendant as he testified, and after listening to his testimony, this court is convinced that he sincerely believed that he was enforcing the law when he stopped plaintiff and issued a citation."[100] But is this a decision for Waters to make in this situation, and if so, how does this augment or undermine the role of the jury in determining such matters? Implicit in this statement is the notion that the state is better equipped to assess the character and conduct of law enforcement than its citizens, and that the state can determine for itself how properly or in what manner the state has acted. In discussing the compensatory damages, which were upheld by the court, Waters claimed, "The jury spoke, and the court concludes that reasonable jurors could reach the verdict that they reached in respect to compensatory damages. *The law simply does not permit this court to substitute its judgment for that of the jury.*"[101] Yet, soon after this statement Waters did just that, he substituted the judgment of the court for that of the jury on the punitive damages issues. And despite the court being "surprised" by the jury's assessment of punitive damages and their request that Officer Chacon write a letter of apology to Nichols, a fact which Waters explicitly commented upon in his Memorandum,[102] it nonetheless stands that the jury did decide to award punitive damages. That they requested a written letter of apology from Chacon should only highlight the significance of their decision and the gravity that they believed this case held. This is the third instance in which the power of the jury was undermined by Judge Waters.

In a written appeal to the Eighth Circuit, Nichols's representing attorney would highlight this incredibly problematic decision of the court, arguing:

> The trial court erred in granting the appellee's Motion for Judgment as a Matter of Law because the record contained sufficient evidence from which the jury could infer that Trooper Chacon acted maliciously when he gave Nichols a ticket for "flipping him off."[103]

In his appeal Norwood stated that the trial judge "improperly invaded the province of the jury," and acknowledged that the district judge "clearly substituted his own assessment of Chacon's testimony for that of the jury,"[104] an act expressly forbidden by *Berry v. United States*[105] and *Reeves v. Sanderson Plumbing Products, Inc.*[106] Norwood would also point out that the request for an apology on behalf of the jury "points to the likelihood that the jury did believe that Trooper Chacon had acted with a spiteful, vindictive, or malicious intention to punish Nichols for his behavior," and that clearly, "the jury inferred something more from Trooper Chacon's behavior than merely a mistaken understanding of the law."[107] In the second argument of his appeal Norwood would claim:

> The trial court erred in granting Chacon's Motion for Judgment as a Matter of Law because reasonable jurors could be outraged that a citizen's free speech rights were infringed by an experienced, well-trained police officer.[108]

Raising the issue of competence, once again using Chacon's outstanding character to highlight the absurd nature of his actions, Norwood argued:

> reasonable jurors could well be outraged that a state trooper with nearly seventeen years' experience did not know the application of the so-called "fighting words" doctrine to police officers and that such an experienced trooper would therefore take Nichols' conduct personally . . . simply because the police officer had the power to punish the appellant and wished to do so. Surely, such conduct merits the award of punitive damages, as an example and a deterrent to other officers who might not otherwise have the necessary self-control in the face of "a significant amount of verbal challenge and criticism."[109]

Yet despite these valid and well-cited criticisms the Eighth Circuit ultimately decided to uphold Judge Waters's decision to vacate the punitive damages award against Chacon. In her rebuttal to Norwood's written appeal Sheri Robinson would argue that due to the fact that no motion was made during the trial on behalf of Nichols the appeal should be barred, and that there was insufficient evidence to support Nichols's claims.[110] To support her arguments she would cite two Eighth Circuit cases[111] and claim that technical discrepancies during the case allowed for the judge to act as he did. Her statement here again demonstrates that, due to a technicality, judicial process in this case was allowed to be undermined. But perhaps more important than this is the sort of precedent this sets for future cases dealing with symbolic expression and First Amendment protection of speech.

A number of scholars have argued that the gesture's relationship to the First Amendment is one that is fairly convoluted, and have documented the courts' continued expansion of the definition of "expressive speech" to include other forms of communication such as flag burning, draft card burning, wearing armbands,[112] arguing that the courts have even entertained the notion of "protest sleeping" as a form of protected speech.[113] Others have criticized the way the courts have handled the issue of what constitutes speech and have argued against classifying speech based on "value,"[114] privileging form over content,[115] and failing to address author intent.[116] Still others have focused instead upon the failure of the "Fighting Words Doctrine" and have argued that obscenity laws are often enforced in arbitrary ways,[117] that the courts have been ambiguous in determining which speech to subsidize and censor,[118] have failed to account for the emotional injury incurred in racial epithets and other forms of hate speech,[119] protected speech objectively more offensive than the speech censored in the *Chaplinsky* case,[120] and have effectively outlined the potential dangers to democracy in deploying such ambiguous jurisprudence.[121] Yet, despite these thorough studies outlining the intricacies of First Amendment jurisprudence, few, if any, of these scholars discuss the issue of punitive damages and the courts' willingness or unwillingness to impose prohibitive sanctions against future abuses of citizens' First Amendment rights. Fewer still have outlined the relationship between First Amendment jurisprudence, the issue of damages, and the precedent the issue of damages sets for future cases.

In this case the Eighth Circuit set a dangerous precedent for future First Amendment jurisprudence and effectively demonstrated the Supreme Court's ability to undermine the power of juries and the judicial process more generally. In vacating the punitive damages award against Chacon the court thoroughly trumped the power of the jury, established that the subjective interpretations of judges during the trial carry more weight than verdicts handed down by juries, and clearly communicated that unfounded arrests of citizens exercising their First Amendment rights are not egregious enough to warrant prohibitive sanctions against law enforcement. The message of the Eighth Circuit is clear: the actions of the state are more heavily protected than the rights of its citizens, effectively confirming Mr. Nichols's statement, garnered during my interview with him and his brother, that "We care more about Civil Rights and the First Amendment than our own fucking government does."[122]

Throughout this paper I have made a sort of hybrid argument

pertaining to both the rhetorical processes at work throughout the trial on damages, so very pivotal to the outcome of this case, and the precedent set forth by the Eighth Circuit in determining this issue and inevitably vacating the punitive damages award against Chacon. I contend that Robinson interpellated Nichols as "The Gesturing Man" so as to undermine his ethos and present him as morally deficient, narrowly limiting the issue to one of unwarranted damages. Norwood engaged in a complex process of identification and dis-identification, framing the issue as one of responsibility, effectively raising the "specter of the state" and warning the jurors of the potential threat posed to the Constitution in their decision. Finally, it is concluded in this paper that the entire judicial process was undermined when the court granted judgment as matter of law and vacated the punitive damages against Trooper Chacon. The significance of the arguments herein should not be understated. In accordance with other legal scholars who have identified the inherent nature of the law as one embodying the fundamental principles and practices of rhetoric, this paper examined the rhetorical practices at play within this case and the rhetorical forms at work within this case that were crucial to the way it would eventually be resolved. Furthermore, legal nuances and technicalities reify the power of the state, undermining judicial processes and setting a dangerous precedent for future cases in the same vein. At the very least this article provides a foundational template for those wishing to engage in future historical or legal research on this matter and should prove informative to those who may once again wish to reawaken and re-instigate the scholarly conversation concerning the middle finger and the First Amendment.

NOTES

1. Admittedly, this gesture has been used in my own social circles to indicate "hello" in an amiable, if not entirely crude, manner.

2. For an exhaustive list of meanings implicit in the gesture as traced through contemporary pop culture, see Ira P. Robbins, "*Digitus Impudicus*: The Middle Finger and the Law," *American University Washington College of Law* 41 (2008): 1403–85. Accessed February 11, 2015. This article is the only law review article that deals explicitly with the use of the "finger" in relation to the Supreme Court and First Amendment protection of said gesture.

3. M. J. Loheed, Matt Patterson, Eddie Schmidt, and Stephanie Hernstadt, "The

History of the Finger," in *The Finger: A Comprehensive Guide to Flipping Off* (Peteluma, CA: Acid Test Productions, 1998), 11.

4. Ibid., 12.

5. Ibid. The play was not, coincidentally, a success, and Aristophanes later augmented the joke to be less vulgar.

6. Robbins, "*Digitus Impudicus*," 1414.

7. Peter Sloterdijk, "Critique of Cynical Reason," *Theory and History of Literature*, ed. Wlad Godzich and Jochen Schulte-Sasse, 3–4. Vol. 40. (Minneapolis: University of Minnesota Press, 1987). This text has served as an excellent guide to those undertaking a study of Cynicism historically and theoretically.

8. Loheed et al., *The Finger*, 13.

9. Or set of names, including, *digitus infimus* (infamous finger), *digitus obscenusus* (obscene finger), *digitus famousus* (finger of fame), *digito destinare* (finger of destiny), *digito petulans* (wanton finger), *digito improbum* (wicked finger), *digito lascivus* (lascivious finger); Loheed et al., *The Finger,* 13.

10. Ibid.

11. Desmond Morris, Peter Collett, Peter Marsh, and Marie O'Shaughnessy, "The Forearm Jerk," in *Gestures: Their Origins and Distributions* (London: Johnathan Cape, 1979), 82.

12. Loheed et al., *The Finger*, 15.

13. For an exhaustive list of variations of the gesture, see Roger E. Axtell, "The Most Popular Gestures," in *Gestures: The Dos and Taboos of Body Language around the World* (New York: John Wiley & Sons, 1991), 30–33.

14. *State v. Anonymous*, 377 A.2d 1342, 1343 (Conn. Super. Ct. 1977); *Mitchell v. State*, 580 A.2d 196, 198 (Md. 1990); *Brockway v. Shepherd*, 942 F. Supp. 1012, 1015 (M.D. Pa. 1996); *Commonwealth v. Kelly*, 758 A.2d 1284, 1285 (Pa. Super. Ct. 2000); *Coggin v. Texas*, 123 S.W.3d 82, 90 n.3 (Tex. App. 2003).

15. Hutchens would later become a bailiff for Judge Klinger in Benton County and was soon after arrested for having child pornography on his computer at the courthouse; after a stint in prison he was released and was again caught for having child pornography. Doug Norwood claimed that he was one of the nicest guys he ever met. Doug Norwood, interview with the author, March 3, 2015.

16. 6. *Nichols v. Chacon*, 110 F. Supp. 2d 1099, 1110 (W.D. Ark. 2000).

17. 7. Ibid.

18. According to a recent interview with Nichols and his brother, Wayne had been forced out of the wrecking service when a new deputy was charged with handling highway clean-up. Prior to that Wayne and his twin brother had been regularly depended upon to tow damaged and inoperable vehicles from Benton County roads. Wayne claims that when the deputy retired he was told by the new officer in charge that he would have to obtain a towing license, join a towing association, and pay regular dues, a requirement that Nichols stated was illegal given Arkansas's "Right-to-Work" laws (Wayne claimed they wanted $150/year, and that he was told that it was best to donate to the trooper fund if they wanted to be considered for the list). The day before the incident, Hutchens had apparently stopped by Nichols's salvage yard and threatened to arrest him and take his tow truck if he should catch him operating without the license. Interestingly, both Nichols brothers claim that

when they were teenagers it was common knowledge that Chacon was "an illegal," and that he was only given his job as state trooper because he was bilingual; Wayne and Dwayne Nichols, interview with the author, April 11, 2015.

19. Nichols was cited with a disorderly conduct charge under Ark.Code Ann. § 5-71-207(a)(3); *Nichols v. Chacon*, 110 F. Supp. 2d 1099, 1110 (W.D. Ark. 2000).

20. *Nichols v. Chacon*, 110 F. Supp. 2d 1099, 1110 (W.D. Ark. 2000).

21. 1 315 U.S. 568 (1942).

22. 2 *Nichols v. Chacon*, 110 F. Supp. 2d 1099, 1110 (W.D. Ark. 2000).

23. Ibid.

24. Doug Norwood.

25. *Nichols v. Chacon*, No. 00-3331WAF, Mem. Op. & J. (W.D. Ark. September 6, 2000), 10.

26. In my interview with Norwood, he claimed that Frank Waters was a very well-respected guy, and that other judges in the state looked up to him, his statements carrying more weight than perhaps was typical; Interview with Doug Norwood.

27. Trial Tr., vol. 2, 4, August 9, 2000.

28. In layman's terms this simply means a request to have judgment determined by the courts (i.e., the judge), effectively trumping the jury's verdict—an issue which has considerable precedent in the Eighth Circuit, and one which we'll soon see became a pivotal one in determining the final outcome of this case; *Nichols v. Chacon*, No. 00-3331WAF, Mem. Op. & J. (W.D. Ark. September 6, 2000).

29. *Nichols v. Chacon*, No. 00-3331WAF, Mem. Op. & J. (W.D. Ark. September 6, 2000).

30. Kenneth Burke, "The Range of Rhetoric," in *A Rhetoric of Motives*, 1st ed. (New York: Prentice Hall, 1950).

31. Louis Althusser and Ben Brewster, trans., "Ideology and Ideological State Apparatuses (Notes towards an Investigation): On the Reproduction of the Conditions of Production," in *Lenin and Philosophy and Other Essays*, 127–86. (New York: Monthly Review Press, 1971), 127–86.

32. Trial Tr. vol. 1, 1–111, August 8, 2000.

33. Ibid., 53.

34. Ibid.

35. Ibid.

36. Ibid.

37. During my interview with Nichols he was quick to point out that his record was and had been clean his entire life, a characteristic his twin brother Dwayne apparently did not share, though his three felony convictions had been successfully expunged; Interview with Wayne and Dwayne Nichols.

38. Rebecca Pilcher, "Gesturing Men Sue Police, Say Arrests Violated Rights," *Arkansas Democrat-Gazette*, November 3, 1999. Regarding reporters: Wayne Nichols initially refused to do an interview with me, though later was gracious enough to do so; he claimed that he had put all of this behind him and that he had been duped and used by the media, first, when a young man, identified only as "Jesop" (Jesop Holloway, a reporter for Fox 24) posed as a college student and then manipulated Wayne's words to write a sensational story, and second, when the local media did a

lengthy camera interview with Wayne and then proceeded to only air a short snippet wherein Wayne was shown claiming that "If the president of the United States rolled up, I'd give him the finger"; Interview with Wayne and Dwayne Nichols.

39. Known simply as "Chris"; Interview with Wayne and Dwayne Nichols.

40. The gesture was displayed to officer Jim Yarber, and unlike Wayne, Chris was arrested and held at the Benton County Jail; charges were dropped against him around March 31, 2000; of note is the fact that the article in the *Democrat-Gazette* references Chris as being of no relation to Wayne; see Andy Davis, "Jury Considers Award in Free-speech Case Judge Ruled Man Was Wrongly Ticketed for Gesture," *Arkansas Democrat-Gazette*, August 9, 2000.

41. Davis, "Jury Considers Award in Free-speech Case Judge Ruled Man Was Wrongly Ticketed for Gesture."

42. Ibid.

43. Trial Tr. vol. 1, 66, August 8, 2000; emphasis mine.

44. Ibid.

45. Althusser, "Ideologies and Ideological State Apparatuses," 174.

46. Ibid.

47. Ibid.

48. Trial Tr., vol. 1, 89, August 8, 2000.

49. Ibid.

50. In an interview with Wayne he claimed that he never wrote Chacon a letter of apology, despite the fact that he and others allude to this letter multiple times during the course of the trial; Interview with Wayne and Dwayne Nichols.

51. As we will soon see, Norwood repeatedly distanced himself from his client and his actions during the trial in a series of complex identifications and dis-identifications before the jury. Emphasis mine.

52. Trial Tr., vol. 1, 89–90, August 8, 2000.

53. Emphasis mine.

54. Trial Tr., vol. 1, 92, August 8, 2000.

55. Ibid.

56. A interview with Doug Norwood openly acknowledges the significance of this case in American law and, indeed, Norwood claimed that he took this case because it could be used in the future in strategic ways. According to Norwood, Chacon was "very good for business," in that he had a particular way of "ruffling people's feathers" and Norwood wanted a trial to end this behavior and effectively set a precedent for law enforcement throughout the county. (Norwood even claimed he represented a client who was upset that he was forced to put out his Cuban cigar when Chacon stopped to help him with a flat tire.) Following the trial Norwood was able to do just that, claiming that he was able to "walk" (settle out of court) 15–20 clients based solely on the precedent set forth in this Eighth Circuit trial; Interview with Doug Norwood. When first approached with this case by Wayne and Dwayne Nichols, Wayne claimed that Norwood leaned back in his chair and said, "I've been waiting for this case for 30 years"; Interview with Wayne Nichols.

57. Emphasis mine.

58. Trial Tr., vol. 1, 88, August 8, 2000.

59. Burke, "A Rhetoric of Motives," 20–21.

60. Ibid., 46.

61. Interestingly, when I first interviewed Norwood this was the way that he described Wayne—as a country boy with long, greasy hair. Norwood also claimed that he was a gentle man, not particularly interested in violence; Interview with Doug Norwood. In my interview with Wayne Nichols these characteristics were confirmed; for example, after describing their large cache of guns and armor piercing rounds, Wayne explicitly claimed that he did not hunt, but rather, preferred to feed the deer on his land (though the neighbor was known to fatally wound them, a fact that upset Wayne); Wayne and his brother also claimed to be thoroughly trained in the art of san soo, Kung-Fu, a style Dwayne claimed was practiced by Steven Segal; Interview with Wayne and Dwayne Nichols. Trial Tr., vol. 1, 82, August 8, 2000.

62. Trial Tr., vol. 1, 82, August 8, 2000.

63. Ibid., 81.

64. Ibid., 84.

65. Ibid.

66. Ibid., 82.

67. Ibid.

68. Ibid., 87.

69. Ibid., 81.

70. Ibid.

71. Ibid., 82.

72. Ibid., 93.

73. Ibid., 93–94.

74. Ibid., 84.

75. Ibid., 85–87.

76. Emphasis mine.

77. Trial Tr., vol. 1, 94, August 8, 2000.

78. Ibid.

79. Ibid., 85.

80. Ibid., 86.

81. Ibid., 17.

82. Wayne claimed that the reason the jury took so long to deliberate is because of one "damned Yankee" on the jury panel who didn't want to give him his due. Interview with Wayne and Dwayne Nichols. Norwood had a slightly different take on the jury, and claimed that there was one particular juror who stood out to him, and that she was "very into that First Amendment thing." Interview with Doug Norwood.

83. Trial Tr., vol. 2, 1–2, August 9, 2000.

84. Norwood claimed that he was "shocked" and had not anticipated the verdict from the jury; Interview with Doug Norwood.

85. Trial Tr., vol. 1, 58–76, August 8, 2000.

86. Ibid., 59–60.

87. Ibid., 60.

88. Ibid., 73.

89. Ibid., 74–75.

90. Ibid., 75.

91. Ibid.

92. Ibid., 77.

93. Trial Tr., vol. 2, 4, August 9, 2000.

94. *Nichols v. Chacon*, No. 00-3331WAF, Mem. Op. & J. (W.D. Ark. September 6, 2000).

95. Emphasis mine.

96. Emphasis mine. *Nichols v. Chacon*, No. 00-3331WAF, Mem. Op. & J. (W.D. Ark. September 6, 2000), 12.

97. Ibid.

98. *Dale v. Janklow*, 828 F.2d 481 (8th Cir. 1987); *Dace v. ACF Industries, Inc.*, 722 F.2d 374 (8th Cir. 1983).

99. U.S. Const. Amend. VI: "In all criminal prosecutions, the accused shall enjoy the right to a speedy and public trial, by an impartial jury of the State and district wherein the crime shall have been committed."

100. *Nichols v. Chacon*, No. 00-3331WAF, Mem. Op. & J. (W.D. Ark. September 6, 2000), 12.

101. *Nichols v. Chacon*, No. 00-3331WAF, Mem. Op. & J. (W.D. Ark. September 6, 2000), 10. Emphasis mine.

102. In a footnote on page 10, Waters writes, "Frankly, the court was surprised by the indignation level expressed by this jury in a question sent to the court during deliberation and in the notation made on the punitive damage verdict form described above, attempting to compel the defendant to apologize, in writing, to plaintiff"; *Nichols v. Chacon*, No. 00-3331WAF, Mem. Op. & J. (W.D. Ark. September 6, 2000), 10.

103. Brief of Petitioner-Appellant, *Nichols v. Chacon*, No. 2000-3331 (8th Cir. November 2000), 19.

104. Brief of Petitioner-Appellant, *Nichols v. Chacon*, No. 2000-3331 (8th Cir. November 2000), 24.

105. *Berry v. United States*, 312 U.S. 450 (1941).

106. *Reeves v. Sanderson Plumbing Products, Inc.*, 120 S. Ct. 2097 (2000).

107. Brief of Petitioner-Appellant, *Nichols v. Chacon*, No. 2000-3331 (8th Cir. November 2000), 24–25.

108. Ibid., 26.

109. Ibid., 28–29; Citing *Houston v. Hill*, 482 U.S. 451, 462, 107 S. Ct. 2502, 2510, 96 L.Ed.2d 398 (1986).

110. Brief of Petitioner-Appellee, *Nichols v. Chacon*, No. 00-3331 (8th Cir. December 13, 2000).

111. *Goff v. Bise*, 173 F.3d 1068 (8th Cir. 1999); *Heating & Air Specialists, Inc. v. Jones* (8th Cir. 1999).

112. Vincent Blasi, "The Checking Value in First Amendment Theory," *American Bar Foundation Research Journal* 2, no. 3 (1977): 521–649.

113. Laurie Magid, "First Amendment Protection of Ambiguous Conduct," *Columbia Law Review* 84, no. 2 (1984): 467–505.

114. Jeffrey M. Shaman, "The Theory of Low-Value Speech," *SMU Law Review* 48 (1995): 297–348. Accessed February 18, 2015. Lexisnexis.

115. Robert Post, "Recuperating First Amendment Doctrine," *Stanford Law Review* 47, no. 6 (1995): 1249. Paul Berckmans, "The Semantics of Symbolic Speech," *Law and Philosophy* 16, no. 2 (1997): 145–76.

116. Joshua Waldman, "Speech and Social Meaning," *Columbia Law Review* 97, no. 6 (1997): 1844–94. Frederick Schauer, "Intentions, Conventions, and the First Amendment: The Case of Cross-Burning," *Supreme Court Review, 2003* (2003): 197–230; Michael J. Mannheimer, "The Fighting Words Doctrine," *Columbia Law Review* 93, no. 6 (1993): 1527–71.

117. Mark C. Rutzick, "Offensive Language and the Evolution of First Amendment Protection," *Harvard Civil Rights-Civil Liberties Law Review* 9, no. 1 (1974): 1–28.

118. Elena Kagan, "The Changing Faces of First Amendment Neutrality: *R.A.V. v St. Paul, Rust v Sullivan*, and the Problem of Content-Based Underinclusion," *Supreme Court Review, 1992* (1992): 29–77.

119. "The Demise of the 'Chaplinsky' Fighting Words Doctrine: An Argument for Its Interment," *Harvard Law Review* 106, no. 5 (1993): 1129–46.

120. Burton Caine, "The Trouble with 'Fighting Words': *Chaplinsky v. New Hampshire* Is a Threat to First Amendment Values and Should Be Overruled," *Marquette Law Review* 88, no. 3 (2004): 441–562.

121. Linda Friedlieb, "The Epitome of an Insult: A Constitutional Approach to Designated Fighting Words," *University of Chicago Law Review* 72, no. 1 (2005): 385–415.

122. Wayne and Dwayne Nichols, interview.

CHAPTER 12

Rhetorical Continuity

Evolution, Creation Science, and Intelligent Design

MATTHEW McNAIR

In 2005, Judge John E. Jones III, a George H. W. Bush appointee presiding over the United States District Court for the Middle District of Pennsylvania, handed down the verdict in *Tammy Kitzmiller et al. v. Dover Area School District*, a case in which the court found the decision of the Dover, Pennsylvania, school board to sticker science textbooks in the district to be one of "breathtaking inanity." In this context, to "sticker" a textbook means to plaster a junior- or high school science primer with a disclaimer noting that many scientific theories—not limited to, but prominently including, the theory of biological evolution—are theories in the conventional sense, that is, mere guesses. Reading the decision of Judge Jones, one can only presume that "breathtaking inanity," in this context, means nothing but.[1]

When the decision in *Kitzmiller* was delivered, the action under scrutiny was only the latest in a long line of attacks on sound science by proponents of creation science, or the idea that all the physical world springs from the supernatural hand of a supreme being, and that science can—and, more importantly, *must*—prove this contention empirically. The *Kitzmiller* debacle was one of two federal cases

decided in 2005 that dealt with the practice of adding creationist disclaimers to science textbooks, which practice was something of a fad
at the time, and at the time of this writing, the last major push by the
antievolution movement to circumvent, via the public schools, the
constitutional prohibition on religious endorsement by local, state, or
federal governments.[2]

The outcome of *Kitzmiller* was as close to a foregone conclusion as
one is likely to get in the realm of constitutional law, and it is unlikely
that any serious observer of the case ever truly doubted that the ruling
would hold for the plaintiffs. Judge Jones, a Republican-appointed,
conservative jurist, used a fairly simple and straightforward eviden-
tiary chain to find the Dover disclaimers unconstitutional. It was a
chain, moreover, laden with precedent, the most obvious and recent
being *Edwards v. Aguillard* (1987), a case originating in Louisiana that
dealt with "balanced treatment," a once-popular creationist demand
that government require public schools to give time, commensurate
with evolution, to creationist viewpoints in the science classroom.
This preceded both the disclaimer fad of the early 2000s, and also
the rise of "Intelligent Design" (ID) theory, itself a more sophisticated
form of creation science. In *Aguillard*, the High Court decreed that
the philosophical underpinnings of creation science were inherently religious in nature, and that regardless of a state legislature's
attempt to scrub sectarian language from a creation-science bill, or of
creation-scientists to denude textbooks of overt religious references,
the presentation of the supernatural as cause for the natural, in a science classroom, unequivocally means an endorsement of religion by
the government.

While Jones relied on *Edwards*, the obvious Supreme Court precedent, in his *Kitzmiller* decision, another case receives prominent mention during what, at times, borders on a jurisprudential diatribe. The
case in question is *McLean v Arkansas* (1982), decided in the Eastern
District of Arkansas by Judge William Overton. The decision in
McLean was never appealed, and the subsequent hearing of *Edwards*
before the Supreme Court has forever relegated its predecessor to second fiddle in discussions of legal precedent when the national conversation turns to proselytizing in the science classroom. Nevertheless, an
examination of the run-up and execution of *McLean* reveals that the

contemporary rhetorical strategies of both creation-science advocates and church-state separatists were tried, tested, and adopted during the *McLean* proceedings. In fact, the rhetorical tactics employed by both sides in *Edwards* so closely mimicked those first used in *McLean* that transcripts of the former read like a rehash of the latter. Finally, William Overton, in his *McLean* decision, so thoroughly debunked the reasoning behind Arkansas's Act 590—the bill that prompted the lawsuit—that the simpatico Supreme Court decision in *Edwards* can actually be seen as watering down the precedent set for the High Court by Overton in *McLean* five years before.

Jurisprudential precedent aside, any student of the First Amendment concerned with the Establishment Clause and the integrity of the nation's public schools would do well to take a close look at the *McLean* proceedings, as the bill that spawned the case and the trial itself mark a turning point in one of the most relevant facets of the contemporary Establishment Clause conversation, and constitute the calcification of rhetorical tactics still in use by activists on both sides of the debate. With that in mind, the present note will provide a very brief history of this American conversation, survey the rhetorical tactics that led to Arkansas Act 590 and *McLean v. Arkansas*, and also examine the forceful and definitive opinion delivered by Judge William Overton, an opinion which, much more than that in *Edwards v. Aguillard*, has provided the philosophical and jurisprudential underpinnings of virtually every subsequent case treating the efforts of anti-evolutionists to circumvent and subvert the Establishment Clause through the engines of science and science education.

The Establishment Clause and the Darwinian Turn

The United States has always been a secular nation by design and by practice, if not by temperament. Beginning with a constitution that acknowledges no higher power than the people governed by that document, the early history of the Republic shows a dogged commitment to secularity in its early years through such documents as the pragmatically secular Treaty of Tripoli in 1797 and the more personable letter Thomas Jefferson sent to the Danbury Baptists in 1802. The former contains a clause in the eleventh article assuring the ruler of

Tripoli that the United States is in no way founded on the Christian religion, and therefore poses no inherent threat, ideological or otherwise, to any of the Islamic governments that then dotted the Barbary Coast.[3] More famously, Jefferson's 1802 letter assures the Danbury Baptists, fearful of religious persecution at the hands of the majority, non-Baptist population, that the words of the U.S. Constitution do indeed protect their right to religious freedom; it is in this letter that Jefferson asserts that the words of the First Amendment, in barring the U.S. Congress from endorsing or prohibiting the practice of this or that religion, has "thus [built] a wall of separation between Church & State."[4] In expressing this sentiment, Jefferson coined a phrase that now encapsulates both a founding principle of the United States of America and also one of its most contentious ongoing conversations.

How can this conversation be so contentious, or even extant, with such firm evidence pointing unambiguously to a strictly secular government? First and foremost, concomitant with indisputable evidence that the Founders intended the government of this country to be entirely free of the influences of state-sponsored religion, there are innumerable pieces of seemingly contradictory evidence that point to a common belief, among the same men, that some form of supernatural force governs the universe. Even in the Danbury letter, Thomas Jefferson—he of the famously abridged Bible, and perhaps the most demonstrably irreligious of the Founders—pays lip service to "the common father and creator of man," just as he gave a cursory nod to a "Creator" and "Nature's God" in the Declaration of Independence.[5] Just as the founding documents of the Republic and the writings of its Founders are replete with evidence of a political entity crafted with wholly secular intent, so too are those same documents chockablock with deference to, or at least recognition of, a force beyond human agency.

From the perspective of the First Amendment, the matter of the Founders' beliefs, lack thereof, or varying degrees of Christian orthodoxy have no bearing whatsoever on anything at all. Rhetorically, however, it would have been folly of the highest order to explicitly reject some form of divine seal of approval for the actions being taken by the colonies during the run-up to the American Revolution. Even in the midst of the Enlightenment, the overwhelming majority of the

American populace—any populace—no doubt harbored any number of strong religious convictions, and in order for the Founders to muster an army capable of giving battle to the most powerful nation on the planet, religious fervor would by necessity play a strong rhetorical role. Indeed, such fervor has historically contributed to revolution, and it is good rhetorical and motivational policy to punch religious buttons in a religious society. However, while in the popular American mythos the colonies were bastions of religious freedom, the reality is that different Protestant sects vied for dominance in colonial America, and dissenters were often harassed, sometimes jailed, and occasionally exiled.[6] This sectarian discord posed a distinct problem for the Founders, but secular reasoning for the revolution resonated across dogmatic lines, and the efforts of pamphleteer-preachers and the erudite, ecumenical Revolutionary leadership carried the day.[7]

In the wake of the Revolution, then, comes the Establishment Clause, and the clear, succinct statement that "Congress shall make no law regarding the establishment of religion, nor prohibit the free exercise thereof." While certainly a landmark and revolutionary bit of law making, the Establishment Clause had a relatively quiet jurisprudential life for nearly two hundred years. Despite rampant sectarianism in the colonial period and lingering animosity following the Revolution, the American populace remained, in matters of religion, more or less homogenous. Christianity was the order of the day—the *de facto* state religion—and "freedom of religion" basically meant that the government couldn't tell you what kind of Christian to be.[8] Consequently, from Ratification until the middle of the twentieth century—circa 1962—the Establishment Clause remained, for all intents and purposes, an untested legal framework.[9]

The fight that took so long to find a full hearing in the judicial system, however, had been brewing since the waning years of the nineteenth century. Underlying the coming storm was an increasingly heterogeneous population—ethnically, politically, and religiously—and a spectacular shift in scientific and religious worldviews. Owing in large part to the influx of nontraditional immigrants and the rise of social crises distinctly urban in nature, mainline Christian denominations began a process of modernization that brought about a shift in earthly focus and a liberalization of dogma, especially as that dogma applied to a literal interpretation of the Bible. As this process gained momentum, a countermovement rose up among those Christians who saw the trend toward modernity as disturbing at best, and most likely heretical.[10] One thing, one idea more than any other, catalyzed and calcified this shift: the theory of biological evolution.

Charles Darwin published *On the Origin of Species* in 1859, and while he was not the first person to posit evolution as an explanatory device, it was his synthesis of his own and others' ideas that convincingly articulated the paradigm-shifting theory to the world. As that world increasingly accepted this theory and began to apply it to disciplines other than biology, its influence spread outside of academia and into society at large. In America, Christian sects increasingly accepted the tenets of Darwinian evolution, which in turn abetted the turn to modernity as outlined above. While the fighting between Christians remained largely in-house until the early 1900s, the rift between conservative and progressive Christian sects, and between Fundamentalist Christianity and the modern world in general, was exposed in tumultuous fashion when the conversation found its way into the public schools, and the war of rhetoric became one of policy. The fight among Christians, sparked by this scientific idea, spread to the country at large as bickering church factions began to see implications of their internal struggle in all walks of life. Seeing these implications through the lens of widespread acceptance of Darwinian theory, and in turn seeing this theory promulgated in the nation's public schools, they perceived in the schoolroom the seeds of the entire world's undoing. This conviction led them to bypass purely sectarian debate and take their case to the state legislatures of the United States, and seek to enforce by legislative fiat what synods and councils and revivals could not: a society that accepted and promulgated a religiously homogenous view of the scientific and empirical world, and the transmission of that worldview to the country's children via the public schools and the science taught therein.

Arkansas and Creationism: Early and Often

Much as *Edwards* overshadows *McLean* in jurisprudential discussions of state-mandated scientific religiosity, so too does the infamous Scopes

Trial overshadow a contemporaneous, and much more important, event in Arkansas. The Scopes case—often referred to as the "Scopes Monkey Trial"—played out in the small town of Dayton, Tennessee, and centered on local high school biology teacher John T. Scopes. Scopes was teaching school in 1925, the same year that Fundamentalist Christian agitators and like-minded state legislators were able to pass a statute that made illegal the teaching of Darwinian theory in the state's public schools.[11] Scopes intentionally ran afoul of the law, and he was consequently arrested and charged with violating Tennessee's new anti-evolution statute.[12] The ensuing trial was an early example of a modern "media circus," and the inclusion of celebrity counsel—Clarence Darrow for the defense and William Jennings Bryan for the prosecution—added to the spectacle, and also foreshadowed similar sensationalistic tactics in later antievolution trials, most notably *McLean*.

The Scopes trial paved the way for later legal shenanigans in the neighboring state of Arkansas by way of the trial's inconclusive ruling. Granting litigants and observer-activists in the conservative, rural state a victory of sorts, the judge in the trial found Scopes guilty, but with an important distinction: Scopes was not convicted for teaching evolution. Instead, by dint of his refusal to teach—or not teach—science as mandated by state law, he was ruled insubordinate to his employer, the state of Tennessee, and given a $100 fine as punishment. Hearing the case on appeal, the Tennessee Supreme Court declined to give a definitive ruling, choosing instead to have the case *nolle prossed*, which precluded the matter of John Scopes and Tennessee's antievolution statute from ever being heard before the High Court.

As the drama of the Scopes Trial was unfolding in Tennessee, private citizens in Arkansas were agitating for a similar measure in that state, with the primary push coming from Baptist minister Ben Bogard. Bogard was lobbying members of the Arkansas legislature to vote for an antievolution statute that was to be proposed in the upcoming session by Representative Astor L. Rotenberry. The measure, HB No. 34, would make it a crime for any state-supported school to teach any "theory or doctrine that mankind ascended or descended from a lower order of animals." The maximum punishment upon conviction was to be a $500 fine that would, presumably, be accompanied by a termination of employment.[13]

While it might be tempting to presume that the legislators of a rural state would, in the 1920s, trip all over themselves in a rush to pass such a bill, the fact of the matter is HB34 was the subject of intense debate and was initially defeated. The introduction of the bill caused an immediate stir, and some members initially called for a month-long postponement on the vote. When a roll-call vote was demanded and granted, the bill's opponents, wary of the political consequences of aligning themselves against the antievolution measure, declined to record their votes. Even with the tacit endorsement of the house, however, the bill returned from the Education Committee with a "do not pass" recommendation.[14] Once again presaging a cornerstone of the contemporary conversation concerning religion-driven legislative fiat and the Establishment Clause in the science classroom, the Arkansas House defied the recommendation of the Education Committee and passed, after some eleventh-hour politicking, Rotenberry's bill.

This legislative victory was destined to be brief, however. Even more so than the house, the Arkansas Senate showed some constitutional foresight when presented with HB34, tabling the measure without a vote and subsequently voting down a substitute motion to put the bill on the calendar. After nearly a month of contentious debate and political jockeying in the Arkansas House, the state's would-be antievolution matter was put to ignominious rest in the Arkansas Senate in roughly sixteen minutes.[15]

It is at this point the antievolution case in Arkansas takes a crucial rhetorical turn, a turn both subversive with regard to the Establishment Clause and prescient with regard to the contemporary debate concerning that founding principle and its appropriate application in public school science classrooms. It should be noted here that submitting to the legislature an unconstitutional bill is not in and of itself unconstitutional; rather, it is the legislature's job to review and repel those measures that tread too heavily on constitutional principles. After a fair hearing in the Arkansas legislature, however, supporters of Rotenberry's bill took their cause to the masses, intending to use the cudgel of majority opinion to subdue clear, if rhetorically difficult, constitutional principles. Abandoning any notion that the defeated HB34 was anything but demagoguery, Rotenberry and Bogard formed in the wake of their legislative defeat the American Anti-Evolution

Association, the stated purpose of which was to organize the people of "Arkansas ... [and] ... every state and every county in every state down to the school districts" in the fight against evolution and the teaching thereof.[16] This was not merely advocacy; under the auspices of the AAA, Rotenberry and Bogard retooled their antievolution bill and reintroduced it, not as a law to the legislature, but as a petition to the voters of Arkansas. Known as Initiated Act No. 1, the measure passed handily, and the teaching of Darwinian theory became illegal in the public schools of Arkansas on November 6, 1928.

The passage of Arkansas Initiated Act No. 1 postdates Tennessee's antievolution statute, but the manner of that passage, especially the tactic of presenting a matter of science and constitutionality to the public at large with no regard for the possible jurisprudential consequence(s), makes the Arkansas incident far more relevant to the contemporary debate. The act put in place a rhetorical canard that antievolutionists continue to exploit to the present day, yet was not identified until the proceedings in *McLean*: that of a supposed tension between the will of the people and the rule of law as it applies to evolution and the science classroom. The consequences of this misrepresentation cannot be underestimated in the debate at hand, as antievolution legislative activists have continued, and continue today, to use the willful misrepresentation of scientific and political definitions to create tensions out of whole cloth, or to exacerbate relatively minor tensions in order to push through a radical and unconstitutional endorsement of Christianity in the public schools.

Ironically enough, the lack of an immediate prosecution also adds to the relevance of Arkansas's antievolution statute. As Tennessee's law had been successfully prosecuted to an extent and then *nolle prossed* by the Tennessee Supreme Court, it had effectively been removed from the national conversation. The Arkansas law, on the other hand, went untested for nearly forty years; in fact, popular sentiment in the rural state made even the *enforcement* of the law unnecessary, as local school boards and educators held largely anti-Darwinian views. It was not until the 1960s, amid the flurry of Establishment Clause cases relating to school prayer, that Arkansas Initiated Act No. 1 had its day in court.

That day came in 1965, when a young science teacher named Susan Epperson agreed to be the plaintiff in a case designed to test the constitutionality of Arkansas Initiated Act No. 1. According to Epperson, it was during that year that Little Rock Central High School adopted a biology textbook that dealt with "the history of man." The history depicted was an evolutionary one, and in the eyes of the Arkansas Education Association (AEA),[17] Epperson and the other biology teachers would be faced with the dilemma of either breaking the law by teaching evolution, or being remiss in their duties as educators by omitting that material. Epperson, singled out by the AEA for her Arkansas roots, her high standing in the community, and the military credentials of her husband, was approached by members of the AEA about a possible challenge to Arkansas's antievolution law. Epperson "knew it was controversial," and when she considered joining the AEA's plan she was fearful of the possible consequences. But when she read Attorney Eugene Warren's brief, she was convinced. "It expressed," she remembers, speaking of the brief, "what I would have said if I had been able to put it into words . . . The way I would have thought about the law, the way it's sort of a detriment to teaching good science." And with that, she agreed to be the plaintiff.[18]

The Epperson team formulated a jurisprudential and rhetorical game plan quite different from that of the Scopes players of 1927. Instead of a sensational, staged "arrest" of an insubordinate teacher, Warren filed a complaint on behalf of Epperson in Pulaski Chancery Court. The judge found for Epperson, ruling Arkansas Initiated Act No. 1 unconstitutional. The case was immediately appealed, but the plaintiffs had successfully placed the matter before the courts without inciting a public outcry for or against the action. And while the Arkansas Supreme Court found against Epperson, the decision handed down by the state bench was a true verdict—not a *noll prosse* order as in *Scopes*—and thus left open a chance for a hearing before the United States Supreme Court. That hearing came in 1968, and the Warren Court made short work of Arkansas's antievolution bill. Writing for a unanimous bench, Justice Abe Fortas said: "Arkansas' [*sic*] statute cannot stand . . . the law must be stricken because of its conflict with the constitutional prohibition of state laws respecting an establishment of religion or prohibiting the free exercise thereof. The overriding fact is that Arkansas' [*sic*] law selects from the body of knowledge a particular religious doctrine; that is, with a particular interpretation of the Book of Genesis by a particular religious group."[19]

As definitive an opinion as Fortas delivered, it would not deter antievolutionist activists for long. *Epperson v. Arkansas* is a Supreme Court precedent, and as such it is an incredibly relevant piece of jurisprudence with regard to Establishment Clause praxis. But *Epperson* cannot claim ultimate importance in the *modern* debate for the simple reason that it was the final and most important chapter of the *old* debate. The decision in *Epperson* provided, once and for all, a federal legal precedent that could and would be used to unequivocally declare unconstitutional any law that blatantly espoused Christian theology and funneled that theology into the public schools via science textbooks; however, the fact of the matter is that Arkansas Initiated Act No. 1, and other "monkey laws" like it, were relics of a dead age. The world, and creationism itself, had moved on. For those who still sought to legislate their faith, the ruling in *Epperson* was motivation and a push for rhetorical adaptation. That adaptation had already surfaced in lower courts by the time *Epperson* was heard before the SCOTUS, and the new way of skirting constitutional prohibitions on classroom proselytizing—so-called creation science—had a cadre of scientists, pseudo-scientists, and Christian apologists busily building a massive corpus of literature that would soon have a proper airing in an Arkansas courtroom.

Creation Science: The New School

The move to adapt the overtly Fundamentalist-Christian rhetoric of creationism to the post-Darwinian scientific paradigm (and to subvert the underlying assumptions of that new paradigm) began not only before *Epperson*, but before *Scopes* as well; the discipline of creation science actually predates the term by which it is described. The advent of creation science can be traced to George McReady Price, a devout Seventh-Day Adventist and self-described "armchair geologist" who published *Illogical Geology: The Weakest Point of the Evolution Theory* in 1906. In it, he used charts, graphs, and scientific jargon to illustrate his ideas, which included a young Earth (6–10,000 years old) and a pioneering articulation of catastrophism, which is the idea that all geological features on Earth can be explained by catastrophic events. Or, more accurately, *one* catastrophic event: Noah's Flood.[20]

Price's rhetorical strategy—using impressive scientific ephemera and vocabulary to awe the uninitiated and inflating or misrepresenting credentials—set the tone for the nascent creation-science movement. He also helped to found the Society for the Study of Deluge Geology and Related Sciences, as well as the American Scientific Affiliation, the latter which held as its mission the "correlation of the facts of science with the tenets of the Christian faith."[21]

Following in the footsteps of Price was John C. Whitcomb, whose 1961 book *The Genesis Flood: The Biblical Record and Its Scientific Implications* regurgitated the Noachian catastrophism of Price and introduced it to a new generation of creation-scientists. Most prominent among these new creation-scientists were Henry M. Morris and Duane T. Gish. As the Warren Court of the 1960s dealt classroom religiosity—including creationism in *Epperson*—blow after blow, the creation-science movement increasingly led by Morris and Gish began to establish a bifurcated rhetorical strategy. Antievolution activists were attacking science education with a cultural impetus, with religiosity freely and overtly mixed into the antievolution statutes they submitted to state legislators; *Epperson* explicitly exposed the folly of this strategy. Morris and Gish, then, teased the two motives apart, with Morris pushing the cultural and ideological underpinnings of creationism and creation science, and Gish—a biochemist—focusing on different creationist explanatory models that might pass muster in a courtroom, if not the scientific establishment.[22]

As stated, Morris was more concerned with the cultural implications of creation science and evolutionary theory, and he once boiled all of science, science education, and the culture that promulgated it to one "ultimate choice," which he defined as "between Biblical Christianity and paganism."[23] Both Morris and Gish were well aware that such rhetoric would hurt the chances of antievolution science education bills in legislatures and/or courts, and agreed that Morris's articulation of creation science should be kept mostly in-house.[24]

Gish's role was more one of ambassador. His 1978 work of creation science, *Evolution: The Fossils Say No!*, is a seminal one, and in it Gish provides a rhetorical framework for the scientific arguments that would be used by creationists lobbying Arkansas legislators to pass the bill that would eventually become Arkansas Act 590, which would in turn precipitate *McLean v. Arkansas*. In *Evolution*, Gish provides a working scientific vocabulary for creation-scientists and creation-science advocates, co-opting the language of mainstream science and using that language to contradict widely held scientific tenets. Gish also simplifies this language, making it more accessible to antievolution activists who, as opposed to dyed-in-the-wool creation-scientists, might have no science training whatsoever. In this form, creation science is defined primarily as what mainstream science is *not*. Thus, in the book, each pillar of creation science is contrasted with a facet of evolutionary theory generally accepted by the scientific mainstream, and points out that said corresponding facet is *not proven* and hence "only a theory."[25] In nonscientific terms, of course, a theory is a guess; for a scientist, a theory is an explanatory model that best links all available evidence. The difference here is that a scientist might disagree with *aspects* of a theory such as evolution, but still agree with the theory itself, as it still links evidence with the greatest degree of efficacy. The antievolutionist, using Gish's simplified jargon, can merely point to this or that facet of evolutionary theory and proclaim that since it has not been proven, then the whole of evolutionary theory is "just a theory," a baseless guess.

Gish also provides a Creation Model (CM), which he defines as an explanatory model that "postulate[s] . . . all basic animal and plant types (the created kinds) were brought into existence by acts of a supernatural Creator using special processes which are not operative today."[26] Distinct biblical allusions aside,[27] it is informative of the overall strategy of the creation-science movement of this era to note the immediate and petulant criticism of evolutionary theory immediately following: "evolution has been *postulated*, but it has never been *observed*."[28] Within the overarching Creation Model, Gish provides three specific models: the Day-Age Theory, Gap Theory, and the Catastrophist/Recent Creation Model. The first two models encompass the widely accepted age of billions of years for the Earth, and the latter is confined to the 6–10,000-year-old Earth of old-school creationism.

The basis for all of these theories is obviously the Bible, specifically the first chapter of Genesis, and the varying degrees to which Gish strays from that text are merely rhetorical dodges meant to pacify those who cannot totally abandon the scientific idea of an ancient

Earth; nevertheless, they provide an important component of the developing scientific rhetorical arsenal of the new creationism, creation science. Gish's work, in the late 1970s and early 1980s, leant an air of science to the religiously based theories of scientific creationism that would ultimately prove adequate to dupe a great number of laypersons and legislators. *Evolution* also hones the creation-science assertion that there is a "controversy" among scientists about the overall validity of evolutionary theory. As mentioned above, a large part of antievolutionists' rhetorical force is derived from fostering tensions where there are none, or exacerbating minor tensions that would otherwise be relatively inconsequential. It has been shown that one of these tensions is between elected officials and the electorate, or more specifically, between generic populism and democratic republicanism. Corollary to this is the American idea of "culture war," a ginned-up struggle between "real Americans" and un-American elites.

The two-prong rhetorical approach of creation-scientists aimed to simultaneously co-opt scientific language and tap into the agitation and fear bred by opposing views of cultural norms when framing the issue of science curricula in the public schools. This strategy reached its stride in the aftermath of the turbulent decades of the 1960s and 1970s, and by playing on the anxieties of a population experiencing a major cultural shift, creation-scientists were able to excite emotions in a wide swath of the populace that went far beyond scientific curiosity. It reached the fever pitch of crusade in many, and caused many more to willingly sacrifice the autonomy of the scientific community to err on the side of cultural tradition. It is into this potent mix of doubt and change that the seeds of Arkansas Act 590 were sown.

Arkansas Act 590

When Eugene Warren and his team planned their case in *Epperson v. Arkansas*, a key component of their strategy was to keep the entire thing, according to Susan Epperson, "an Arkansas effort."[29] This would seem sound strategy, especially considering the rural South's traditional mistrust of elite outsiders. As the creation-science movement grew to national proportions, however, it became less and less likely that any case dealing with the same would be entirely local; in fact, the national proselytizing of the creation-science movement had motivated at least one grassroots supporter to action far above and beyond petitioning his local school board or legislature. This one man—Paul Ellwanger— would in fact be the catalyst that got the *McLean* ball rolling.

Paul Ellwanger was a respiratory therapist living in South Carolina when he founded the organization known as Citizens for Fairness in Education (CFE). Ellwanger, along with being the founder, listed himself as "Director and National Coordinator for Balanced Treatment Legislation Promotion."[30] The ultimate goal of CFE was to rid public schools of scientific education that utilized evolutionary theory, and replace it with science that was based upon Paul Ellwanger's personal interpretation of the Bible. Ellwanger, while rabidly ideological and overtly theocratic in his personal and CFE correspondence, was pushing a balanced treatment approach to eradicating evolutionary education. While pure creationism had been swept aside in *Epperson*, balanced treatment had yet to have its full day in court, and the work of creation-scientists like Duane Gish made the prospect of a successful balanced treatment bill plausible. Not content to lobby only his home state, Ellwanger enlisted attorney and antievolution activist Wendell Bird in the cause, and Bird helped Ellwanger draft a model bill, which Ellwanger then shopped from state to state, legislature to legislature.[31]

Ellwanger concentrated his bill-shopping efforts in the conservative, religious South, and it was in Arkansas that he finally got some solid traction from local activists. He first presented the bill to state senator John Lisle. Lisle, a member of the Baptist Church, probably seemed a likely candidate for sponsorship, but when Lisle was presented the bill by a local cohort of Ellwanger's in 1981 and subsequently read both the bill and what Lisle characterizes as "all of Duane Gish's literature," he refused to sponsor Ellwanger's legislation. Characterizing the proposed bill "unconstitutional" and concerned with an issue that had been decided "a number of times," Lisle was convinced that adoption of Ellwanger's balanced treatment legislation would have the effect of forcing Arkansas schoolchildren to "study Duane Gish's religious views," and that furthermore, the language of the bill could be construed to mandate balanced treatment in not just science classes, but in any class that discussed science, even tangentially.[32]

Ellwanger had better luck with state senator Jim Holsted, a member of the Methodist Church.[33] This is not to say that Holsted was a champion of the balanced treatment bill, or even gave it too much thought. Although he would later defend what he saw as the constitutionality of Arkansas Act 590, it appears that he never expected it to pass. Contemporary to the passage of Act 590 (originally SB482), Holsted is on record as saying of the bill that he "never expected to get it out of the House,"[34] and a quarter century later maintained that he "didn't really think it would pass ... both houses," and going on to say that the bill constituted "pretty radical legislation; there was a lot of controversy on it ... really, my intent was [to encourage the legislature to] look at the [science] curriculum and see what was being taught and make some adjustments."[35]

In fact, a consistent theme of the passage of SB482 is the widespread presumption, among those that voted for the bill and those that later denounced it (oftentimes one in the same), that the bill would not pass. This casts dubious light on the assertion by some that SB482 was purely a bill to promote science education, because if that was clearly the function of the bill, then it would be unreasonable to presume that the bill would fail on account of controversy or constitutional concerns. Indicative of this contradiction, and perhaps a more honest take on the situation, is the comment of state representative Bill Clark, who said after the general session that SB482 "is a terrible bill, it is worded so cleverly that none of us can vote against if we want to come back up here [to the Capitol]." Representative Clark had voted for the passage of SB482.[36]

It would appear that this duplicity—a veneer of scientific authority masking a bill obviously, if implicitly, pushing a theistic cultural agenda—is the fruition of years of work on the part of organized creation-scientists and cultural warriors in the wake of *Epperson*. Coincidentally, it was in Arkansas that this improved rhetorical strategy was given its first trial run, and the passage, challenge, and ultimate defeat of Arkansas Act 590 would codify the script for every future constitutional battle in the science classroom.

Opinions differ as to the degree of inside help that SB482 had in making it onto the legislative docket during the 1981 general session. Then attorney general Steve Clark believes that "the wheels were greased by someone,"[37] while former state senator John Lisle is convinced that "it was a done deal" before the bill even came up for a vote.[38] Regardless, the record shows that the bill was indeed introduced late in the session, and it appears to have subsequently been placed ahead of bills filed earlier. The bill's House of Representatives sponsor, Cliff Hoofman, had also gotten a promise from Governor Frank White that he, the governor, would sign the bill if it passed,[39] although White himself maintained a staunch know-nothing stance in the wake of the controversial signing. In one subsequent press conference, White insisted that while he was "a Christian," and as such "believe[s] what the Bible says," he nevertheless had "no commitment" to either evolution or creation science and had no need "to rationalize [Act 590] with the separation of church and state."[40]

Whether the legislators that were allegedly shocked when the bill passed were indeed duped by the creation-science movement's new-and-improved rhetoric is immaterial at this point. And while it certainly seems dubious that legislators would vote for a "terrible bill" and then claim to be taken aback when that same terrible bill wound up in a very expensive court battle, it is not too charitable to presume that none of the legislators voting for SB482 could foresee the national spectacle that would come from their par-for-the-course round of pandering. It is important to remember that in 1981, Arkansas was still a political and media backwater, with the rise to national prominence of Bill Clinton, along with the exponential economic growth of the state's northwest corridor, still a decade away. According to state senator Holsted, who sponsored the balanced-treatment bill, he "never realized [Act 590] would have the national implications it did," presuming instead that the legislature would "set up a model system and . . . get something that'll work and the people will be pleased with it and maybe some other states will use it. I never realized it would do what it did."[41]

McLean v. Arkansas

SB 482 passed the Arkansas Senate by a vote of 22–2 and the Arkansas House by a vote of 69–18, and was signed into law by Governor Frank White on March 19, 1981. Arkansas Act 590, as it was then officially

known, was only on the books for about two months before it was
challenged in court. The plaintiffs filed an official complaint on or
about May 27, 1981. This marks not only the official kickoff of *McLean
et al. v. Arkansas Board of Education et al.*, the most important rhetorical event in the modern debate over the separation of church and
state in the science classroom, but also the real commencement of
debate on the bill that caused all the trouble. As the bill ran its course
in legislature with little debate and scant news coverage, the general
public was not well informed when the trial brief was filed. This follows the pattern set in *Epperson*, but unlike that earlier case, *McLean*
was destined to be sensationalized and played out in the local and
national media; as such, in the run-up to the trial it was the task of
both sides to present their case not only to Judge William Overton,
but also to the masses.

Unlike Arkansas Initiated Act No. 1, the law in the Epperson affair,
Act 590 was a statute worded to express the intention of academic freedom, ostensibly using law to disrupt the supposed monopoly intolerant
Darwinian scientists held on tax-supported classrooms. By taking a cue
from the Epperson team, however, the plaintiffs in *McLean* were able to
dictate the paradigms from first filing to final ruling. Rather than float
a prosecutable test-case, as in *Scopes v. Tennessee* (1925), the plaintiffs
sought an immediate declaratory ruling. In so doing, the anti-590 camp
was able to dictate the terms of debate and construct a rhetorical paradigm that would have to be countered rather than defended.

The creation-science movement had spent the last two decades
developing two distinct rhetorical attacks to employ against secular
science education: scientific and cultural. By passing their model bill
in a conservative southern state, antievolution activists had assured
an audience that would be amenable to religious undertones of said
legislation. On the other side, much as Susan Epperson was a model
plaintiff in *Epperson v. Arkansas* (1968) on account of her personal
faith, so too were the plaintiffs in *McLean* well suited to the rhetorical fight on grounds of religion. The plaintiffs were in fact a group of
ministers who considered Act 590 an unacceptable encroachment by
government on religious freedom. Ken Hicks, the bishop of United
Methodist Church in Little Rock, describes a "very ecumenical" meeting of ministers that found Act 590 to have "religion oozing out of

it," and being used by activists to foist their own religious views on Arkansas schoolchildren. The ministers ultimately enlisted the help of the ACLU and filed suit against the implementation of Act 590.[42]

Unlike Arkansas Initiated Act No. 1, which expressly forbade a widely accepted scientific framework to protect a religious idea, Act 590—like the majority of the new creation-science rhetoric—was bereft of overtly religious language. Antievolution activists had abandoned the honest-but-foolhardy tactic of announcing religious motivation. Instead, Act 590 was itself presented as a safeguard against the establishment of religion, and as a protection for academic freedom. Rhetorically, the act and the literature surrounding it implied that creation science, like Darwinism before it, was a persecuted theory. In order to "protect academic freedom by providing student choice,"[43] then, the legislature must intervene. The act also contained another hallmark of the new creation-science rhetoric: the use of a legal argument that, while weak, holds great rhetorical power by dint of its esoteric legalistic veneer. This disingenuous use of elitist argument with an egalitarian façade is part and parcel of the new creationism's rhetorical strategy, and while infuriating to the intelligentsia, plays well to the faithful and the general public.

This argument particularly concerns the establishment of "secular religion" by the state, and is easier to support, superficially, than the delicate argument required of the McLean camp. In section VI of Act 590, one of the legislative purposes of the act[44] is to prevent "establishment of Theologically Liberal, Humanist, Nontheist [sic], or Atheist religions." According to some creationist literature,[45] the legal argument for this rests in *Torcaso v. Watkins* (1961),[46] which found unconstitutional the religious test required of elected officials in Maryland. The creationist spin on this case is that it effectively establishes secular humanism as a religion. Extrapolating that atheism and evolution are tenets of this new "religion," antievolution activists contend that teaching evolution in science classrooms is itself a violation of the Establishment Clause. By invoking the idea(l) of student choice and the goal of "ensuring freedom of religious exercise for students and their parents" and "freedom of belief and speech for students,"[47] the defendants in *McLean* protectively positioned Act 590 behind several important Supreme Court rulings.

Noting the rhetorical and jurisprudential strength of this position, ACLU counsel Eric Naiman advised the McLean camp to be wary of any argument centering on academic freedom. He proposed instead the plaintiffs argue that the marketplace of ideas applies only to professionals, in this case the university-level scientific mainstream, and that it was this professional community that had determined evolutionary theory to be the most sound, and therefore the theory most appropriate for pre-college instruction. This counters the creationists' contention that it is government censoring their opinion—which it was not, as no law-forbidding deity-neutral creation-science instruction had ever been on the Arkansas books[48]—and presents creationism as a failure in the marketplace of ideas. By that token, Act 590 would constitute an arbitrary interference by the state in the affairs of science educators, which is obviously an unconstitutional exercise of state power.[49]

In the actual complaint, the plaintiffs took pains to dub Act 590, the official title of which is "Balanced Treatment for Creation-Science and Evolution-Science Act," as the "Creationism Act," referring to it as the latter for the duration of the complaint and the trial. This served the rhetorical purpose of explicitly linking Act 590 to the outmoded creationist rhetoric of past legal battles. This also robs the act of the egalitarian phrase "balanced treatment." Alleging abridgement of academic freedom, the plaintiffs offered that rather than give over classroom time to a pseudo-scientific theory abhorrent to their professional sensibilities, many instructors would teach neither evolutionary theory nor creation science.[50] This would run contrary to the right of access to information afforded students by SCOTUS precedent.[51]

The plaintiffs also asserted that the "creationism act" is informed primarily by religion, thereby putting it afoul of the First Amendment via the Establishment Clause. In the complaint, they contend that creation science is in fact not science, but religion, and that Arkansas Act 590 has no secular legislative purpose, its primary effect being to promote a particular tenet of a particular religion, specifically the idea of special creation as explained by a Fundamentalist Protestant reading of the Book of Genesis. From a scientific standpoint, the plaintiffs argued that since creation science relied on an omnipotent creator working outside the bounds of physical reality it was not falsifiable, and therefore could not be science.

The defense's primary claim was that the case was not a legitimate one, as the plaintiffs contended that the statute itself is unconstitutional on its face and warranted a constitutional challenge before it was applied. By that logic, the defense claimed that Act 590 was beyond adjudication as a "statute [that] is unambiguous on its face" and therefore "should be applied as worded." Furthermore, the defense contended that a legislature, "in passing a statute, knew what it [the legislature] intended, was aware of the rules of statutory construction, and that the statute fully expresses that intention."[52] This is a sound point, should the judge agree that the language of the bill is in fact above reproach, but if that argument is ineffective and the case goes to trial—and *McLean*, of course, ultimately did—the conceit becomes not only weak rhetorically, but in fact becomes burdensome, as it bases all subsequent arguments on a premise disproved by the very trial in which said arguments are being aired.

Interpolation: *McLean* and the Rise of the Religious Right

One interesting circumstance of Act 590's passage is the manner in which Arkansas's then attorney general Steve Clark found out about it. While the state AG doesn't have to sign off on a bill under consideration in the legislature, tradition holds that bills with the potential for controversy are shown to the person who will be charged with defending them should there be a court challenge. According to Clark, he found out about the law from a newspaper reporter after Act 590 had already been signed by the governor. Upon being appraised of the law by a reporter, Clark offered his first impression and honest opinion, saying he had some "qualms" about the law. This statement would, according to Clark, come back to haunt him.[53] Indeed, that innocuous statement instigated a coordinated, vocal, and pervasive condemnation of Clark by antievolution activists; this campaign of vilification was a key component of the public's perception of Act 590 and *McLean v. Arkansas*, and followed the pattern of exploitation and exacerbation practiced by creationists with regard to perceived tensions, minor or practically nonexistent, between the public, their elected officials, and constitutional law.

The creationist campaign to discredit Attorney General Clark is of vital importance to the current debate, for two reasons: one, this "creationist campaign" was conducted not by creation-scientists but the Religious Right, a social and legislative activist group just coming into its own in the early 1980s, and in the *McLean* affair the group demonstrated for the first time the ability to coalesce conservative Christians of all denominational stripes into a coherent voting bloc; and, two, the campaign was conducted via the medium of cable television, signifying the onset of the instantaneous, twenty-four-hour news cycle, the skillful manipulation of which is now a key component of both conservative and liberal social movements.

Pat Robertson, one of the archetypes of modern televangelism, was already hosting *The 700 Club* in 1981, and was keeping an eye on the antievolution proceedings in Arkansas through a paid news stringer. When Robertson heard of Clark's "qualms" comment, he took it as a signal that Clark would not be fully committed to the ideological cause underlying Act 590, and began to prepare his rapidly growing following for action. When *McLean* was officially filed, Robertson was ready. Initially denigrating Clark and his team, all young men in their early thirties, as looking "like a bunch of weathermen," he declared them in over their heads and sent representatives of his organization to Arkansas to insist that Clark hand over the reigns of the defense, telling Clark he didn't "have the resources to defend [the law]" and that he had "given pause" to the Robertson constituency with the "qualms" comment.[54]

Robertson had arranged for creationist attorney Wendell Bird, who had helped to author the model bill from which Act 590 sprang, to step in, but Clark refused to accept outside interference in the matter. This did not sit well with Robertson and his organization, but when it was revealed that Clark had allowed a dinner with him to be auctioned off to benefit the ACLU the smear campaign went into high gear. Clark explains:

> The ACLU had a fundraising event. My office was contacted . . . and [the office staff] donated a lunch with me. I actually didn't know it; it was auctioned away for fifteen bucks, a real hot-ticket item—you know, who wants to eat with Clark?—but, just before trial began, Reverend Robertson had a reporter here who dis-

covered this, and they went on air . . . saying I had sold out to the "other side," that [I] . . . was supposed to be representing the "Christian view" [and] . . . was deliberately throwing the trial.[55]

According to Clark, his initial reaction was, "he's a TV preacher—who cares." But by the second or third day of the trial, Robertson had successfully motivated scores of people from all over the country to descend on Little Rock, Arkansas, and their presence turned the trial into a raucous arena of protest and counter-protest. The Robertson devotees regularly jammed the capitol's phone lines, and the entire spectacle thrust the state and its balanced-treatment act into the national spotlight. This was, of course, exactly what Clark and the governor did not want.

The general consensus among Robertson and the Religious Right was that Clark should be fired for selling out to secular left-wing interests. Judging from Clark's description of the bedlam at the capitol, Governor Frank White might well have been amenable to such a suggestion. At any rate, White was in a fix, for he was the focal point of a virtually unprecedented nationwide effort attempting to goad him into removing an elected official.[56] Clark, of course, was an elected official and so subject to the people of Arkansas, not the governor.

Regardless, Robertson had successfully exerted his burgeoning influence, and would continue to do so for the duration of the trial. Says Clark of the rise of Robertson and his ilk, and their activism during *McLean*:

> It was just a situation where we had lots of people that *had* to be heard . . . the Moral Majority was part of that . . . it was more powerful than any organization preceding it. They had broadcast capabilities that were nation-wide. That sort of ability to motivate, to activate—it wasn't just *motivate*, but *activate* people, in the 24-hour news cycle—the news cycle at that time was believed to be two or three days, not 24 hours or hours and minutes as it is now. There was no internet, there was no cable television of any consequence . . . so here [Robertson] comes . . . on *The 700 Club* at nine o'clock in the morning, and by five o'clock it's a firestorm . . . that was powerful. It was a way that had just not been seen before . . . before that, you just thought of causes that were natural

disasters, wartime, things like *that* would rally people instantly. My first reaction was "it's just some TV preacher, who cares? There's not that many people that watch TV preachers." I was wrong.[57]

McLean, cont.

As noted above, the strongest pretrial argument for the defense was the illegitimacy of the plaintiff's case, an argument immediately rendered moot when the case did indeed go to trial. At this point, the re-tooled rhetoric of the creation-science movement was pitted against that of both scientists and progressive Christians, and the results were nothing short of disastrous for the defense. As the ruckus kicked up by Pat Robertson and like-minded culture warriors consistently eroded the thin veneer of scientific legitimacy creation science had cultivated over twenty years, Steve Clark and the defense counsel faced not only a withering barrage of public criticism from both sides of the issue, they likewise fought an uphill battle, rhetorically, in the courtroom, as they faced an opposing counsel stocked with more labor, more time, and far better witnesses than the defense could ever hope to produce. As the basic premise of the state's argument was obviated by the trial itself, the Clark team was forced to rely on the rhetorical arguments of the creation-science movement, a movement that faced a distinct disadvantage in the marketplace of ideas outside of its own insular world.

From a scientific viewpoint, the core problem with creation science is not that creation-scientists believe in a creator—in *McLean* testimony and interviews, a significant number of evolutionists professed religious beliefs that include a god or creator—but that creation-science activists have no positive evidence; that is, the sole purpose of the creation-science movement is not to explain, but to merely debunk evolutionary theory. For example, in a written debate with Duane Gish, Isaac Asimov charges that "the creationist argument consists entirely of pointing out 'flaws' in evolutionary theory [with] not one word in *support* of the 'Creator.'"[58]

This is not to say that the defense did not present scientists in support of their case; they did, and some were even biologists that had published in peer-reviewed journals. Unfortunately for the defense, however, nearly all of these scientists belonged to one or another creation-science organization, which organizations invariably require members to sign pledges of faith; under even routine questioning, the religious motivations behind each and every statement made by the witness becomes apparent, and the argument falls. For every scientist with such heavy rhetorical baggage, the plaintiffs could produce another scientist, equally credible, that would also profess a religious faith and yet not only decline to sign such a pledge, but go on record as to the compatibility of religion and science, and to the scientific failings of creation science.[59]

The defense fared no better in their choice of religious experts. A prime example of this is Norman Geisler, a professor of systematic theology at Dallas Theological Seminary. Geisler was the lead witness for the defense, and his argument hinged on the idea that only belief *in*—not merely belief in the *existence of*—a creator or god constituted religion. By this line of reasoning, Geisler testified that scientists who were wholly committed to evolutionary theory—that believed *in* the theory—were indeed practicing religion. This is an esoteric argument at best, and hamstrings one of creation science's primary rhetorical appeals, i.e., its common-sense simplicity. This is in contrast to a string of highly charismatic witnesses for the plaintiffs, including Stephen Jay Gould and theologian Langdon Gilkey, the latter of which caused Steve Clark to speculate that "[Gilkey] and the Lord are so tight that they have coffee in the morning."[60]

Attempts by antievolution ideologues to insert their religious beliefs in schoolrooms by dint of legislatively controlled science education always depend, at their core, on the manipulation of language and the misrepresentation of science. On these counts, the testimony that perhaps best encapsulates the victorious argument in *McLean* comes from William V. Mayer, at the time of *McLean* a forty-year teaching veteran and the director of the Biological Science Curriculum Society. In his deposition, Myers not only repackages and re-presents the plaintiffs' case, he simply and succinctly debunks some of the most pervasive misconceptions exploited by the creation-science movement and antievolution activists.

First and foremost, Myers confronts the canard that evolution is a "theory, not a fact." He explains that in the parlance of the scientist, a theory is "a synthetic explanation of the facts ... that is subject to change as we learn more about a topic. This exposes both the disingenuousness of creation-science rhetoric, and also its teleological *modus operandi*: instead of seeking to explain data, creation-scientist activists bent on legislating science seek only to prove a belief, and to justify and validate a foregone conclusion.[61] Ultimately, Mayer argues that the tenets of creation science "are blatantly religious and ... poor science. [Creation-scientists] deliberately misrepresent ... they make the [misleading] statements even if they know better."[62]

Ultimately, Judge William Overton found the arguments of the plaintiffs to carry the day, and he ruled for McLean et al. on January 5, 1982. Merely handing down the decision, however, would not make *McLean* the landmark case that it is; instead, it is Overton's definitive articulation of the differences between science and creation science, and of what science *is*, that make *McLean* the ultimate linchpin in the jurisprudential history of the Establishment Clause in the science classroom.

Invoking the wall of separation coined by Jefferson in 1802, Overton sets about systematically dismantling the claims made by the defense in support of Act 590. One of the defense's strongest legal supports was the constitutional requirement that a judge consider only the legislative purpose of a bill, and not the intent of individual legislators or a collective legislature. Act 590, unlike earlier antievolution laws, invokes no overtly religious principle. However, Overton determines that while courts must give "great deference" to a bill's statements of legislative purpose, the court is not *bound* by said legislative purpose and is legally permitted to "consider evidence of the historical context of the Act, the specific sequence of events leading up to passage of the Act, departures from normal procedural sequences, and contemporaneous statements of the legislative sponsor."[63] All of these precedent-supported points inform a legal framework for examining the evidence present in *McLean* that so obviously points to a dishonest attempt by a few persons to foist a government-sponsored religious curriculum upon schoolchildren via legislative fiat.

Along with this justification concerning Act 590's historical and philosophical underpinnings, Overton contends that even if the defendants "are correct and the Court is limited to an examination of the language of the Act, the evidence is overwhelming that both the purpose and effect of Act 590 is the advancement of religion in the public schools." He goes on to point out that through the creation-science movement's willful misrepresentation of evolutionary theory's basic tenets, those involved with that movement have sought to create from whole cloth a divisive, dualistic pedagogy that unnecessarily posits a zero-sum choice between religion and science or, as the creation-science movement would have it, creation science or evolution-science. Overton therefore concludes that the "emphasis on origins as an aspect of the theory of evolution is peculiar to creationist literature," and although "the subject of origins of life is within the province of biology, the scientific community does not consider origins of life a part of evolutionary theory." Thus, according to Overton, the two-model approach demanded by creation-science philosophy and mandated by Act 590 is a "fallacious pedagogy" prefaced upon a "contrived dualism."[64]

Perhaps most important with regard to precedent, Overton also uses his decision in *McLean* to establish a five-pronged test to conclude if a theory mandated by state curriculum should indeed be considered science: (1) The theory must be guided by natural law; (2) It must be explanatory by reference to natural law; (3) It must be testable against the empirical world; (4) Its conclusions must be tentative and subject to change; and (5) It must be falsifiable. Along with these explicit criteria, Overton also notes that, generally, science is "what is accepted in the scientific community and is what scientists do."[65]

Finally, Overton declares that while "no doubt a sizable majority of Americans believe in the concept of a Creator or, at least, are not opposed to the concept and see nothing wrong with teaching schoolchildren the idea," the fact remains that

> the application and content of First Amendment principles are not determined by public opinion polls or by a majority vote. Whether the proponents of Act 590 constitute the majority or the minority is quite irrelevant under a constitutional system of government. No group, no matter how large or how small, may use the organs of government, of which the public schools are the conspicuous and influential, to foist its religious beliefs on others.[66]

Conclusion

McLean went unappealed, and aside from the $400,000 in taxpayer dollars that were wasted, the law and the trial had little immediate impact on the day-to-day lives of Arkansans or anyone else. As a piece of jurisprudence, however, *McLean* has far-reaching implications, and if not for its termination in the lower courts, would be considered the ultimate precedent in Establishment Clause law as that law is applied to the science classroom. As the introduction to this note has shown, *McLean* is still cited as precedent in such discussions, as the rhetoric used in antievolution crusades and legislative efforts is to this day the rhetoric first given a full hearing in *McLean v. Arkansas*.

The actual SCOTUS precedent in this matter belongs to *Edwards v. Aguillard* (1987), a case challenging a Louisiana balanced-treatment law that was itself based upon the very same model bill, authored by Paul Ellwanger and Wendell Bird, that spawned Arkansas Act 590. The case itself is largely a repeat of the arguments presented in *McLean*; furthermore, Justice William Brennan's majority opinion and Justice Lewis Powell's concurring opinion, while once again dealing creation science a defeat, do less to codify the definition and breadth of the Establishment Clause in such cases than does William Overton's decision in *McLean*. In fact, as a result of Justice Brennan's failure to approach the scientific inaccuracies of creation science, the court's opinion in *Edwards* can be seen as one that erodes, rather than buttresses, the precedent laid down by William Overton five years before; softening the language of rejection, Brennan opines that "under the Act's requirements, teachers who were once free to teach any and all facets of this subject are now unable to do so . . . the Act fails to even ensure that creation science will be taught."[67] Rather than draw upon Overton's definition of science and rejection of thinly veiled religious dogma, Brennan has instead codified the High Court's sympathy with religion-infused pseudoscience, even as the bill championing such pseudoscience is rejected as unconstitutional.

And so, while *Edwards* will always be cited as Supreme Court precedent, it comes on the heels of *McLean* and waters down the former's stronger and clearer decision. When *Edwards* was argued before the High Court, the tactics of both camps had already been established, fielded, and refined in Arkansas five years previous. These rhetorical tactics, as evidenced in cases such as *Kitzmiller v. Dover* (2005) and *Selman v. Cobb County* (2005), are still in use today. *McLean* did not require *Epperson* to exist, and *Edwards* would not exist without *McLean*. This one case that barely registers in the popular imagination nonetheless stands alone as the very crux of Establishment Clause debate as it is argued in legislatures and courtrooms, and also schoolrooms—those most conspicuous and influential of the organs of government—today.

NOTES

1. John E. Jones III, *Kitzmiller, et al. v. Dover Area School District* 400 F. Supp. 2d 707 (2005).

2. The other was *Selman v. Cobb County School District* 449 F. 3d 1320 (2006). A virtually identical case out of Georgia's Northern District Court (Atlanta Division), *Cobb* was also decided in favor of the parents bringing suit against the school district. The case was appealed to the Eleventh Circuit in 2006; the court of appeals remanded the case.

3. "Treaty of Tripoli," http://avalon.law.yale.edu/18th_century/bar1796t.asp (accessed June 18, 2011).

4. "Letter to the Danbury Baptists," http://www.loc.gov/loc/lcib/9806/danpre.html (accessed June 18, 2011).

5. "Declaration of Independence," http://www.archives.gov/exhibits/charters/declaration_transcript.html (accessed June 18, 2011).

6. Thomas L. Tedford and Dale A. Herbeck, *Freedom of Speech in the United States*, 5th ed. (State College, PA: Strata Publishing, 2005).

7. Bernard Bailyn, *The Ideological Origins of the American Revolution* (Cambridge, MA: Harvard University Press, 1967); Garrett Ward Sheldon and Daniel L. Dreisbach, eds., *Religion and Political Culture in Jefferson's Virginia* (Lanham, MD: Rowman & Littlefield, 2000).

8. Excepting, of course, the Mormons, whose capitulation, under societal and governmental duress, to monogamy constitutes a whole other study, and is far beyond the purview of the present note.

9. This is not to say that religious expression did not fall under the scrutiny of the High Court during this long stretch. Indeed, there were numerous Supreme Court cases that dealt with religion before the 1960s, especially a spate of rulings involving Jehovah's Witnesses, e.g., *Chaplinsky v. New Hampshire* (1942), that were handed down in the years leading up to and during World War II. These cases, while landmark rulings that laid the basis for what continues to be prevailing First Amendment jurisprudential theory, are more properly classified as free-speech cases as opposed to Establishment Clause cases. While a notable exception is *Everson v. Board of Education of the Township of Ewing* (1947), it was in 1962 that the Supreme Court, under Chief Justice Earl Warren, began delivering decisions that fundamentally changed the relationship between churches and the state as that relationship is realized through the public school system. In that year the decision in *Engel v. Vitale* did away with state-mandated prayer in public school, with *Abington v. Schempp* (1963) reinforcing that ruling.

10. Nancy T. Ammerman, "North American Protestant Fundamentalism," in *Fundamentalisms Observed*, ed. Martin E. Marty and R. Scott Appleby (Chicago: University of Chicago Press, 1991), 1–56.

11. Tenn. Code Ann. §49-1922; Tenn. Acts 1925.

12. Edward J. Larson, *Summer for the Gods: The Scopes Trial and America's Continuing Debate Over Science and Religion* (New York: Basic Books, 1997). Despite the modern-day impression of interloping Yankee ACLU activists, the Scopes arrest and prosecution was actually a scheme cooked up by Dayton's town fathers to bolster the failing economy of their once-booming mining town.

13. Leo Thomas Sweeney, "The Anti-Evolution Movement in Arkansas" (M.A. thesis, University of Arkansas, 1966).

14. Ibid.

15. Ibid. The bill nearly sputtered back to life numerous times during the 1927 session, but each tactic employed by the antievolutionists to remove the bill from the table was countered by equally deft maneuvers on the part of the opposition.

16. Sweeny, "Anti-Evolution," 73. In the interest of ideological context, it is informative to note that, according to charter, membership in Rotenberry's and Bogard's group excluded "Negros [sic] and persons of African descent, atheists, infidels, agnostics, such persons as hold to the theory of evolution, habitual drunkards, gamblers, profane swearers, despoilers of the domestic life of others, desecrators of the Lord's Day and those who would depreciate feminine virtue by vulgarly discussing sex relation[s.]"

17. The Arkansas Education Association, or AEA, is a teachers' union, and not affiliated with the Arkansas Department of Education, which is an instrument of the state government. For more on the Arkansas Department of Education, see http://www.arkansased.org. For more on the Arkansas Education Association, see http://www.aeaonline.org.

18. Susan Epperson, interview with author, May 29, 2007.

19. *Epperson v. Arkansas,* 393 U.S. 97 (1968).

20. Willard B. Gatewood Jr., "The Decline and Revival of the Evolution Controversy," Paper presented at the Charles W. Oxford Lecture, University of Arkansas, Fayetteville, February 24, 1983.

21. Gatewood, "Decline."

22. Gish, a prolific author and regular speaker on the creationist debate and lecture circuit throughout the 1970s, 1980s, and early 1990s, holds a Ph.D. in biochemistry; it is not the norm for creation-scientists during this period (or, generally, at the time of this writing) to have advanced degrees in the biological sciences; it is much more common for those creation-scientists with advanced degrees to hold said degrees in nonbiological sciences such as engineering or mathematics. Still, it should be noted that while Gish is a biochemist—an area of special importance in the modern creation/evolution debate—his principal works, such as *Evolution*, pertain to areas outside his specialization, in this case paleontology and geology. The tendency to use an advanced degree to lend credence to authoritative statements outside of one's discipline *is* common among creation-scientists.

23. Henry Morris, *A History of Modern Creationism* (San Diego: Master Books, 1984), 77.

24. University of Arkansas Special Collections, "Creation Science Papers," Series 6; see also Bill McLean, deposition, *McLean v. Arkansas* (1982).

25. Duane T. Gish, *Evolution: The Fossils Say No!* (San Diego: Creation Life Publishers, 1978).

26. Ibid., 11.

27. I.e., the capital "C" in "Creator" and use of the word "kinds."

28. Gish, *Evolution*, 13 (emphases in the original). The criticism of this point as "petulant" if further justified on page 17 of *Evolution* as Gish, while defending a theory of human origins that has its central and only impetus an omnipotent supernatural being, complains—without a hint of irony—that the theory of evolution "is so plastic that it is capable of explaining everything."

29. Susan Epperson, interview with author, May 29, 2007.

30. Paul Ellwanger, deposition, *McLean v. Arkansas* (1982).

31. University of Arkansas Special Collections, "Creation Science Papers." Manuscript collection 701, Box 7.

32. John Lisle, interview with author, May 20, 2007. Lisle also notes in this interview that should creation science have been mandated by one or more state legislatures, Duane Gish would have stood to make a substantial profit as one of the very few authors actively creating creation-science works that might be used as textbooks in a balanced treatment scheme.

33. I note the religious affiliations of both Lisle and Holsted as a matter of historical curiosity. After the sect's beginnings in England and the American colonies as staunch church-state separatists and fairly radical Protestant freethinkers, Baptist congregations eventually came to be affiliated with antievolutionist sentiment, including the Arkansas Initiated Act No. 1 affair. Methodists, on the other hand, were generally a more progressive sect in American history, and tended to side with those religious groups that accommodated evolution into their worldview. The case of Arkansas Act 590, and of Lisle's and Holsted's affiliations and positions on Ellwanger's bill, runs contrary to contemporary conventional wisdom.

34. Stephen A. Smith, "Scientific Creationism in Arkansas: A Study of Public Opinion, Public Persuasion, and Public Policy," *Communication Law Review I* (1982): 13–17.

35. Jim Holsted, interview with author, December 6, 2006.

36. Smith, "Scientific Creationism in Arkansas."

37. Steve Clark, interview with author, November 2, 2006.

38. John Lisle, interview with author, May 20, 2007.

39. Cliff Hoofman, interview with author, October 20, 2006.

40. *Arkansas Democrat*, March 20, 1981.

41. Jim Holsted, interview with author, December 6, 2006.

42. Ken Hicks, interview with author, May 25, 2007.

43. Arkansas Act 590, title.

44. It is important to note that "legislative purpose" is quite a different matter than "legislative intent." "Intent" is the personal motivation of a lawmaker or a lawmaking body, and is an illegal consideration in court. "Purpose" is the desire *effect* of a bill, and is a legal consideration. This precedent is laid out in *Lemon v. Kurtzman* 403 U.S. 602 (1971).

45. See, e.g., Norman L. Geisler, Creator in the Courtroom: "Scopes II" The Controversial Arkansas Creation-Evolution Trial (San Diego: Creation Life Publishers, 1982).

46. See also *United States v. Seeger* 380 U.S. 163 (1965); *Welsh v. United States* 398 U.S. 333 (1970).

47. Arkansas Act 590 (Section VI).

48. Steve Clark, interview with author, November 2, 2006.

49. Eric Naiman, "Brief on Academic Freedom," Creation Science Papers, Series 5, Box 28, University of Arkansas Special Collections.

50. *McLean v. Arkansas* (1982), Complaint. This fear can be shown to be well founded, as during deposition the bill's sponsor, Jim Holsted, concluded that teaching neither theory would be "just fine." Furthermore, during the 2001 General Session of the Arkansas Legislature, state representative Jim Holt (R-Springdale) proposed a bill that would mandate just that: a complete abandonment of any theory of origins or development. It should be noted that the actual origin of life is not a concern of biological evolutionary study. The conflation of evolution and origins is a consistent rhetorical misrepresentative tactic of antievolution activists.

51. See, e.g., Tinker v. Des Moines 393 U.S. 503 (1969); Bigelow v. Virginia 421 U.S. 809 (1975); Virginia State Board of Pharmacy v. Virginia Citizens Consumer Council 425 U.S. 748 (1976).

52. *McLean v. Arkansas* (1982), Defense brief. Creation Science Papers, University of Arkansas Special Collections.

53. Steve Clark, interview with author, November 2, 2006.

54. Ibid.

55. Ibid.

56. This effort might reasonably be compared to the John Birch Society's efforts to impeach Chief Justice Earl Warren in the 1950s. See Charles Ogletree Jr. "Judicial Activism or Judicial Necessity: The DC District Court's Criminal Justice Legacy," *Georgetown Law Journal* (March 2002.) The kicker here is that Clark is an elected official of the state of Arkansas, and his detractors are, for the most part, citizens of other states. Further, the idea that this movement could legally remove Clark is patently ludicrous, and the simplification of legal precedent and the basic rules governing government itself is once again indicative of the misleading and anti-intellectual rhetoric employed by antievolution activists and their ilk.

57. Steve Clark, interview with author, November 2, 2006.

58. *Science Digest*, October 1981.

59. Matt McNair, "Another Brick in the Wall: The Rhetoric of Creationism, Science, and Education, and the Fate of the Establishment Clause in the Science Classroom" (M.A. thesis, University of Arkansas, 2008).

60. Steve Clark, interview with author, November 2, 2007.

61. This would exclude those scientists who are "creation-scientists" inasmuch they are scientists who also happen to believe in a creator of some kind. The misrepresentation of their nominal colleagues' work and personal beliefs is yet more evidence of the disingenuousness inherent in the legislative-activist wing of the creation-science movement.

62. William V. Mayer, deposition, *McLean v. Arkansas* (1982).

63. William Overton, decision, *McLean v. Arkansas* (1982).

64. Ibid.

65. Ibid.

66. Ibid.

67. Justice William Brennan, Opinion of the Court, *Edwards v. Aguillard* (1987).

CHAPTER 13

Doe v. Human

The Establishment Clause and Bible Story Time

AFSANEH N. ROE

The State of Arkansas adopted legislation by Initiated Act 1 of 1930 to require "That every teacher or other person in charge shall provide for the reverent daily reading of a portion of the English bible without comment in every public tax supported school up and to including every high school in the state in the presence of the pupils, and prayer may be offered or the Lord's prayer repealed." While such a mandate reflected the will of the majority of voters in 1930 (For Act No. 1, 69,694, Against Act No. 1, 53,460), the United States Supreme Court later held in *Abington School District v. Schempp*, 374 U.S. 203 (1963) that mandatory Bible readings were "religious exercises, required by the States in violation of the command of the First Amendment that the Government maintain strict neutrality, neither aiding nor opposing religion." Nonetheless, the court's decisions are not self-enforcing, and determined local officials often ignore the law of the land and continue to aid and promote the dominant religion through popular, but clearly unconstitutional, practices in the public schools.

As the discussion erupted early on, "the struggle to accommodate one person's right of religious expression while not infringing on another person's right to be free from religious coercion has existed since our Founding Fathers first drafted the Bill of Rights. . . . In no arena has that battle raged more intensely than in our public schools."[1]

According to Adam Laats writing in the *Journal of Religious History*, Evangelicals have "measured their power by their influence in public institutions, especially public schools" and as the rise of Supreme Court rulings have continued to fall out of their favor, this was seen as a growing problem for society to many.[2] In *McCollum v. Board of Education*, which now is a foundation for lawsuits of its kind, a woman brought suit on behalf of her young son in a case against religious public education in Champaign, Illinois.[3] In *McCollum*, Protestant, Catholic, and Jewish instructors were entering into public schools and teaching classes during school hours.[4] The court ruled that religious instruction should stop being available on public school property during school hours and it was also seen as a violation of the First Amendment of the United States Constitution.[5] Though it was what they considered voluntary, the ruling stated that "pupils compelled by law to go to school for secular education are released in part from their legal duty upon condition that they attend the religious classes."[6] Many saw this as another fundamental turning point in successfully separating church and state, while others saw this as a societal downfall. As reported by *Time* magazine, twenty-eight top religious leaders at the time released a statement in response to the U.S. Supreme Court decision, stating that it would "greatly accelerate the trend toward the secularization of our culture."[7]

In the 1963 case *Abington School District v. Schempp*, the Supreme Court ruled 8–1 that Bible readings and the recital of the Lord's Prayer were unconstitutional in public schools.[8] Schempp's request to integrate other religions into the Bible reading sessions was not accepted by staff, which led to the case. Some in the public saw this decision as an attack on many Evangelic Christians and many saw this as a way to "kick God out of public schools" while also kicking "evangelicals out of the American mainstream."[9] This decision surely altered the way public schools were supposed to be treating religious activities.

Cases have continued to flow into the American courts, but the fight has seemed rather intense in the South. After the Bible Act was passed in 1930, the Bible became a normal part of education for many in Arkansas; others began speaking up for their constitutional rights. For example, in the early 1970s, the court case of *Goodwin v. Cross County School District*, in which a parent maintained that religious practices such as Bible distributions, minister presentations, and student prayer were a direct violation of the First and Fourteenth Amendments.[10] Additionally, in 1982 a judge in Little Rock banned "creation science" from public schools in Arkansas and held that it was "purely and simply a religious crusade to sneak the *Bible* into U.S. classrooms."[11]

These suits set the stage for the 1989 case of *Doe v. Human* in Gravette, Arkansas, a town no larger than 1,500 people at the time.[12] Students were not required, but had the "opportunity" to attend, an elective class over teachings of the Bible during school hours. Dodie Evans, the former owner and editor and chief of the *Gravette News Herald*, stated that the classes were "started in 1939 by a woman who moved to Arkansas from Ohio to help story time in rural areas. She taught at my school, and after she passed, other teachers took her place."[13] This continued for years, as many in the community found value in this tradition. Christi McLaughlin, a student at Gravette Elementary during 1965–1970, shared her experience with the Bible class:

> I loved Bible story time, as did my friends. For one thing it was a fun break from math and science. I remember it most for Bible stories that she'd read to us and sing songs like "Jesus Loves Me," but we might have also had an opportunity to memorize an easy Bible verse to recite the next time we got together. I don't think the lady that came to share bible stories with us was a teacher or even an employee of the school, but more like a guest speaker who came around once a week. Since we were a part of the standard curriculum each day, it was more like a special topic class that was offered when they could.[14]

The classes were attractive to students who wanted a break from the mundane repetition of core classes. It was a different way of learning that integrated "fun" into the school day. As McLaughlin shared more of her story, she recurrently referred to this class as "*Bible* story time," and clarified that she did not remember having a "separate Bible class" to attend. The distinction that she made, even years later, is that this gathering did not feel like a classroom setting, but more so, it was a period to enjoy story time, songs, and games. This reference is key in understanding how the students were prompted to perceive the elective class—not as religious education at all.

Due to the fact that the students were not required to go to class, there were *limited* options for those whose parents wanted to opt out. McLaughlin stated, "If parents did not want their children to attend Bible story time, it was perfectly fine. They could simply make that request, and it would be honored. Those students would just go to the office and work on homework or something."[15] In giving parents the chance to remove their child from such classes, the school was able to maintain a facade that it was honoring other religious beliefs. The question is whether the school could maintain such a belief of correctness when "perfectly fine" turned into isolation and partiality. Without doubt, it can be easy to assume that an elementary student would choose to stay in Bible story time with the majority of her/his classmates rather than being sent to the principal's office to do more work (or experience future blanket or implied ostracism). Nonetheless, this course continued for several years with no questioning of the propriety of the course by students, teachers, administrators, or parents and, from McLaughlin's perspective, this included most of the school.

Years later, it became clear that those who did not approve of the class were not given much of a voice. In 1982, a woman who worked at Gravette Elementary for five months, as a long-term substitute teacher, became greatly disturbed when she found out her third-grade students were attending the Bible class. She first attended the once-a-week class, because it was a requirement that one certified teacher be in the room at all times with the volunteers. She explained her troubled experience of observing the class for her first and only time:

> We were supposed to maintain discipline and make sure no one got rowdy. The little ladies from the church, the holiness church, would have little flannel boards and black boards and they would teach their lesson. I only went once. . . . I remember the lesson they were giving because it bothered me so greatly. The day I was there, they taught the children the song "be careful little eyes what you see . . ." *They were third graders!* Then they talked about the sinful nature and how you looked at things that were

dirty and you became dirty. You heard things that were sinful and wrong and you became sinful and wrong.[16]

As she continued in her story she found that this class was not what she was expecting. Though she began her observations with much discomfort, she stayed longer to see where the class was heading. It was not until she felt that fear was being implanted into her students at such young ages that she knew she needed to say something. She responded:

> This is where I finally had it, they made the kids hold their hands in front of their face, and think about all the things those hands could do that were sinful, like touch things they shouldn't touch, steal, and hurt someone. To me, I thought these little kids are going to be afraid of their hands! They are going to be terrified of all the things and feel bad, and it just got me. So I went to the principal, and I was livid.[17]

The fun games and songs that McLaughlin spoke about were what rushed this teacher to the principal's office to discuss her accusations against the class. When she confronted the principal about her concerns, he expressed to her that there was competition with the private Christian school in town and "in order to [keep] those children into a public school system, they had to let the ladies come in and do this class."[18] To the principal, it seemed there was no other option, and as long as they gave an outlet for parents to dismiss their students from the class, it was constitutional. Though, the backlash of opting a student out did not seem to occur to this principal as it did to this substitute teacher. She shared a little about her response to the principal and her experience with a student whose parents also did not approve:

> They were not going to stop it. It bothered me so much I didn't have to attend anymore. But I also didn't want the kids to have to attend. I was just about as upset about the little boy in class whose parents wouldn't allow him to attend. That's something else they explained you know parents have the option, when we send a note home they can send a note back saying they don't want their child to attend and that child doesn't have to, they can go to the library instead. So I said, you're excluding them? And he said, "Well that's how we handle it."[19]

Overall, the administration did not consider the true implications of the rules set in place. This teacher found herself being the only one who was standing up for the boy studying in the library by himself while the rest of his class learned about the Bible. She explained:

> At the end of this class, the ladies would always give out treats and cookies . . . The students would come back to class and be bragging about what they got, and he didn't get any. Which made it even worse, so I started bringing special treats for him so that he and I could have a party. I didn't make him go to the library by himself anymore.[20]

This teacher continued to demonstrate bravery as she spent the rest of her semester refusing to attend a class she believed was unconstitutional and supporting a young student who became isolated due to religion. The seclusion and ostracism that this little boy experienced was a consequence of his pursuing constitutional rights as a minority voice in the school community. Her story continued with sharing that a few other teachers had agreed with her, but overall most agreed with the reasoning given by the principal. Though this teacher was just one courageous voice that was willing to stand up to the norm of Gravette's educational system, a lawsuit years later attempted to bring Bible classes to an end in public schools.

In 1989, parents of a Gravette Elementary student filed suit against the Gravette School District "asking for injunctive and declaratory relief, asserting that defendant school district and school officials violated the First and Fourteenth Amendments by allowing volunteers to teach Bible classes during regular school hours."[21] These parents, who went by the placeholder names John and Mary Doe, kept their identity a secret, knowing that the response to this case would not be a positive one. According to Attorney Jim Lingle, who represented the couple, the family "had a child in the elementary school, and they were afraid for the child's well-being and even for their own safety if their names came out."[22] It was not until later in the court proceedings that it became apparent that their decision to hide their identity proved to be a wise one. Just before the case went to court, the local newspaper began writing about the accusations being made in the town. Dodie Evans, editor and chief of the *Gravette News Herald* at the time, wrote several columns addressing the case. On July 9, 1989, about a month before the case, he wrote:

> The Gravette school board and more particularly, the Gravette Christian community are being faced with decisions concerning the continuous Bible Story Classes and the Gravette Elementary School. The decision making process is going to be painful. On the one side, the court system, from past experience, has been unkind to such traditional practices no matter how noble, or moral or uplifting for a community. On another hand, it's a community operating under a tradition, which has continued with overwhelming approval for more than a century, is now confronted by unknown persons who voiced their objections. Finally, the school board must weigh the possible costs and consequences of the decision they make, knowing in advance they are in a no win situation.[23]

Just a week later, the school district held a meeting regarding the case, and it was announced in the July 26 article of the *Gravette News Herald* that the district voted to fight to keep the school's "Bible story time."[24] It was agreed that the school district would not spend any tax dollars on the court case. The community would band together, and court fees would be paid through donations. The lead defendant, Paul Dee Human, was the superintendent for the Gravette School District. Though Human had not personally attended any of the "relevant sessions," he argued that the instruction was "not religious and that it [was] not sectarian."[25] To further this argument, Human continued to share in court that the Bible readings were meant "to help [the children] determine their value system and help them become better persons" and continued by stating, "the *Bible* is the foundation of Western Culture."[26] Understanding that Human had never attended a Bible class, he was incapable of knowing firsthand what was being taught and how the lessons were implemented. The argument continued as Mrs. Elsie Smith, one of the volunteers who taught the Bible classes at the time, expressed that she taught stories for the students' "moral and ethical values, to make children better citizens."[27] It is important to define what exactly makes up a good citizen. From the plaintiff's argument, the defining issue would be a biblical foundation.

Kelly Evans, a Gravette student who attended the school four years after McLaughlin, shared that the one song she remembered singing the most was "Trust and Obey."[28] Trusting and obeying seemed to be a consistent trend in the Bible class and the song is a religious hymn. Obedience seemed to go hand in hand with good citizenship, but trusting in the "truth" seemed contradictory. Mrs. Smith testified in a confident manner that what she taught in class were "statements of fact, not statements of religion."[29] She attempted to distinguish between the two, but for the defendants, it was only a refusal to see past their personal belief system and a determination to spread the "good news."

Attorney Jim Lingle shared what it was like trying to communicate with the defendants:

> They could not see beyond themselves. They were not teaching religion, they were teaching truth—the Bible is literally true and to hell with you if you don't believe that. They had no tolerance, and really no conception of the idea that some people or any good people could believe anything different from what they did. That was the hardest part for me. I don't think they ever got it. To them, they were being persecuted.[30]

After over fifty years of teaching Bible classes, also known as "Story Time," the town was finally receiving legal pushback. The court's discussion revolved around what the school's motives were with regard to the class. To help further the principles behind determining the outcome of the case, *Lemon v. Kurtzman* of 1971 was referenced.[31] In the referenced case, it was declared that "in order for a governmental unit successfully to avoid a claim that it is establishing religion, it must appear that the challenged government activity has a secular purpose, neither advances nor inhibits religion, and does not foster an excessive entanglement with religion."[32] According to Human, their attempt to develop good citizens made the distinction. In the case summary it is noted that Gravette's school officials were indeed "partly motivated by secular purposes in allowing the *Bible* classes to be taught."[33] Though, considering the Bible classes as strictly secular was not the case.

During the first hearing, the court believed the motives of the class were to teach the fundamentals of Christianity and because the "instruction takes place during regular school hours and on school property" it could easily be perceived through a child's mind, that these classes are inseparable to the core curriculum.[34] Before the final hearing, the court issued a preliminary injunction in which the Gravette School District and its officials were to "cease its practice with respect to Bible instruction."[35]

With just three months before the next hearing, the community began responding in frustration. The newspaper in Gravette shared a glimpse of this tension right before the case by reading:

> The initial reaction to the situation is one of frustration and anger and thoughts of retaliation. These in themselves are contrary to the principles taught in the classes. The frustration occurs partially because the accusers remain unknown. Traditionally our judicial system teaches the accused in this case, the school is accused of doing wrong by offering the classes, has the right to face the accuser. The first response that comes to mind is that whatever respect a person has for one another with an opposing belief that respect dies with anonymity. The founders of our nation did not bury their heads behind hoods. In fact, plundered their signatures in the face of British superiors. Should we expect anything less from today's self-proclaimed martyrs?[36]

It was hard for a community that wanted answers for many in the community to understand why someone would hide his identity. They did not realize that as the minority voice the Doe family was protecting itself from the town's ridicule and retaliation. Their attorney, however, did not have the security of anonymity. Soon after the first ruling, Lingle began noticing hateful messages that were not just targeting him but also his family. His mother, a resident of Rogers, Arkansas, at the time, received a letter from someone asking how she could raise such a "monster."[37] On the contrary to those sending letters to his mother, or faxing messages to his office addressed to "Lucifer," Lingle shared that some unlikely townspeople were supportive through the adversity. He stated:

> I was a little surprised, but not a lot, at the hatred toward me. But a lot of people were nice, like for example, one thing that surprised me—a Catholic priest came up to me and said, "You're doing the right thing" and walked off. And a minister from the church of the Nazarenes had said, "I can't come out and say this in public, but you're doing the right thing."

It was one thing for Lingle to receive hatred, but it was another to see that he was now becoming the voice for a minority too afraid to speak out. With at least 96 percent of students attending the Bible class at the time,[38] it was clear that the majority of the town saw Lingle and the case as a threat.

Rumors of who the family could be quickly spread soon after the case was filed. Lingle shared that though there were assumptions of who they were, he does not believe anyone knew for sure.[39] Dodie Evans remarked that a couple accused of being the "Doe Family" by people in the community asked him to write a news story to clear their name.[40] Without doubt, this case was causing turmoil, which led numerous people to outwardly support the Christian majority.

Lingle held that the family was not against the Bible, or even against Christianity. According to him, his clients were not aware of the classes until their child came home and told them. He shared that "they really, really, did not want their children having that kind of instruction, and they were Christians, just of a different bend."[41] Kelly Evans, the student from a decade earlier, shared that she "had a couple of Jehovah's Witness classmates, and they would just go to the library during that time." [42] Though the defendants' faith was not pointed out in the court case in order to protect the family's identity, it seemed that the misunderstanding was much deeper than just upholding religious fundamentals. The purpose of the case was not to suppress religious freedom, but an attempt to place religion in its proper sector and out of public, government-supported education.

On August 16, the headline in the *Gravette News Herald* read: "Board Votes to Move Story Time Off Campus," as an act of the school's evasion.[43] Dodie Evans explained, "Since the classes were not held by ministers, but by a couple of individual ladies who conducted them, the board voted to move the story sessions off campus with children that were approved by their parents to attend them."[44] Though the classes did not start immediately due to the court order to cease Bible teachings completely until the next hearing, it was in the works to raise enough support to do so. Voices from all over the area were rising up in support of the Gravette School District. Kim Hendren, who had served on the Gravette City Council, Gravette School Board, and Arkansas Senate, shared this statement: "The issue is whether the local school board will control the school and not the federal courts."[45]

The full hearing was on November 2, 1989. During the hearing the school district continued to argue that "the practices were constitutional because they were nondenominational, were secular in nature, and were voluntary."[46] The description of a voluntary class is defined through the case that parents could arrange for their child to spend time in the "library, in tutoring sessions, or in other, unspecified instructional situations" instead of the Bible classes.[47] Though this may sound reasonable at first thought, it is clear that this system can easily lead to isolation and discrimination when it pertains to only 4 percent of the population.

Lingle also found himself confused at the backward motion he felt the Christian community was taking by supporting these courses. He remarked, "One thing that confounds me is that it used to be that fundamentalist Christians would have been on the other side of things. They would not have wanted someone else teaching their kids religion. Now they have become the *quote* majority. It has completely changed."[48] Christians have had a history of public Christian education, and now in America there was meant to be a clear separation of the two. Though, to the majority of Gravette, Arkansas, the Establishment Clause was anything but clear and certainly not convenient.

The plaintiff argued that the Bible story time was unconstitutional under *McCollum v. Board of Education* and *Lemon*.[49] In return, the defendants argued the exact opposite, and believed their case was distinct from *McCollum* and was constitutional under the guidelines of *Lemon*. The defendants contended that their case was different from *McCollum* due to their nondenominational teachers, absence of church sponsorship or affiliation, and not requiring attendance to classes.[50] Though the defendants struggled to support these distinctions, the court perceived many of their arguments as irrelevant, due to the fact that a nondenominational title still claims Christianity and the notion of voluntary was void due to peer pressure. The odds continued to fall for the defendants when they continued to share that their motives were primarily secular by "building character, forming moral values, and developing a truly educated person."[51] By their terms, the Bible was the foundation of all education because it is truth. In that regard, Lingle remarked: "I was a bit surprised that they took the approach they did and just said 'God said it and I believe it!' 'This is not religion, this is truth!' Their blinders were so thick."[52] Call them blinders, or call them deep convictions, the defendants in this case were determined to prove their Bible classes as constitutional and a practice of "equal access."[53]

After breaking down what a typical Bible class would incorporate, it became harder to see how such environments would have solely secular motives. The defendants believed that completely prohibiting the Bible from public schools "would violate freedom of speech and religion, as well as the right of Gravette parents to educate their children."[54] Though the school district believed they were simply exercising their rights, the decision was to make the preliminary injunction permanent because classes either "advanced or inhibited religion."[55] The court addressed that though the volunteer teachers had the right to converse over religious topics, they had "no right to teach a religious course during school hours on public school grounds."[56] The decision was made, and Gravette was not going to sit still about it.

Just days later, the local newspaper was flooded with stories in regards to the case. The November 8 issue of the *Gravette News Herald*'s headline read: "Story Time Ruled Illegal."[57] The rhetoric was strong in Gravette, as *Story Time* was exactly how the classes were portrayed to families who supported them. Dodie Evans shared that though many typically overlook a small town, this case "brought in the reporters."[58] As recorded in *USA TODAY*, just two weeks after the trial, "Bible classes began this week in donated trailer on private lot near elementary school. Judge had ruled classes taught in public school for 51 years were unconstitutional."[59] Due to the agreement that no money from the school board would be used to fund the trial or any activities surrounding it, locals funded the trailer. The school board sent out 500 petitions to be signed by parents to allow their children to attend the Bible classes, and 250 were returned.[60] What was once 96 percent of the school was now half of the population. This did not stop the perseverance of the community to continue fighting the cause.

In November, it was decided by the school district to appeal the case, and many in the community voiced their support to contribute funds all the way to the Supreme Court.[61] In November, $20,000 of donations were received, but the board still questioned whether enough funds could be raised.[62] Publications were reporting: "Donations will finance Gravette School Board appeal of ruling against on-campus *Bible* classes, officials said. Appeal to U.S. Supreme Court could cost $100,000."[63] After hesitant deliberation, the school board decided to postpone.[64] Though questions of moving forward were arising, strong voices began to partner with the school district's attempt to appeal the case. In January, Arnold Murray, a Gravette minister who conducted a nationwide television ministry, announced that people everywhere should "help fight the battle" guaranteeing enough money to press forward.[65]

A year after the first case, the headline of the *Gravette News Herald* read: "Bible Case Appeal to U.S. Supreme Court" where more than $40,000 has already been paid for legal fees with more to come.[66] The school district still believed they could slightly restructure the class and return them back to the school through the appeal. It was not until March of that year that the Gravette School Board received news that the Supreme Court refused to hear the case. On May 1, the Gravette School Board decided not to pursue anything further in the court system and made an announcement to the town: "We have made a gallant effort, and while disappointed in the Supreme Court decision, we are still fortunate in that we can offer released time for the students to attend classes off campus."[67] While many were dissatisfied with the court ruling, those "fighting the good fight" did not see it as a complete loss. In response to the Supreme Court decision, the mobile trailer where Bible classes had been held the past year was transitioned into a chapel built by Kim Hendren on his property near the school.[68] While this appeared contradictory to the law, the *Gravette News Herald* reported that Lingle's clients were not looking to challenge the offsite practice.[69]

Though the court case ruling meant to craft an end to the violation of the First and Fourteenth Amendments, Gravette continued to do what the majority felt was right: to conduct Bible story time on their terms. As James Madison shared in a letter to Thomas Jefferson, "Repeated violations of those parchment barriers have been committed by overbearing majorities in every State. In Virginia I have seen the Bill of Rights violated in every instance where it has been opposed to a popular current."[70] Likewise, Dodie Evans believed that a court case itself could not change a half-century tradition.[71] This proved to be correct; the Gravette school system remained in their practice of Bible story time, and they continue to this day. The popular voice did not face defeat, but found freedom in evasion. Regardless of the ruling of *Doe v. Human*, the result proved that a government could not enforce the Constitution easily when it is not in line with what the majority desires. The offsite loophole brought an answer that satisfied the majority of the community. To this day, Lingle does not regret standing for what he believed was the right thing to do, adding that during the fight, "God [was] on our side."[72]

NOTES

1. Tom Bennett and George Foldesy, "Our Father in Heaven: A Legal Analysis of the Recitation of the Lord's Prayer by Public Schools Coaches," *Clearing House: A Journal of Educational Strategies* 81, no. 4 (2008).

2. Adam Laats, "Our Schools, Our Country: American Evangelicals, Public Schools, and the Supreme Court Decisions of 1962 and 1963," *Journal of Religious History* 36, no. 3 (2012).

3. McCollum v. Board of Education, 333 U.S. 203 (1948).

4. Ibid.

5. "Religion: On School Time or Off?" *Time*, March 22, 1948.

6. McCollum v. Board of Education, 333 U.S. 203 (1948).

7. "Religion: Separate-or Secular?" *Time*, July 19, 1948.

8. *Abington School District v. Schempp*, 374 U.S. 203 (1963).

9. Laats, "Our Schools, Our Country."

10. *Goodwin v. Cross County School District*, 394 F. Supp. 417 (E.D. Ark. 1973).

11. *McLean v. Arkansas Board of Education*, 529 F. Supp. 1255 (E.D. Ark. 1982); "'Creation Science' a Ploy to Sneak Bible into U.S. Schools, Judge Rules," *Globe and Mail* (Toronto, Canada), January 6, 1982.

12. United States Census Bureau. Gravette, Population (1980).

13. Dodie Evans, interview with author, April 13, 2015.

14. Christi McLaughlin, interview with author, April 15, 2015.

15. Ibid.

16. Anonymous (by request) Gravette substitute teacher, interview with author, March 28, 2015.

17. Ibid.

18. Ibid.

19. Ibid.

20. Ibid.

21. *Doe v. Human*, 725 F. Supp. 1499 (1989).

22. Attorney Jim Lingle, interview with author, March 28, 2015.

23. Dodie Evans, "Off the Cuff," *Gravette News Herald*, July 9, 1989.

24. Dodie Evans, "Off the Cuff," *Gravette News Herald*, July 26, 1989.

25. *Doe v. Human*, 725 F. Supp. 1499 (1989).

26. Ibid.

27. Ibid.

28. Kelly Evans, interview with author, April 15, 2015.

29. *Doe v. Human,* 725 F. Supp. 1499 (1989).

30. Attorney Jim Lingle, interview with author, March 28, 2015.

31. *Lemon v. Kurtzman,* 403 U.S. 602 (1971).

32. *Doe v. Human,* 725 F. Supp. 1499 (1989).

33. Ibid.

34. Ibid.

35. Ibid.

36. Dodie Evans, "Off the Cuff," *Gravette News Herald,* July 9, 1989.

37. Attorney Jim Lingle, interview with author, March 28, 2015.

38. *Doe v. Human,* 725 F. Supp. 1499 (1989).

39. Attorney Jim Lingle, interview with author, March 28, 2015.

40. Dodie Evans, interview with author, April 13, 2015.

41. Attorney Jim Lingle, interview with author, March 28, 2015.

42. Kelly Evans, interview with author, April 15, 2015.

43. *Gravette News Herald,* August 9, 1989.

44. Dodie Evans, interview with author, April 13, 2015.

45. Ibid.

46. *Doe v. Human,* 725 F. Supp. 1499 (1989).

47. Ibid.

48. Attorney Jim Lingle, interview with author, March 28, 2015.

49. McCollum v. Board of Education, 333 U.S. 203 (1948).

50. Ibid.

51. Ibid.

52. Attorney Jim Lingle, interview with author, March 28, 2015.

53. *Doe v. Human,* 725 F. Supp. 1499 (1989). The School District "did not argue at the hearing that they were obliged to allow Bible classes under the 'equal access' rule of *Widmar v. Vincent,* 454 U.S. 263, 102 S. Ct. 269, 70 L. Ed. 2d 440 (1981), nor did they produce testimony from which the court could determine whether the *Widmar* principles were relevant here.

54. Ibid.

55. Ibid.

56. Ibid.

57. "Story Time Ruled Illegal," *Gravette News Herald,* November 8, 1989.

58. Dodie Evans, interview with author, April 13, 2015.

59. "ARKANSAS," *USA TODAY,* November 17, 1989.

60. Dodie Evans, interview with author, April 13, 2015.

61. Ibid.

62. Ibid.

63. "ARKANSAS," *USA TODAY,* November 21, 1989.

64. *Gravette News Herald,* December 20, 1989.

65. Dodie Evans, "Off the Cuff," *Gravette News Herald,* January 10, 1990.

66. *Gravette News Herald,* January 30, 1991.

67. Gravette News Herald, May 1, 1991.

68. Ibid.

69. *Gravette News Herald,* February 1991.

70. James Madison to Thomas Jefferson, October 17, 1788. *The Founders' Constitution.* Volume 1, Chapter 14, Document 47.

71. Dodie Evans, interview with author, April 13, 2015.

72. Attorney Jim Lingle, interview with author, March 28, 2015.

CHAPTER 14

Pulpit Politics

Politics and Sermons of Robert E. Smith and Ronnie Floyd

KATTRINA BALDUS JONES

Blame our ancestors. The collision of faith and politics has been at the forefront of presidential campaigns for decades, and in the last two elections, Arkansan religious leaders Robert E. Smith and Ronnie Floyd have used the pulpit to express their political preferences. In 2004, Ronnie Floyd told a national audience on Fox News Channel that he had simply been encouraging his followers to "vote God, His ways, His will, His Word" in sermons—*not* endorsing a presidential candidate.[1] However, God looked strikingly similar to George W. Bush in a projected image sitting behind the podium of the First Baptist Church of Springdale. Four years later, Robert E. Smith of Little Rock became the first Arkansas pastor to sign "The Pulpit Initiative," a plan that sought to challenge a 1954 IRS rule prohibiting pastors from officially endorsing political candidates in their sermons.[2] Although the Separation of Church and State has long since been a heated topic for debate, Arkansas's involvement and influence in particular regarding pulpit politics have been making headlines across the nation. In order to fully understand Arkansas's role in pulpit politics, we must carefully examine the controversial sermons of Dr. Ronnie Floyd and Bishop

Robert E. Smith, corresponding statewide and national public reactions, and each sermon's impact on rights of religious organizations.

Review of the Literature

Despite the tight-knit relationship between religion and politics, religious leaders' decision to voice their opinions from the pulpit regarding presidential preferences is not devoid of repercussions. Religious leaders' official endorsement of political candidates puts their churches at risk of violating their tax-exempt status with the IRS.[3] Churches, integrated auxiliaries of churches, and other religious organizations may be legally organized under state law in several ways, including but not limited to unincorporated associations, nonprofit corporations, corporations sole, and charitable trusts.[4] Accordingly, aforementioned organizations qualify for exemption from federal income tax under the Internal Revenue Code (IRC), section 501(c)(3) and are usually eligible to receive tax-deductible contributions.[5] Furthermore, all IRC section 501(c)(3) religious organizations and churches must obey certain rules in order to maintain their tax-exemption statuses. The most significant stipulation that religious organizations and churches must abide by is as follows: "[Churches and religious organizations] must not participate in, or intervene in, any political campaign on behalf of (or in opposition to) *any* candidate for public office."[6] While the prevalence of the correlation between faith and politics may have been present in the past two elections, the public endorsement of any political candidate running for elective office is illegal according to the IRS. Moreover, the IRS tax guide clearly explicates the ramifications of *any* political campaign activity:

> Contributions to political campaign funds or public statements of position (verbal or written) made on behalf of the organization in favor of or in opposition to any candidate for public office clearly violate the prohibition against campaign activity. Violation of this prohibition may result in denial or revocation of tax-exempt status and the imposition of certain excise tax.[7]

Contrary to IRS standards, religious advocates of political endorsement by religious institutions abide by a different set of guidelines. According to the Bill of Rights in the United States Constitution, the First Amendment reads:

> Congress shall make no law respecting an establishment of religion, or prohibiting the free exercise thereof; of abridging the freedom of speech, or of the press; or the right of the people peaceably to assemble, and to petition the Government for a redress of grievances.[8]

Thus, a controversy is born; while the IRS asserts that religious affiliates may not use the pulpit to promulgate political agendas, the First Amendment states that all people have the right to freedom of speech. Furthermore, Congress cannot lawfully intervene with the practice of religion. The First Amendment can serve to not only justify the behavior of many U.S. citizens, but is also exercised—some would say abused—by our own president. Separationists (advocating the separation of church and state) claim that the reemergence of the relationship between religion and government was demonstrated to the American people for eight years during the Bush administration.[9] Furthermore, Bush's repeated use of "religious rhetoric" attracted many evangelical Christians, thus condoning similar behavior in churches and religious institutions across the United States.[10]

Although there have been public reactions supporting both sides of the story, there is a paucity of literature extensively investigating the specific rhetorical devices employed in religious sermons. In fact, two of the most controversial and outspoken religious figures in the past two presidential elections were Arkansas's own pastors, Bishop Robert E. Smith and Dr. Ronnie Floyd. On Independence Day in 2004, Ronnie Floyd, pastor of both the First Baptist Church in Springdale and the Church at Pinnacle Hills in Rogers,[11] delivered and broadcasted a sermon in which he allegedly endorsed George W. Bush via national television.[12] Shortly thereafter, Floyd posted the sermon on his personal website where Laura Kellams, well-respected reporter of the *Arkansas Democrat-Gazette*, quickly discovered it.[13] After watching Floyd's sermon, Kellams notified Reverend Barry Lynn, executive director of Americans United (AU) for Separation of Church and State, a liberal watchdog group advocating for the legal enforcement of separation of church and state.[14] Kellams frequently explored "the role of churches in American politics"[15] in her research for the *Gazette* and, upon viewing Floyd's sermon, called attention to Barry Lynn and AU to take action.[16]

Subsequently, Lynn proclaimed that Floyd's sermon was comparable to a Bush campaign commercial, overtly endorsing Bush and in turn denigrating Senator John Kerry.[17] In response to what he perceived to be ill-placed partisan politics, Lynn wrote a letter to the Internal Revenue Service, informing the organization about Floyd's unmistakable promulgation of George W. Bush for president, and his resultant violation of IRC 501(c)(3).[18] While the sermon elicited relatively adverse public reactions and was showered with media attention, Floyd continues to successfully practice in both of his church campuses in northwestern Arkansas. To better understand the implications of Floyd's endorsement of George W. Bush, interpretations of the First Amendment, and the rights of religious leaders, we must investigate Floyd's rhetorical devices and revisit the social criticisms and opinions surrounding the 2004 sermon.

Fast-forwarding by four years, Arkansas elicited additional media interest in the 2008 election when Bishop Robert E. Smith of the Word of Outreach Christian Center in Little Rock was the first Arkansas pastor to sign what is known as "The Pulpit Initiative," a strategic litigation plan instigated by the Alliance Defense Fund (ADF), a conservative, Christian legal alliance formed to fight for religious freedoms.[19] The Pulpit Initiative seeks to restore the rights of religious leaders and pastors to speak "Scriptural truths" from the pulpit without jeopardizing their church's tax-exempt status.[20] Although Bishop Smith was unable to participate in "Pulpit Freedom Sunday" on the Sunday originally designated due to airfare delay, he publicly endorsed Senator John McCain the following Sunday on October 12, 2008. Citing the First Amendment as their alibi, more than thirty pastors nationwide participated, "flagrantly violating a 54-year-old Supreme Court Ruling that prohibits tax-exempt churches from publicly endorsing politicians."[21] Erik Stanley, attorney for the ADF, claimed that if the IRS gave trouble to any of the churches involved, the ADF planned to "sue the IRS in federal court."[22] By the same token, Bishop Robert E. Smith's sermon was also discovered by reporters at the *Arkansas Democrat-Gazette*, to which Barry Lynn wrote another letter to the IRS exposing his violation of tax laws.

Because contemporary media outlets have sufficiently addressed both Ronnie Floyd and Robert E. Smith and the ongoing debate surrounding pulpit politics, it is imperative that we examine public perceptions, the specific rhetorical strategies employed in each sermon, and similarities and differences evident in each. Furthermore, in light of its modernity and pertinence to ubiquitous controversies, it is also critical to analyze both of the pastors' sermons in relation to the First Amendment. Finally and perhaps most importantly, we must adequately address the public reaction to both Smith's and Floyd's sermons, in an attempt to understand popular conceptions of "pulpit politics" and the function of the First Amendment. Thus, such undertakings give rise to the following research questions:

1. What rhetorical strategies were employed in both Robert E. Smith and Dr. Ronnie Floyd's presidential endorsement sermons?

2. What similarities and differences in each of these religious leaders' sermons were present?

3. What were the public reactions to and criticisms of the sermons, and how do these reflect popular understandings of the First Amendment?

Methodology

In order to answer the proposed research questions, I employed a multitude of historical methods, including oral history interviews, the examination of contemporary media sources, and a comparative rhetorical analysis of the teachings of Dr. Ronnie Floyd of Springdale and Dr. Robert E. Smith of Little Rock, Arkansas. First and foremost, I explored contemporary media outlets in Arkansas to uncover the public reactions of each sermon, including several articles featured in the press archives of Americans United from 2004 and 2008, newspaper articles, blog posts, and editorials published in the *Arkansas Democrat-Gazette* and the *Arkansas Times*. Additionally, I navigated both pastors' personal websites to obtain church background information and short biographies. In order to study the implications of the sermons on the *national* level, I reviewed in-depth interviews posted with each pastor on network television station websites (e.g.,

Fox News and NPR). Furthermore, I also consulted sources regarding relevant rhetorical means by which to frame and analyze the data.

Upon contacting Dr. Robert Smith in Little Rock, I was able to obtain a DVD of his October 12, 2008, sermon entitled "The Issues, The Republic, The Candidates" with relative ease, which I transcribed to the best of my ability. In addition, I conducted a personal interview with Dr. Smith in All Things Whatsoever Christian Center in Lowell, Arkansas, in which Dr. Smith provided a reconstruction of the event, including clarifications, intentions, and perspectives regarding his October 12, 2008, address. Unfortunately, I was not able to conduct a personal interview with Dr. Ronnie Floyd of Springdale, despite countless efforts put forth to contact him. Multiple emails and phone calls went unanswered. However, I *was* able to get a hold of Mr. Rob Boston, spokesperson and contributing writer for AU's Press Center, who directed me to the Press Archives on AU's website. There, I located Dr. Floyd's July 4, 2004, sermon and compiled a transcription from AU's press releases and articles. Upon receipt of *both* sermons, I conducted a comparative rhetorical analysis of the two sermons in which similarities, differences, and rhetorical strategies were examined. Finally, I reviewed the public reactions and popular understandings surrounding the religious leaders' messages. The following sections illustrate such findings.

Rhetorical Strategies

For many, casting a ballot in the 2004 presidential election portrayed a sense of patriotism and political involvement, but for some, it also embodied a sentiment of biblical morality.[23] According to surveys distributed to those who voted in the 2004 election, George W. Bush won 79 percent of the 26.5 million evangelical Christian votes in November 2004, representing "Christian activists [who] led the charge that GOP operatives followed and capitalized upon."[24] In vehement disagreement with pro-choice and same-sex marriage, Christian religious leaders felt compelled to encourage congregants to vote. Ronnie Floyd of Arkansas, for example, attested that Christians desperately needed to get involved: "[Same-sex marriage] touches every segment of society, schools, the media, television, government, churches. No one is left out." [25] Thus, in light of perceived Christian obligation and political exigency, Floyd took partisan politicking to the pulpit.

ETHOS

Originating as an Aristotelian appeal, *ethos* can be defined as "the persuasive appeal of one's character."[26] Ethos appeals are rhetorical tools governed by ethics, morals, values, standards, principles, or one's conscience.[27] According to Aristotle, ethos is established by means of how knowledgeable, authoritative, and benevolent a speaker appears to be about his or her subject.[28] Upon authoring eighteen different books, nationally broadcasting weekly sermons, and speaking at two different church campuses with nearly 16,000 congregants,[29] Ronnie Floyd has established a respectable reputation, and a strong rapport with his community,[30] thus qualifying him as a worthy candidate for credibility. What's more, Floyd's credibility in the conveyance of his Christian faith is easily transferrable to not only his political agenda, but ultimately contributes to his overall rhetorical repertoire. Hence, he is able to use the credibility he has implicitly earned (e.g., through establishing a good reputation) in conjunction with the explicit credibility he integrates into his Sunday sermons. For example, consider the following excerpt in which Floyd alludes to the above-mentioned decline of evangelical Christian voters supporting George W. Bush:

> In the presidential election of 2000, a Barna Research poll observed that 57 percent of the evangelical vote went to George W. Bush, while 42 percent went to Al Gore . . . According to the polls, conservative Protestant turnout dropped from 19 percent of the vote in 1996 to 15 percent in the year 2000. In the 2000 election, President Bush received among evangelicals about 4 million fewer votes than Bob Dole received in 1996. Amazingly, George W. Bush defeated Al Gore by a margin of only 537 votes [in Florida].[31]

First and foremost, Floyd exemplifies the concept of being a *knowledgeable* speaker by means of reciting specific, succinct statistical information in which he delivers quick facts that are relatively easy for his congregants to follow. Secondly, Floyd reiterates ethos through the verbal citation of the sources from which the statistics were obtained. Finally, Floyd demonstrates authority in this segment of his sermon through benevolence, which he ascertains through the word "amazingly" in the final sentence of the quotation, in an attempt to soften his audience through the element of flattering, awe-stricken language. Therefore, in expressing that George W. Bush is "amazing" in being able to overcome so many obstacles, he attempts to elicit perceptions of benevolence and kindness among his congregation. Thus, Floyd employs ethos according to the criteria prescribed—and effectively—insofar as the strategies executed accomplish the persuasive goal he had originally intended upon.

Although Bush won nearly 80 percent of all evangelical Christian votes back in 2004,[32] the outcome of the 2008 presidential election not only proved to be vastly *different* from 2004 in what turned out to be one of—if not *the* most—historical election in United States history to date. About eight months before the election, a Godtube.com poll result revealed that nearly 44 percent of Christian voters supported two of the nation's pro-choice Democratic candidates, Barack Obama and Hillary Clinton.[33] What's more, Obama continued on to win the 2008 presidential election with substantially more evangelical Christian votes than anyone expected, with what some touted as a "faith-based appeal."[34] In light of the notion that "the evangelical movement is changing," as noted by McCain's constituents at a 2008 Republican fundraiser,[35] politically active pastors like Bishop Robert E. Smith looked beyond economical struggles and resisted putting faith on the backburner. Ultimately, Smith sought to preserve the deep-seated bond between Christianity and conservativism. While Floyd capitalized on his character and credibility through ethos, Smith presented emotional appeals as a means to bolster political action among his congregants.

PATHOS

A term also crafted by Aristotle, *pathos* refers to "an appeal to one's emotions."[36] Further, pathos is centered on sympathy, compassion, sentimentality, and the heart.[37] Pathos appeals are often employed to evoke an emotional response from a listener or audience member, as pathos is the "category by which we can understand the psychological aspects of rhetoric."[38] In preparation of his "Pulpit Freedom Sunday"[39] sermon, Smith incorporated a plethora of pathos strategies; however, guilt and fear emerged as the two most effective appeals and are addressed herein. About three-quarters of the way through his sermon, Bishop Smith addressed same-sex marriage in extensive detail, by way of illustrating the Bible's opposition to homosexual activity. Below, Smith incorporates a particularly callous, emotionally charged appeal:

> [Sodomy] is worthy of death and [...] should be punishable by the death sentence. [Also], one who makes it convenient, those who legislate in favor of it, all the way to the Supreme Court Justices—to abortion clinics, to those who say "go get one cause I don't want it" [are all equally guilty].[40]

In the passage above, Smith asserts that even people merely *associated* with abortion in any way, shape, or form—whether it be an innocent bystander, someone who has entertained the mere *thought* of what it might entail, or a doctor who performs one—should be subject to equally harsh punishment. Further, he implies that any person who is simply affiliated with someone who is pro-choice should cut off such ties and feel immediate remorse and guilt. What's more, the first sentence in the sermon encapsulates an intense, malicious message: if any person engages in sodomy, then they should be *executed*. When asked in an interview to elaborate on this statement, Smith supported his assertion in saying, "Sodomy *should* be punishable by death. With same-sex [relations], one cannot reproduce a life. Where is the humanity, then? You have total perversion. Anarchy."[41] In his response, he proposes that to be homosexual is to be *inhuman*, perverse, and anarchic. Worst of all, *after* evoking ill perceptions and social anarchy, Bishop Smith attests that a homosexual person should be cold-bloodedly *murdered* for their sexual orientation. This is an *extremely* disturbing and foreboding concept for congregants—regardless of sexual preference, thus instilling a fear in them *so* powerful that they have *no* choice but to believe homosexuality is wrong. In sum, Bishop Smith effectively evokes daunting feelings of guilt and fear through his intense, graphic language.

EXIGENCY

To begin his sermon, Ronnie Floyd employed the strategy of exigency through his religious rhetoric, so as to accentuate the dire need for voters to prevent anti-Christian legislation (e.g., abortion or same-sex marriage). "I believe this will be one of the most critical elections in U.S. history," stated Floyd in his July 4, 2004, sermon.[42] Floyd illustrates a sense of exigency among his congregants by virtue of the words "critical" and "history," implying that the current political situation warrants immediate attention and action. In hopes to cultivate Christian voting, Floyd questioned, "Why would evangelical Christians stay at home and not practice the responsibility of Christian citizenship, when God's word, which we say we believe, calls us to stand up in our citizenship?" Here, Floyd suggests that Christians have a "responsibility" and therefore an obligation to represent their Christian faith in the voting booth. In so doing, Floyd establishes a sense of *duty* to God and moral allegiance to the Christian faith as a whole. Further, Floyd is in fact *accusatory* in his words, mocking his congregation in saying that they "say" they believe in the word of God, but suggests that one cannot possibly be following the exigent words of God if he or she "stay[s] at home" and does not execute God's will on the ballot. Consequently, Floyd's impetus for prompt action on behalf of God through the incorporation of exigent language ultimately serves as a vehicle for a compliant, faith-driven citizenry.

Correspondingly, political circumstances *also* warranted swift action in the eyes of Robert E. Smith in the 2008 election. Similar to Dr. Floyd, Smith also employs the rhetorical strategy of exigency in his sermon in 2008, advocating for active Christian involvement in the upcoming election: "This is such a volatile, controversial election [. . .]," asserted Smith, "policy-making is particularly important this year." Like Floyd, Smith attempts to foster a sense of emergency among his audience, paralleling Floyd's terminology by using "important" instead of "critical" to heighten worshippers' attention. Additionally, Smith incorporates the idea of instability and unpredictability of the election's outcome by saying it is "volatile" and "controversial," thereby motivating congregants to vote to avoid a potentially dangerous situation. What's more, Smith also parallels Floyd's reminder to his congregants of their moral *obligation* and duty to the church as a means to motivate them to vote wisely:

> In elections, men are bound to vote for the candidate to the best of their knowledge. They are required to vote based on faith. If I

don't have faith, I can't vote. For the Christian, voting expresses the mind of God on issues and persons.[43]

Here, Smith not only expresses the urgent need for Christians to vote—demanding that we are "bound" as men—but more importantly, he also asserts that such men must vote based on Christian morals and ideals. Moreover, Smith also utilizes this strategy toward the end of his 2008 sermon in declaring, "God is concerned with the men in office."[44] Again, this statement reiterates the demand for Christians to become politically active, so as to evade the inevitable danger that may ensue if apathy persists. Smith is conveying the message that God has given his "disciples" direct orders and that it is time for the true Christians to comply. Thus, both Floyd and Smith stressed exigency in the rhetoric of their sermons; they assert that Christians must appropriately and immediately demonstrate their faith by virtue of voting for whomever candidate their pastor deems fit.

"OTHERING"

Upon eliciting feelings of political emergency and a pressing need for Christians to preserve their faith in the 2004 election, Floyd integrated the rhetorical strategy of "othering," by way of his recurrent reference to "one candidate" versus "the other."[45] In accordance with the "self/other-nexus" of identity theory, one's identity can be constructed through establishing what some*thing* or some*one is*, or *is not*; that is, clear-cut distinctions are made between one entity and another so as to illustrate important differences.[46] Thus, we are subject to Ronnie Floyd's othering through his unabashed demarcation of presidential candidates in his July 4, 2004, sermon:

> One candidate believes that the United States is at war with terrorism. The other believes we're not at war at all, but in a lawsuit. One candidate believes in the sanctity of an unborn life, signing legislation banning partial-birth abortion and declaring that human life is a sacred gift from our Creator. The other believes in abortion on demand, voting six times in the United States Senate against the ban and insisting there is no such thing as a partial birth.[47]

In this excerpt, Ronnie Floyd establishes "the other" by continually utilizing the phrase "one candidate" to refer to the candidate in which he *does* support, while "the other is the candidate he *does not* support. In so doing, Floyd assembles an "Us vs. Them" mentality, implying that the moral configuration of "one candidate" is *so* drastically different from that of "the other" that the two are in essence *at battle* with each other. Floyd appears to be making a calculated effort not only to pinpoint the key differences between the two presidential candidates, but also to position one *against* and in fact, *over* "the other." Further, he also ridicules "the other" by virtue of condescension; in that, he mocks this unfavorable contender in the first sentence of this excerpt by suggesting that "the other" is incapable of understanding what a war on terrorism truly is, and on the contrary has confused the country's (then, current) situation of warfare with a mere "lawsuit." Finally, he comparatively praises "one candidate" while disparaging "the other" by virtue of explicit allusions to instances in which the estranged candidate supported anti-Christian legislation.

To elaborate further, in examining the campaign platform of both candidates, one discovers the following: *Bush* supported the war on terrorism, while Kerry opposed it; *Bush* supported banning partial-birth abortion and thus believed in "the sanctity of an unborn life," as declared by Floyd above, and Kerry voted against the ban on partial-birth abortion. Thus, in accordance with the self/other dichotomy, Floyd essentially alleges that "one candidate" is morally superior, intrinsically smarter, and holistically more Christian than "the other." In sum, "one candidate" is George W. Bush, while "the other" is John Kerry.

Partitioning the two candidates amplifies certain distinctions between the qualities of the two individuals, one of whom he has alienated and deemed unworthy and anti-Christian—all by means of a repetitive, somewhat unpleasant reference to an "other."

POWERFUL LANGUAGE: ABSOLUTES

Conversely, Bishop Smith does *not* implement othering as his chief rhetorical tool in his 2008 sermon, despite aforementioned similarities in exigent messages. By contrast, Smith employs a multitude of powerful language and often speaks in *absolute terms* when preaching to his congregation. In fact, one might argue that this rhetorical strategy is more effective in its execution than the employment of othering; in that, othering approaches arguments more circuitously, perhaps rendering the language more *powerless* rather than *powerful*. Notwithstanding the risk of logical fallacies, speaking in absolutes *can* present a false sense of certainty if employed as a "totalizing statement."[48] However, words like "don't," "must," and "cannot" can be effectively used and oftentimes make the speaker's words seem forceful and potentially indisputable. For example, Smith employs powerful verbal language in his contention that women do not (nor anyone, for that matter) have the right to perform an abortion:

> A woman is said to have the rights and authority over her own body. Well, that's the lie the serpent told Eve. I have news for women today—especially Christian women—a Christian woman does *not* have the rights over her body. It is *not* your independent property. [God] says: "You are *not* your own—I have purchased you." A woman does *not* have the right, by God or by her husband, to go and get an abortion.[49]

The language used in this excerpt is markedly bold, albeit controversial, thereby eliciting the effect of irrefutability in the communication of absolute terms. More specifically, Smith includes the above italicized word, "not," four different times in this segment of his sermon, covering all bases with a commanding, assertive edge in his arguments. Further, he does not allow room for disagreement or refutation in any way, and strategically neglects to utilize contractions of any kind, hence congealing his assertions. Although he has objectified females in the process, Bishop Smith successfully amalgamates a classic biblical reference (e.g., Adam and Eve), the omniscience of God (as a "purchaser"), and his fervent pro-life convictions—all through the expression of powerful, absolute terms.

In a similar vein, Smith upholds absoluteness as a rhetorical cue to denigrate those who support abortion: "A person who commits, or submits to, agrees with, or legislates in support of abortion *cannot* believe in God, much less say they are a Christian."[50] Here, Smith perpetuates his disdain for abortion and all those associated with it by means of powerful language. Effectively, Smith avoids abbreviations, contractions, disclaimers, and tag questions, and instead speaks in absolute terms such as "cannot," so as to motivate his audience to preserve their Christian faith by voting for the candidate who opposes abortion. Why? Because, according to Bishop Robert E. Smith, "If I don't have faith, I can't vote."[51] Thus, his sermon is infused with absolute statements embedded in biblical faith that often render his arguments quite compelling.

Public Controversy: Support vs. Opposition

Regardless as to whether or not the clever rhetorical devices employed by Bishop Smith or Dr. Floyd were carefully calculated or simply intrinsic to their leadership and devotion to the Christian faith, extensive media coverage suggests that both sermons elicited not only ample public attention but more importantly, public *controversy*—in both the religious and political arena. Notably, in Smith and Floyd's resurfacing of the historic link between church and state, tax privileges were compromised; notoriety replaced popularity, and constitutional law was called into question. All things considered, the two sermons under examination evoked a public outcry, in turn bolstering the nationwide divide between pulpit politicking, interpretations of the First Amendment, and legitimacy of IRS tax codes.

Vote IRS

Every superman has his kryptonite. In spite of having two megachurches and a mini-Christian enterprise attracting over 16,000 supporters[52] with an unremitting allegiance to his work, Ronnie Floyd is *not* considered to be a hero by all northwestern Arkansans. Indirectly, in fact, Arkansas's perhaps most widely read publication, the *Arkansas Democrat-Gazette*, is arguably *the* organization responsible for precipitating national attention to Floyd, and consequently active interest by Americans United. Consequently, Floyd's churches' tax-exempt status was compromised and his sermon was subject to high volumes of public and legal scrutiny.

Taking a side, the *Gazette*'s own Pat Lynch, a free-lance columnist and radio broadcaster in central Arkansas for the past twenty years, questioned Floyd's all-too-revealing political agenda:

Floyd is playing with fire and he knows it. Politics and power are the most potent mood-altering substances, and their abuse can be more than intoxicating. He is a good man, I am sure, and First Baptist is a fine and faithful congregation, but nice people still occasionally make big mistakes.[53]

Interestingly, Lynch compares Floyd's political power to an intoxicating, abusive drug. In so doing, he implies that Floyd's congregation is *dependent* upon him and thus are likely to be heavily influenced— perhaps even unknowingly so—by his assertions. Thus, he argues that Floyd is subjecting congregants to his political "intoxicants," ultimately dictating their voting decisions on Election Day. Notwithstanding the likelihood that Floyd *is* probably a "good man," Lynch acknowledges that he is crossing a line as his political words are not devoid of consequences, nor are they devoid of potential "side effects."

Reporters were not Floyd's only kryptonite. In fact, a multitude of residents across the state—and nation for that matter—were in fervent opposition to Floyd's ill placement of his presidential preferences. Edward Hejtmanek, a resident of Fayetteville, Arkansas, writes of his disagreement with Floyd for campaigning for Bush, indicating that he (Hejtmanek) seeks to preserve the value of separation of church and state:

> It is difficult to understand the hypocrisy of local minister Ronnie Floyd. His campaigning for President Bush from the pulpit is in violation of the spirit of the constitutional separation of church and state. [. . .] I call upon thinking members of the Springdale congregation to hold Floyd accountable for hypocrisy.[54]

In this letter to the editor, Hejtmanek firmly expresses his belief that the words preached by Ronnie Floyd violate the Constitution; while he may be entitled to convey the "word of God" through social issues, he claims that he has breached that right and is "campaigning for Bush." Further, he encourages Floyd's congregation to look past their allegiance to their beloved pastor, Christianity—even their political affiliation—to recognize that Floyd is obligated to not only God, but also to the *law*, which states that he can*not* endorse a political candidate on the pulpit.

In a similar vein, one of Ronnie Floyd's detractors recalls the sermon on a well-visited *Arkansas Times* blog post, attesting that Floyd's messages were a clear violation of separation of church and state:

We can all remember the July 4, 2004 service when Ronnie told
us to "vote God" while showing Bush's picture on the giant screen
behind him. This WAS a campaign for Bush and Ronnie Floyd
lied by denying it. It's all about motives. He may have stayed in
bounds as far as the written law goes, but it's all about motives
and Ronnie pushed the envelope. By denying it, he lied, plain and
simple. He should realize it and apologize for it. Unfortunately,
the whole church suffered for it.[55]

As shown above, Bill the blogger believes that in staying "in
bounds as far as the written law goes,"[56] Ronnie Floyd was able to
get away with preaching his political views on the pulpit. Further,
he describes the sermon as a "campaign" for George W. Bush, which
would clearly violate IRC code (5)(c)(3), thereby making his sermon
not only a "lie," but more importantly, illegal. Mirroring this Arkansan
resident's convictions is Reverend Barry Lynn, executive director of
Americans United, who was outraged upon viewing the nationally
televised sermon, using similar terminology to describe the sermon:
"Pastor Floyd's presentation seemed more like a Bush campaign commercial than a church service."[57] Thus, in accordance with AU's mission,[58] Lynn wrote a letter to the Internal Revenue Service on July 20,
2004, in which he illustrated his perception of the transparency of
Floyd's endorsement of George W. Bush:[59]

> It is clear that Floyd's message was intended to intervene in the
> election on behalf of Bush. The pastor's description of the can-
> didates' stands and their personal religious beliefs was obviously
> aimed at encouraging congregants to cast ballots for Bush. The
> church is known for its stands on social issues and its opposi-
> tion to legal abortion and gay rights. By lauding Bush's stands on
> these and other issues and attacking Kerry's, Floyd was plainly
> telling his congregation to be sure to vote for Bush.[60]

Here, Lynn asserted that Floyd was quite blatantly encouraging
his congregation to vote for Bush, not to mention that the church did
not keep their views on social issues a secret—views of which coincided strikingly well with those of the Bush administration. Further,
Rob Boston, a writer for AU's Press Center, reiterates the assertions
made by his director, posing the question, "What was Floyd's message
Sunday morning [on July 4, 2004]? It was obvious: Vote for Bush."[61]

Vote Floyd

No doubt about it: "vote God" is a vote for Ronnie Floyd. Those who abide by his political criteria believe that they are abiding by God, and therefore comply with his prescribed political preferences. Many of his supporters claim, in congruence with his own teachings, that his politicking from the pulpit is not only excusable, but that to evade political matters is to evade Christian obligation. One supporter illustrates this notion in an editorial from the *Arkansas Democrat-Gazette*:

> Christian leaders have the duty to lead their flocks to behave responsibly in all areas of life: personal, corporate, and political. In a society based on government by the people, if Christians and others of deep moral conviction divorce themselves from the political process, the vacuum will be filled by men whose world view is purely secular.[62]

Based on the statements above, this Floyd supporter believes not only that Christians are obliged by God to morally invest in politics, but also suggests that Christians are entitled to practice politics in "all areas of life." Furthermore, this editorial implies that Christians should be awarded the "privilege" to pitch political messages from the pulpit, hence condoning Floyd's behavior and disregarding IRC code (5)(c)(3).

In addition to obligation to Christianity and allegiance to one's pastor, congregants also justify Floyd's sermon by virtue of the First Amendment. In fact, some of strongest arguments in favor of Ronnie Floyd are contentions embedded in the First Amendment, thus suggesting that the government is prohibited from interfering with religious practices. For example, Gwen Carpenter of Magnolia, Arkansas, offers her interpretation of constitutional rights in a *Arkansas Democrat-Gazette* letter to the editor following Floyd's sermon:

> Does the constitution deny Christian pastors their right to free speech and free exercise of religion? No, but it does say this: Congress shall make no law denying anyone freedom of speech and to practice religion. [...] Did pastor Ronnie Floyd [misuse] his constitutional rights? Of course not. Did he break a law? I think not.[63]

Here, Carpenter claims that pastors have the right to speak freely about *all* issues on the pulpit, and that Congress has *no* right to control what is being said inside church walls. Furthermore, she asserts that, under this amendment, Congress *cannot* intervene with the freedom of speech by any person—pastors included—nor can they interfere or prohibit religious activities. Based on this understanding, Floyd did not break a law or practice ill use of the Constitution; conversely, he adhered to his right to free exercise of faith.

Also on board with Floyd is fellow pastor James Dobson, founder and chairman of *Focus on the Family*, who appeared before the congregation at Floyd's First Baptist Church in Springdale in September.[64] In his address to the congregation, he reiterated Floyd's concern for an urgent need[65] for evangelical Christian voters in the 2004 election, as well as his undying support for Floyd.[66] Dobson and four other religious leaders reported that they were 100 percent supportive of Ronnie Floyd, to which Dobson turned to Floyd and said, "You do not stand alone. We stand shoulder to shoulder with you."[67]

Additionally, in August 2004, Governor Mike Huckabee reportedly told an interviewer that Floyd had *not* violated IRS regulations.[68] He continued: "[But] did he make it pretty clear where he was coming from? Probably so. Most pastors do." What's more, while AU and many others have accused Floyd of violating tax laws, he does *not* explicitly state which candidate he will be voting for in his sermon. Laura Kellams of the *Gazette* reported the following upon viewing the televised message:

> Floyd never mentioned Bush, a republican, or Kerry, his Democratic challenger, by name. He told members of his congregation to "vote God" in November and contrasted the candidates' positions on abortion and religion, among other issues, while pictures of the candidates were displayed behind him alternately as he discussed each candidates' views.[69]

Although Floyd displayed an *image* of George W. Bush, albeit somewhat larger, he also had an image of John Kerry. Hence, many of his supporters believe that he did not violate the tax code, as he did not specifically state the name of the candidate he planned to vote for. Instead, favorers adhere to the First Amendment, assessing his message as timely, necessary, and completely lawful.

The Pulpit Initiative: Four Years Later

Four years after the unforgettable controversy precipitated by Ronnie Floyd, Bishop Robert E. Smith of Little Rock followed in his footsteps, interlocking his political agenda with his faith in the public eye. Although his sermon in the 2008 election did not generate as much publicity as Floyd's, Smith believes that was due in part to Floyd's "predominantly white mega-church" and "user-friendly ministry."[70] Conversely, his participation in the Pulpit Initiative along with thirty-two religious leaders in the United States [71] elicited nationwide media coverage, as he was the only Arkansan pastor on board.

What's in a Name?

Thanks to the *Arkansas Democrat-Gazette*, Bishop Smith's sermon "The Issues, the Republic, [and] the Candidates"[72] was brought to the attention of Americans United, to which Barry Lynn wrote another letter of complaint to the IRS—and this time, his letter was slightly different. Perhaps the single most important distinguishing characteristic of the two sermons in question is this: Floyd hinted, suggested, implied—and alluded to—his political support of George W. Bush on the pulpit; by contrast, Bishop Smith concluded his sermon with the following statement: "I will be voting for John McCain and Sarah Palin."[73] Thus, while Floyd's sermon may have conjured up a few more national reactions, Bishop Smith deliberately, explicitly stated the exact name of the candidate(s) who he was going to vote for on Election Day. Thus, there was no confusion; Smith knowingly broke the rule. In fact, according to David Stell, IRS spokesman:

> It is not IRS regulations, rather it is the *law* (Title 26, United States Code, Section 501(c)(3)*) that prohibits all Section 501(c)(3) charitable organizations, churches and religious organizations, from directly or indirectly participating in, or intervening in, any political campaign on behalf of (or in opposition to) any candidate for elective public office.[74]

It does not get much more cut-and-dry than that. Stell and the IRS have a solid argument against the sermon: Smith *directly* participated in the endorsement of McCain; in turn, he violated section 501 (c)(3) and is therefore subject to loss of his church's tax-exempt status and an excise tax.

During an interview on *All Things Considered* on National Public Radio, Barbara Hagerty introduces the show by describing Pulpit Freedom Sunday: "To preach a sermon that endorses or opposes a political candidate by name [is] a flagrant violation of a law that bans tax-exempt organizations from involvement in political campaigns."[75] Here, Hagerty attempts to remain as objective as possible in her frame of the initiative; however, as previously stated, a religious leader *cannot* explicitly state the *name* of the political candidate he or she supports or opposes based on IRS section 501(c)(3).[76] In response to this controversy, Ohio pastor Eric Williams of North Congregational United Church of Columbus expresses his belief that pulpit politicking is an easy way for pastors to influence public policy:

> I ask myself, "Hmm. Why would a religious leader want to oppose a candidate? Why would a religious leader want to stand up and ask for my support for a candidate who's running for office?" They want to gain influence in the governmental process. [. . .] My concern is that an extreme segment of the Christian faith today is seeking to establish themselves as the public religion of our nation.

Williams proposes that Christian pastors could monopolize government, and subsequently the outcome of elections. Furthermore, he warns that if we (as a nation) continue to look the other way when religious leaders like Bishop Smith endorse candidates in church, we risk allowing voters—Christian voters in particular—to serve as the primary vehicle for political change. In so doing, Williams also believes that we are jeopardizing the separation of church and state.

Putting IRS codes and reporters aside, Arkansas residents had a different kind of opposition to Smith's sermon on *Arkansas Times*'s Arkansas Blog, featuring Smith's involvement in the Pulpit Initiative:

> I don't like this at all. My dislike has nothing to do with separation of church and state or the tax deductibility of contributions. My dislike stems from the fact that I have gone to church my whole life and do not want a pastor telling me this one candidate is mandated by God over another candidate [. . .] To me, it weakens and cheapens the role of the church. It also leaves a door open for the church to be controlled by a political party.[77]

The first blog entry illustrates an important reaction among the public: some people want to keep it *separate*. More specifically, congregants who support their pastors may see eye to eye on understandings of the Bible, religious ideals, and even how to live by "the word of God";[78] however, a religious individual may *not* want to be pressured, shamed, or coerced into prescribing to the same political preferences as their pastor. In sum, even in a place of worship and obligation, some want a *choice*. In that way, compliance and allegiance to one's faith could be sustained, while political beliefs could be checked at the door of the church.

The Man with a Plan

Sufficed to say, upon investigating media resources and "public opinions," surrounding Bishop Smith's participation in the Pulpit Initiative, there appears to be substantially fewer followers and supporters. Not surprisingly, however, one organization that coincided well with the contentions of Bishop Smith was the Alliance Defense Fund (ADF) who implemented the Pulpit Initiative.[79] According to ADF, Smith reserves the right to engage in political endorsement in worship:

> The goal [. . .] is to restore the right to pastors to speak freely from the pulpit, even for or against a candidate for office if they so choose, without fear of censorship by the government or worrying about jeopardizing their church's tax exempt status; [. . .] all churches [should] once again [be able to] speak out according to their faith about candidates. Through the courage of individual churches, freedoms of speech and religion will be restored to many more.[80]

Here, we see the unremitting support of and self-serving interpretation of the First Amendment; the ADF claims that all religious organizations and their constituents are entitled to speak freely about politics on the pulpit. According to this passage, Smith is no exception and in fact has the right to speak frankly and freely about candidates —names and all. Smith agreed, confirming these statements in an interview:

> The state in *no way* should interrupt or hinder faith. The state should not interfere with the expression of faith—only Judeo-Christian principles can dictate faith, and only biblical faith can

help the law. [...] The church should not be subject to ANY taxation.[81]

Interestingly, Smith believes that although the *government* should *not* interfere with faith, the government would actually *benefit* from faith. Either way, he believes that he has the constitutional right to stand on the pulpit and endorse any candidate he sees fit, no matter what the IRS says.

In terms of Arkansans' opinions, not all oppose Smith's involvement in the initiative. In fact, some support the idea of resurrecting the power of the First Amendment, which would diffuse the authority of the IRS:

The First Amendment is a protection for churches against the state:

> Congress shall make no law respecting an establishment of religion or prohibiting the free exercise thereof. According to that amendment, congress cannot enact any law that prohibits a church—or its pastor—from endorsing a candidate or any issue. And that calls into question the IRC statute.[82]

Although supporting the amendment from this direction supports political agendas purported by pastors (e.g., Smith), evangelical Christian faith as interpreted by Smith knows no laws nor amendments: his actions are governed solely by the "word of God." Therefore, when asked if he planned to continue politicking on the pulpit, keeping tax exemptions in mind, he replied:

> Would I tell people that one candidate was a sinister man and the antichrist? If you see destruction coming, you must warn the people. I expect that several churches will be forced to forfeit their tax-exemption statuses in the future. I am willing to take that risk—to me, it is worth the cost.[83]

Conclusion

All things considered, the separation of church and state is one of the most divisive and conflict-ridden issues most certainly in the state of Arkansas, but also throughout the nation. Insofar as we become highly cognizant and conscientious of religious leaders' critical role in progressive policy transformation, we can consequently make our own contributions to what promises to be an eternal and enthralling debate for years to come.

NOTES

1. Erin Curry, August 2, 2004: "Ronnie Floyd, on Fox News, discusses pulpits and politics." http://www.bpnews.net/bpnews.asp?ID=18792 (Accessed February 22, 2009), 1–7.

2. David Coon (October 9, 2008): "Arkansas Blog: Pulpit Politics." http://www.arktimes.com/blogs/arkansasblog/2008/10/pulpit_politics.aspx (Accessed February 19, 2009).

3. Curry, "Ronnie Floyd, on Fox News," 1.

4. Internal Revenue Service, "Tax Guide for Churches and Religious Organizations" [Online]. Available from http://www.irs.gov/pub/irs-pdf/p1828.pdf (Accessed February 21, 2009), 1–28.

5. Ibid., 2–3.

6. Ibid., 5.

7. Ibid., 7.

8. Charters of Freedom, "The Bill of Rights: A Transcription," The U.S. National Archives & Records Administration. http://www.archives.gov/exhibits/charters/bill_of_rights_transcript.html (Accessed February 18, 2009), 1–3.

9. Barry Lynn, "Uncivil Religion: Bush and the Bully Pulpit," Church and State 71 (2003): 23.

10. Ibid., 23.

11. Ronnie Floyd, "Ronnie Floyd: Reaching Northwest Arkansas, America, and the World for Jesus Christ," 2009. http://www.ronniefloyd.com/ (Accessed February 21, 2009).

12. Americans United for Separation of Church and State (September 24, 2008). "Arkansas Church's Partisan Politicking Needs IRS Investigation, Says AU." http://www.au.org/site/News2?abbr=pr&page=NewsArticle&id=6827 (accessed February 17, 2009), 1–2.

13. Frank Fellone, "News Treated as Such," Arkansas Democrat-Gazette, Editorial, August 10, 2004. Retrieved from Lexis-Nexis Academic Database on February 20, 2009. 1–2.

14. Americans United, 1.

15. Fellone, "News Treated as Such," 1.

16. Americans United, 1.

17. Ibid.

18. Ibid., 2.

19. Alliance Defense Fund: Defending Our First Liberty, "The Pulpit Initiative: Frequently Asked Questions," http://www.alliancedefensefund.org/userdocs/Pulpit_Initiative_FAQ.pdf (Accessed February 20, 2009), 1–3.

20. Ibid., 1.

21. National Public Radio, "Faith Matters: Political Endorsement from the Pulpit," October 10, 2008. http://www.npr.org/templates/story/story.php?storyId=95594731 (accessed February 21, 2009), 1–4.

22. Ibid., 2.

23. Alan Cooperman and Thomas B. Edsall, "Evangelicals Say They Led Charge for the GOP," *Washington Post*, November 8, 2004. http://www.washingtonpost. com/wp-dyn/articles/A32793-2004Nov7.html (Accessed March 20, 2009), 1–4.

24. Ibid., 1.

25. Ibid., 2.

26. AP Language and Composition: Exam Preparation Resources, 2002. See http://www.bookteacher.org/AP%20Language%20and%20Comp%20Prep.htm for AP Rhetoric and Writing Resources. (Accessed March 25, 2009), 1–21.

27. Ibid., 2.

28. Gideon Burton, "The Forest of Rhetoric: *Silva Rhetoricae*," 2001. http:// rhetoric.byu.edu/. (Accessed March 23, 2009), 1–3.

29. Floyd, "Ronnie Floyd."

30. Ibid., see "About" tab on top of website.

31. Transcription of July 4, 2004, sermon by Dr. Ronnie Floyd, obtained from Americans United for Separation of Church and State Press Archives, "Baptist Pastor Promotes Bush in Nationally Televised Sunday Sermon," July 20, 2004. http://members.au.org/site/News2?abbr=pr&page=NewsArticle&id=6827 (Accessed February 22, 2009), 1–2.

32. Cooperman and Edsall, "Evangelicals Say They Led Charge for the GOP," 2.

33. Diane Shader Smith and Megan MacLeod, "Stunning Poll Results Reveal That Nearly Half of Christian Voters Support Pro-Choice . . . ," February 4, 2004, from www.Godtube.com, posted on http://www.reuters.com/article/pressRelease/idUS117227+04-Feb-2008+PRN20080204 (Accessed February 23, 2009).

34. Liz Halloran, "Obama Campaign Is Making Progress with Evangelical Voters: McCain Leads with the Group but the Democrat Is Doing All the Right Things," *US News*, July 17, 2008. http://www.usnews.com/articles/news/campaign-2008/2008/07/17/obama-campaign-is-making-progress-with-evangelical-voters. html. 1-2 (Accessed February 20, 2009).

35. Ibid., 1–2.

36. AP Language and Composition, 2.

37. Ibid., 2.

38. Burton, "The Forest of Rhetoric," 2.

39. Coon, "Arkansas Blog," 1.

40. Bishop Robert E. Smith Sr., "The Issues, the Republic, the Candidates." DVD of sermon at Word of Outreach Christian Church delivered and recorded on October 12, 2008. (Self-transcribed.)

41. Bishop Robert E. Smith, interview with author, Lowell, Arkansas, May 2, 2009.

42. Floyd sermon: July 4, 2004, 1.

43. Ibid.

44. Ibid.

45. Ibid., 2.

46. Iver B. Neumann, "Self and Other in International Relations," *European Journal of International Relations* 2, no. 2 (1996): 139–74.

47. Floyd sermon: July 4, 2004, 1.

48. AP Language and Composition: Exam Preparation Resources, 2002. See

http://www.bookteacher.org/AP%20Language%20and%20Comp%20Prep.htm for AP Rhetoric and Writing Resources (Accessed March 25, 2009).

49. Smith sermon: October 12, 2008.

50. Ibid.

51. Ibid.

52. Ronnie Floyd, 2009, Personal website.

53. Pat Lynch, "Pastor Floyd Crosses the Line," *Arkansas Democrat-Gazette*, Op-Ed column, August 5, 2004. Retrieved from Lexis-Nexis Academic Database on February 20, 2009. 1–2.

54. Edward Hejtmanek, "Bush's Policies at Odds," *Arkansas Democrat-Gazette*, Letter to the Editor, August 12, 2004. Retrieved from Lexis-Nexis Academic Database on February 20, 2009.

55. Bill, comment on "Pastor Violates IRS Code" blog on *Arkansas Times* website. Comment posted on June 30, 2006, at 9:23 A.M.

56. Ibid.

57. Americans United for Separation of Church and State, "Arkansas Church's Partisan Politicking Needs IRS Investigation, Says AU," September 24, 2008. http://www.au.org/site/News2?abbr=pr&page=NewsArticle&id=6827 (Accessed February 17, 2009), 1–2.

58. Visit Americans United for Separation of Church and State's official website to learn more about the organization: www.au.org.

59. Americans United, 1.

60. Ibid., 1–2.

61. Rob Boston, "Church Service or Campaign Commercial? Partisan Production at Southern Baptist Congregation in Arkansas Raises Federal Tax Law Questions," Americans United, 2004. http://www.au.org/site/News2?page=NewsArticle&id=6927&news_iv_ctrl=0&abbr=cs (Accessed February 22, 2009).

62. George Schroeder, "Let Faith Fill Vacuum," *Arkansas Democrat-Gazette*, Editorial, August 28, 2004. Retrieved from Lexis-Nexis Academic Database on February 20, 2009. 1.

63. Gwen Carpenter, "Free Speech Protected," *Arkansas Democrat-Gazette*, Editorial, August 25, 2004. Retrieved from Lexis-Nexis Academic Database on February 20, 2009. 1.

64. Laura Kellams, "Marriage Gets Attention at Pulpit Leaders: Increase Political Activity," *Arkansas Democrat-Gazette*, Arkansas section, September 20, 2004. Article retrieved from Lexis-Nexis Academic Database on February 20, 2009. 1–2.

65. Refer to pp. 000–000 herein for a rhetorical discussion of Floyd's "exigency" strategy in his July 4, 2004, sermon.

66. Kellams, "Marriage Gets Attention," 1.

67. Ibid., 1.

68. Laura Kellams, "Pastor Denies Accusations of Politicking Group Critical of Sermon Contrasting Bush, Kerry," *Arkansas Democrat-Gazette*, Arkansas section, August 2, 2004. Article retrieved from Lexis-Nexis Academic Database on May 1, 2009. 1–2.

69. Laura Kellams, "IRS Complaint Going Nowhere, Springdale Pastor Says," *Arkansas Democrat-Gazette*, Northwest Arkansas section, September 16, 2004. Article retrieved from Lexis-Nexis Academic Database on May 1, 2009. 1–2.

70. Bishop Robert E. Smith, interview with author, Lowell, Arkansas, May 2, 2009.

71. See Alliance Defense Fund, 1–3.

72. Title of Bishop Robert E. Smith's sermon delivered to his congregation for "Pulpit Freedom Sunday" on October 12, 2008, at Word of Outreach Christian Church.

73. Ibid.

74. Frank Lockwood, "Bishop Defies Law, Lambastes Obama," *Arkansas Democrat-Gazette*, Religion section, November 1, 2008. Retrieved from Lexis-Nexis Academic Database on April 29, 2009.

75. Barbara Hagerty, "Pastors to Preach Politics from the Pulpit," *All Things Considered*, National Public Radio, September 24, 2008. http://www.npr.org/templates/story/story.php?storyId=95594731 (Accessed February 21, 2009), 1–4.

76. IRS Tax Guide, 5–7. (Refer to p. 3 of this document for more IRC section 501(c)(3) stipulations.)

77. Anonymous, comment on Arkansas Blog, "Pulpit Politics," *Arkansas Times*: http://www.arktimes.com/blogs/arkansasblog/2008/10/pulpit_politics.aspx. Comment posted on July 18, 2006, at 3:03 P.M.

78. Smith sermon: October 12, 2008.

79. Alliance Defense Fund, 1–2.

80. Ibid., 3.

81. Smith to author, personal interview in Lowell, Arkansas, May 2, 2009.

82. Skypilot, post on "Pulpit Politics" Arkansas blog. *Arkansas Times.* Comment posted on October 10, 2008, at 7:12 A.M.

83. Smith to author.

Appendix

December 13, 1968
Public Relations Committee
Students United For Rights
and Equality (S.U.R.E.)
Southern State College
Magnolia, Arkansas

Reverend James Schoenrock
College View Baptist Church
2111 N. Washington
Magnolia, Arkansas

Dear Sir:

On Sunday morning, December 8, 1968, a small group of Southern State College students went to your church to attend worship services.

After the students were seated in the sanctuary, they were approached by a man, presumably a member of your congregation, they followed the man, at his request, into a room off the lobby, he asked them to leave the church. The reason he gave for asking these students to go somewhere else to worship was that the College View Baptist Church is not an integrated church and its members are not ready for integration.

The action of these college students in exercising their right to freedom to worship in a church of their choice was a purely individual action. However, since the promotion of social understanding and human rights are among the primary purposes of our organization, we feel obliged to inquire into the situation.

Action such as that taken by a man in your church on December 8 is not in accord with the basic tenets of Christianity, as you must be even more aware of than we are. Therefore, we respectfully, request some explanation from you.

We ask you to let us know whether or not the man who escorted the students out of your church was a church official, or whether his behavior reflected a purely personal bias. We also wish to know whether your church has an official policy concerning the freedom of college students to worship among you without regard to race, creed, color, or national origin.

Sincerely yours,

Steven J. Bouley
Chairman, Public Relations
Committee

Bjm

Contributors

PAULA KILLIAN AGEE (M.A., communication, University of Arkansas) is director of Diversity, Leadership, and Organizational Development at Tyson Foods.

JOSH BERTACCINI earned a dual B.A. in broadcast journalism and English studies from Syracuse University in 2002. He obtained his M.A. in communication from the University of Arkansas in 2014. Josh has worked professionally in sports broadcasting for the past fifteen years.

DAVID R. DEWBERRY (Ph.D., University of Denver) is an associate professor of communication at Rider University. He has served as the editor of the *Communication Law Review* and *First Amendment Studies*. In 2013, the National Communication Association awarded him the Franklyn S. Haiman Award for Distinguished Scholarship in Freedom of Expression.

REBEKAH HUSS FOX (Ph.D., Purdue University) is an associate professor at Texas State University where she teaches courses in rhetorical methods, organizational rhetoric, environmental communication, and extremist rhetoric on the Internet.

RYAN GLISZINSKI is a course instructor at the University of Arkansas, Fayetteville. He recently received his M.A. in communication from the University of Arkansas and is looking forward to continuing his independent research in First Amendment studies.

CAROLINE M. HEINTZMAN (M.A., University of Arkansas) is a communications practitioner. She was a visiting scholar at both Oxford and Cambridge Universities, studying the history and philosophy of freedom of speech. During her undergraduate years, she interned for the United States Senate. Caroline is passionate about protecting our First Amendment rights.

KATTRINA BALDUS JONES (M.A., University of Arkansas) is a facilitator and manager of global programs in Global Leader Development at Walmart Stores, Inc., where she facilitates a wide array of leadership courses such as coaching, confrontation, change, and emotional intelligence.

JAMIE KERN received her master of arts in communication from the University of Arkansas. She is currently employed at the U of A as the assistant director for Transfer Central in the Office of Admissions. She enjoys drinking wine and playing with her two cats.

ANDREW LONG graduated from the University of Arkansas with a B.S.B.A. in computer information systems in 2003, and with his M.A. in communication in 2005. He then attended Law School at the University of Oklahoma, graduating with his J.D. in 2008. He currently lives with his wife, Laura, and their daughter Maddie in Oklahoma City.

MATTHEW McNAIR (M.A., University of Arkansas) is the environmental review coordinator for the Arkansas Department of Parks & Tourism. He is a Ph.D. candidate (geography) at the University of Oklahoma, but has not ruled out beating his mortarboard into a plowshare. He maintains a great disdain for sneaky classroom proselytizing.

DAVID N. MORRIS (M.A., University of Arkansas) is a freelance writer and musician. In 2003 he won the Pi Kappa Delta National Tournament for NPDA Debate. He currently performs with the Fayetteville, Arkansas, based rock band The Inner Party.

AFSANEH N. ROE (B.A., University of Arkansas) is a current master's student of communication at the U of A. She researches leadership communication and teaches public speaking at the University of Arkansas.

CORTNEY SMITH is a doctoral candidate in rhetoric and public culture at Indiana University. Her interdisciplinary dissertation combines rhetoric, Native studies, and history to explore how contemporary Native art counters the dominant and hegemonic narrative of the Vanishing Race Myth.

STEPHEN A. SMITH (Ph.D., Northwestern) is Professor Emeritus of Communication at the University of Arkansas. He taught courses in freedom of speech for more than thirty years at the university.

ALLIE TAYLOR (B.A., University of Arkansas) is a master's candidate of media studies/mass communication at the University of Arkansas. She has taught public speaking courses, currently is a research assistant, and serves as a graduate student liaison. She also serves as vice chair of the city of Fayetteville Telecommunications Board.

Index